ASPECTS OF ANTIQUITY

Naphtali Lewis
General Editor

The Statue of Augustus at Prima Porta.
Heroic portrayal of Augustus as Imperator,
the most famous of some 150 known
sculptured portraits of Augustus.
Courtesy of the Vatican Museum

Augustus Caesar, son of a god, will establish a golden age again.
VERGIL, *Aeneid*

A golden age will arise in the whole world.
VERGIL, *Eclogues*

This was the life that existed on earth in the golden age of Saturn.
VERGIL, *Georgics*

THE
GOLDEN
AGE OF
AUGUSTUS

MEYER
REINHOLD
with the assistance of Paul T. Alessi

SAMUEL STEVENS
Toronto & Sarasota
1978

US Edition
Samuel Stevens & Co.
Cloth: 0-89522-007-5
Paper: 0-89522-008-3

Canadian Edition
Samuel-Stevens, Publishers
Cloth: 0-88866-585-7
Paper: 0-88866-586-5

Library of Congress Catalogue Card Number 77-83161

Library of Congress Cataloging in Publication Data
Main entry under title:

The Golden age of Augustus.

Bibliography: p.
Includes index.
1. Rome — History — Augustus, 30 B.C.-14 A.D. —
Addresses, essays, lectures. 2. Augustus, Emperor of
Rome, 63 B.C.-14 A.D. — Addresses, essays, lectures.
3. Rome — Intellectual life — Addresses, essays, lectures.
I. Reinhold, Meyer, 1909 -   II. Alessi, Paul T.
DG279.G6   937'.07   77-83161
ISBN 0-89522-007-5
ISBN 0-89522-008-3 pbk.

Jacket Design by Peter Maher
Book design and typography by Dreadnaught

Printed and Bound in The United States of America

Samuel-Stevens, Publishers
554 Spadina Crescent
Toronto,Ontario M5S 2J9

Samuel Stevens & Co.
PO Box 3899
Sarasota, Florida 33578

For Matthew and Andrew Barrett *Nepotibus Caris* MR

And *Parentibus Dilectis* PTA

CONTENTS

PREFACE

The half century during which Augustus dominated, administered, and moulded the life of Rome and its far-flung empire belongs to that small cluster of eras, such as the Periclean Age, the Elizabethan Age, and the Age of Louis xiv, which mankind has come to regard as among the most lustrous and creative in the annals of the world. Contemporaries were swift to characterize the reign of Augustus as a "Golden Age," and there was a "widespread belief that a new page had been turned in the history of mankind."[1]

The Augustian Age was indeed extraordinary — even unique — in many ways. Augustus' regime was the longest continuous hold on power by anyone in Rome's long history: for almost sixty years he was at the center of political power, and he bestrode the Roman world as its sole ruler for almost fifty. The constitutional forms he devised controlled its vast empire for centuries. It is not far from the mark to conclude that he saved Greco-Roman civilization from disintegration, and guaranteed its survival for hundreds of years to come. In place of acute world instability and war-weariness, he created confidence in Rome's ability to maintain order and in her equity toward the rest of the world; he reconciled especially the Greek East to Roman rule and unified the empire. To the provinces he appeared as defender of civilization against the barbarians; to Rome and Italy, as protector of their priority and privileges in the empire and restorer of their ancestral moral values.

The Augustan Age was a remarkable time, too, of creativity in literature and the arts — despite the powerful presence and intrusion of the ruler. The spur of patronage, and the deep commitment to the regime by writers like Vergil and Horace, combined to release an outpouring of brilliant literary masterpieces that rank among the greatest classics of world literature.

ix

Augustus' zeal for the eternal city as an imperial showcase generated an urban building program unequalled by any previous Romans. But for all the princely sums he spent on the capital, the construction he fostered was imperial and civic in character; there were no allocations, for example, for public housing for Rome's population of about a million.

Yet Augustus was not a great general of the calibre of Alexander the Great or Julius Caesar, nor a brilliant political theorist, nor a great religious leader, nor an intellectual, nor even, indeed, a charismatic statesman. What then accounts for his great success, for his long hold on power, and for the acclaim he received? Suffice it to say that he was essentially an astute pragmatic politician, a consummate administrator, and master of the art of the possible in Roman affairs. It has often been asked whether Augustus was a truly sincere statesman or a cunning hypocrite. Was he the power-hungry leader of a faction, or indeed the "prince of peace," and "savior of mankind," as he was called by contemporaries? Were men so war-weary and crisis-weary that they were willing to be deceived?

His success was, in part, due to his skill in applying elastic methods — to his deftness in accommodating opposing forces, combining necessary innovations with the restoration of old, traditional practices, and creating acceptable myths for the Romans and the inhabitants of the empire. As a result, the paradoxes of the age are indeed as enigmatic as the character of Augustus himself: his "restoration of the republic" standing side by side with his introduction of an hereditary monarchy; his proclamation of the *Pax Augusta* ("Augustan Peace"), with his aggressive policies of conquest that resulted in annexations of more new territory than was added by any other Roman leader in history; the myth of one national family, with the fostering of an elitist hierarchy; the myth of liberty, with the dominant power of one man, the *princeps;* the myth of national consensus, with the existence of vigorous pockets of opposition to Augustus; the myth of a new moral order, with widespread materialism and moral corruption; the myth of the consent of the governed through elections, with the establishment of a dynasty; the myth of checks and balances, with the overriding authority of the *princeps;* the myth of a return to simplicity and moderation, with the unrestrained luxury spending of the age, together with the fabulous wealth of the emperor, his family, and associates.

For the empire as a whole, Augustus made Rome the efficient policeman of the world and restored confidence in life and property. He assured the continuity of "diversity-within-unity" in the empire. Beyond that, he offered no world-wide program or policies to satisfy the moral and spiritual needs of a far-flung, pluralistic society. Though the world looked to him as the source of justice and as a providential leader, he vigorously fostered a culture that was elitist, hierarchic, plutocratic, designed to gratify a small minority of the population. True, he presented himself to the world as imbued with the cardinal virtues of military prowess, justice, clemency, and duty. But he offered it neither wisdom nor the gentler virtues. And his regime was patently paternalistic, providing benefits to a passive people, leaving little room even to Romans for differences and a voice in their own destiny. But, unlike the great monarchs of the Eastern kingdoms, some of whom bore the title "king of kings," Augustus, in Roman terms, was *princeps* ("first citizen"), *princeps senatus* ("ranking senator"), *pater patriae* ("father of his country"), *patronus* ("super-patron") of powerful patrons of numerous clients, and *salvator* to the Latin-speaking, *soter* to the Greek-speaking ("savior" in either language) of the world. In his own personal life a simple style prevailed; verbal pageantry took the place of regal insignia and display.

The "Augustan Age" as a high point in literature and art was revived in England in the first half of the eighteenth century, when the patronage and the moral and nationalistic tone of literature in the reigns of Charles ii to George ii were identified with the Augustan Age of Rome. More recently, Robert Frost, at the inaugural of President John F. Kennedy in 1961, prophesied "the next Augustan Age." But one of the great ancient historians of our time, conceding Augustus' many great accomplishments, reminds us that "as he never thought of real liberty, so he never attained to the profound humanity of men who promote free life."[2] And it was John Stuart Mill who warned that "a good despotism in a country at all advanced in civilization is more noxious than a bad one."[3]

Still, like all supremely significant ages in man's history, the Augustan Age displays polyvalent features. In the end, students

xi

must work out for themselves — out of the rich, many-faceted sources for the period — their own evaluations of Augustus and the world order he created. It is simplistic to denounce him as a cynical despot; it is equally so to eulogize him as "the savior of the world." It is instructive to know that even at the crest of widespread optimism during the Augustan Age there were perceptive Romans who harbored — and expressed — a sense of melancholy pessimism. The hollowness of the vaunted ideal of a return to the purer national past, to its simplicity and "Roman virtues," stood exposed in the face of Rome's grandeur, power, and wealth; Augustus' call to the Roman ruling class to sacrifice themselves for the sake of Rome's long-range imperial mission was blunted by the prevailing, deeply held yearnings for personal happiness. Even if few among Rome's elite were compassionately concerned about the cost to the rest of the empire of the good life provided to a tiny layer of the population, was the guarantee of order assured by Augustus worth the price they themselves had to pay — their own liberty?

In the preparation of this collection of sources, all translations of Greek and Latin texts were made by the editor with contributions by Paul T. Alessi. The latter wishes to acknowledge with thanks the assistance provided by a Research Initiation Grant of the University of Houston.

SOURCES
FREQUENTLY CITED

ADA. *Acta Divi Augusti,* Part I (Rome 1945). Official documents of Augustus and the Senate.

CIL. *Corpus Inscriptionum Latinarum* (16 vols., Berlin, 1862 –). A collection of over 100,000 Latin inscriptions.

Dessau, ILS. H. Dessau, *Inscriptiones Latinae Selectae* 3 vols. (Berlin, 1892 to 1916). Over 9,000 selected Latin inscriptions.

Dio Cassius. Cassius Dio Cocceianus (ca. 155 to ca. 230 AD), who after a long and distinguished public career wrote, in Greek, a vast *History of Rome* up to 229 AD. Though rhetorical, annalistic, and not always critical, Dio's history is especially valuable as the fullest account we have of the Augustan Age.

Ehrenberg-Jones. Victor Ehrenberg and A.H.M. Jones, eds., *Documents Illustrating the Reigns of Augustus and Tiberius.* 2nd ed. (Oxford, 1955).

FIRA. *Fontes Iuris Romani Antejustiani.* 2nd ed. 3 vols. (Florence, 1940 to 1943). Vol. I: laws, decrees of the Senate, edicts of officials, enactments of emperors; Vol. II: literary sources, from jurists and codifications; Vol. III: legal documents and transactions.

Frontinus. Sextus Julius Frontinus (ca. 30 to 104 AD), distinguished Roman administrator, whose voluminous practical writings include *Aqueducts of Rome,* a guide to governmental regulations concerning their use.

Horace. Quintus Horatius Flaccus (65 to 8 BC), one of the distinguished authors of the Augustan Age, member of Maecenas' literary circle. His works include: *Epodes,* and *Satires* (in two books), written during the last decade of the Republic; *Odes,* four books of exquisitely crafted lyric poems on a great variety of topics; the *Secular Hymn,* written in 17 BC for the Secular Games; and *Epistles,* two books of essays in verse in the form of letters. Horace's works provide "inside" glimpses into the relig-

xiii

ion, politics, and social and intellectual life of the time. After a surge of enthusiasm for Augustus about 30 BC, when he applauded his clemency, moderation, and moral program, Horace turned away from the *princeps'* pragmatic political methods dictated by expediency.

IGRR. *Inscriptiones Graecae ad Res Romanas Pertinentes* 3 vols. (Paris, 1906 to 1927). A valuable collection of thousands of Greek inscriptions dealing with Roman matters.

Ovid. Publius Ovidius Naso (43 BC to 18 AD), member of Rome's smart set. Non-political, brilliant, sophisticated, frivolous, irreverent, Ovid was temperamentally "un-Augustan." His works include: *Amores,* love poems; *The Art of Love,* on seduction and sexual intrigue; *Metamorphoses,* (in fifteen books), a collection of myths unified under the theme of change; *Fasti,* a calendar of Roman holidays; *Tristia* and *Letters from Pontus,* written in his place of exile on the Black Sea.

Pliny the Elder. Gaius Plinius Secundus (23/4 to 79 AD), distinguished political figure and prolific author. His sole extant work is the *Natural History,* in thirty-seven books, an encyclopedic collection of information on a wide variety of subjects.

Propertius. Sextus Propertius (ca. 54−47 to 16−2 BC), member of the literary circle of Maecenas. He wrote elegiac poetry (in four books) during the first decade of the Principate, expending a good deal of his versatile talent on love poems to his mistress, "Cynthia." Propertius had no deep commitment to Augustus, though patriotism and pride in empire elicited from him some poems on national and Augustan themes.

SEG. *Supplementum Epigraphicum Graecum* (Leiden, 1923−). Newly discovered Greek inscriptions reported periodically.

Seneca the Elder. Lucius Annaeus Seneca (ca. 55 BC to 40 AD), writer on rhetoric who collected numerous excerpts from the declamations he had heard at Rome during the late Republic and the early Principate, under the title *The Orators' and Rhetors' Aphorisms, Divisions, and Colors.*

Seneca the Younger. Lucius Annaeus Seneca (ca. 4 BC to 65 AD), son of Seneca, the rhetorician. He was a prolific and versatile author, whose works include philosophical and moral tracts, as well as tragedies. Seneca was an adherent of the Stoic philosophy.

xiv

Strabo. Greek author (ca. 65 BC to ca. 21 AD) of *Geography*, in seventeen books. This is a storehouse of information on geography, military, political, and economic affairs.

Suetonius. Gaius Suetonius Tranquillus (ca. 69 to ca. 150 AD), author of numerous works, including *Lives of the Twelve Caesars*, from Julius Caesar to Domitian. Despite their anecdotal, antiquarian, and scandal-mongering interests, Suetonius' lives contain much valuable data.

Tacitus. Cornelius Tacitus (ca. 55 to ca. 120 AD), eminent Roman lawyer and senator. After the death of Domitian he turned to the writing of the history of the Principate. Especially valuable for the Augustan Age is his great work, *Annals*, in eighteen books, covering imperial history from 14 to 68 AD. He should be read, however, with caution because of his rhetorical style, moral evaluations of historical events, cynicism, and nostalgic bias for an aristocratic republic.

Tibullus. Albius Tibullus (55–48 to 19 BC), elegiac poet, member of Messalla's literary circle. He was neutral in politics, preferring a secure private existence in the country, where he devoted himself principally to writing elegiac poetry on erotic themes.

Velleius. Velleius Paterculus (before 19 BC to after 30 AD), who after a long political and military career became an amateur historian, writing a *Roman History*, up to 30 AD. He was an enthusiastic supporter of the imperial family, especially Tiberius.

Vergil. Publius Vergilius Maro (70 to 19 BC), the greatest author of the Augustan Age, and one of the greatest figures of world literature. He was the leading light of Maecenas' literary circle. Vergil achieved instant fame with his *Eclogues* (or *Bucolics*), ten pastoral poems of exquisite taste and beauty. His didactic poem *Georgics*, acclaimed the most perfect poem in the Latin language, was effectively a program of return to national dedication and shared communal values. Vergil's fame rests mostly on his masterpiece, the *Aeneid*, a patriotic, nationalistic, and philosophical epic, in twelve books. Though it is cast in the form of a myth — for 1,500 years the most famous myth of the western world — it embodies the distinctive themes of the age: peace, shared values, dedication to country, moral revitalization through revival of ancestral Roman virtues, pride in empire, and commitment to Augustus. Yet the *Aeneid* is full of doubt and pessimism, "the epic of grief" it has been called.

THE GOLDEN AGE OF AUGUSTUS

Mother Earth (or Italia) symbolizing the fertility of the age in children,
animals, crops. From the Altar of the Augustan Peace.
Courtesy of Fratelli Alinari, Rome

PROLOGUE
1
WHITHER ROME?

A decade or so before the Principate of Augustus, Vergil and Horace responded to the uncertainties of the Roman condition with diverse judgments about Rome's future — Horace's tinged with pessimism and despair, Vergil's full of Messianic anticipation and radiant hope for a "Paradise regained." The two poems — both unique in Roman literature — complemented each other consciously, but we do not know which was written first. Vergil's *Fourth Eclogue* was later heralded by Christians as a prophecy of the birth of Christ. Actually, we do not know what sort of poem it was (wedding poem; birthday poem?) or even whether a specific child was intended. In age-old Eastern tradition the birth of a "wonder child" as savior child-king was believed to usher in a better time. Noteworthy is that Vergil hovers between a vision of a savior as warrior (like Achilles) or civilizer (like Hercules), and that in the "Golden Age" he envisages political power and poetic power will support each other.

Horace, *Epodes* no. 16

A second generation is now being wasted by civil wars, and Rome herself is crumbling from its own power, she whom neither the neighboring Marsi[1] had the power to destroy, nor an Etruscan force under threatening Porsena, nor the courageous bravery of rival Capua,[2] nor savage Spartacus, nor the Allobrogian Gaul,[3] untrustworthy in time of revolution; nor did barbaric Germany with her blue-eyed youth conquer her, nor Hannibal hated by parents. We, an impious generation of accursed blood, will destroy her, and once more our soil will be occupied by wild beasts. Alas, the victorious barbarian will stand upon the ashes, and under resounding hoof the horseman will trample down the city; in arrogance the conqueror will scatter (oh horrendous sight!) the bones of Romulus now protected from winds and the sun's rays.

All of you perhaps, or the better part of you, seek what is the

5

preferable to the following: just as the citizenry of Phocaea[4] swore an oath and fled in exile from their fields and the hearths of their fatherland, and left their shrines to become the habitat of boars and predatory wolves, you will go wherever your feet will carry you, or wherever across the seas the south or the boisterous southwest wind will summon you. Is this your decision? or does someone have a better proposal? why do we delay under favorable auspices to board a boat? But let us take this oath: that, when rocks lifted from the depths of the sea float, return home be not forbidden, and that there be no disdaining to shift sail back toward home when the Po shall wash the peaks of Mt. Matinus,[5] or when the lofty Apennine will jut out into the sea, when unnatural passion will couple monstrous beings in a new kind of lust, so that tigers will wish to yield to deer, and a dove will mate with a hawk, and a trusting herd will not fear growling lions, and the goat now sleek will enjoy the salty sea.

Sealing with curses these things and whatever else will cut off sweet return, let us, the citizen body, all of us or at least the part that is better than the untrainable mass, be off; may the weak and hopeless lie upon their ill-fated beds. But you who have manliness, remove this womanish grief, and speed off beyond the shores of Etruria. Widespreading Ocean awaits us; let us seek the fields, the happy fields and the rich islands of the blest, where yearly the earth unplowed yields grain, and the vineyard unpruned continually blooms, and the branch of olive never fails to sprout, and the dark fig adorns its native tree, honey flows from the hollow oak, from high mountains water lightly springs on splashing foot. There goats ungoaded come to their milk pails, and the flock willingly returns with udders swollen, and at evening the bear does not growl as he circles the sheepfold, and the earth does not puff up high with vipers, nor do diseases infect the flock, no sweltering rage from any star scorches the herd. In our happiness we will be more astonished that the rainy southeast wind does not wash away the topsoil with flooding showers, and fertile seeds are not burned up in dried clods, because the king of the gods on high moderates each season. Not here did a ship driven by Argive oars[6] strive to come, nor a shameless Colchian[7] set foot here; not here Phoenician sailors swung their yards nor the toiling crew of Ulyssess. Jupiter marked out those shores for a devout people, ever since he debased the golden age with bronze; first with bronze, after that with iron he hardened the ages, from which a happy escape is granted to the devout, as I am mantic poet.

Vergil, *Eclogue* no.4

Muses of Sicily,[8] let us sing somewhat loftier themes. Shrubs and lowly tamarisk do not please everyone. If we sing of woods, let them be worthy of a consul.

The last age of Cumaean[9] song has now come; the great series of ages is born anew. Now too the Virgin[10] returns; the kingdom of Saturn returns; now a new lineage is being sent down from lofty heaven. Only do you, O chaste Lucina,[11] shed favor on the boy being born, under whom the iron age shall first cease and a golden race will arise in the whole world: now your Apollo reigns. Your consulship, O Pollio,[12] yours will thus initiate this glorious era and the splendid months will begin to advance; under your leadership, if any traces of our sin remain, obliterated they will free the lands from constant fear. He will receive the life of the gods and will see heroes associating with the deified, and they will view him, and he will rule over a world made peaceful by the virtues of his father.

But for you, child, the earth without cultivation will produce its first little gifts, ivy meandering everywhere about with primrose plants, and bean stalks mixed with smiling acanthus. Goats of their own accord will bring home udders swollen full with milk, and the herds will not fear mighty lions. Of its own accord your cradle will pour forth charming flowers for you. The serpent too will die, and the treacherous poisonous herb will fade away; Assyrian balsam will spring up everywhere. But as soon as you will be able to read of the renown won by heroes and the deeds of your father, and to understand what manliness is, little by little the field will grow yellow with soft wheat, the blushing grape will hang from untended brambles, and the hard oaks will exude dewy honey. Nevertheless, a few traces of our ancient sin will surface, bidding men to test the sea in vessels, to fortify towns with surrounding walls, and to cut furrows in the earth. Then there will be a second Tiphys[13] and a second Argo to carry chosen heroes; there will be a second round of wars too, and once more a mighty Achilles will be sent to Troy. After this, when the passage of time strengthens and makes you a man, the traveler will abandon the sea, and the wooden ship will not exchange merchandise; every land will bear everything. The ground will not endure hoes, nor vines the sickle. Then too the strong plowman will unyoke the collars from his oxen; and wool will not learn how to deceive by varying colors, but on its own accord the ram in meadows will change his fleece now to sweetly blushing purple, now to a bright yellow hue; spontaneously crimson will clothe the pasturing lambs.

"Ages like these, run on," the Fates, in agreement on the fixed will of destiny, exclaimed to their spindles. Enter on your great honors (the time will soon come), O dear offspring of the gods, mighty descendant of Jupiter! Look! the world nods under curved weight; look at the lands, the tracts of the sea and the deep heaven. Behold how all things rejoice in the approaching era! May, then, the last part of a long life remain for me and as much inspiration as will be sufficient to relate your deeds: neither Thracian Orpheus nor Linus[14] will excel me in song, although his mother, Calliope,[15] may help the one, Orpheus, and his father, the handsome Apollo, help the other, Linus. Even Pan,[16] if he were to compete with me and Arcadia were judge, even Pan, were Arcadia judge, would declare his defeat.

Begin, little boy, with a smile to recognize your mother (your mother endured ten long months of impatience), begin, little boy: those who have not smiled for a parent a god has never honored with his table, nor a goddess with her bed.

I

AUGUSTUS PRINCEPS: THE NEW ORDER

For 500 years the Roman people lived under a republican form of government; for about half that time the city of Rome ruled an empire of ever-growing size. In the last century of the Republic, Rome and its empire were mortally endangered from within and without. The disorders of the "Roman Revolution," the threats to the integrity of the empire, and the profound fears for life and property everywhere came to an end with the victory of Julius Caesar's adopted son, Octavian. With the suicides of Antony and Cleopatra in Alexandria in Egypt in 30 BC, Octavian, at the age of thirty-three, was master of an empire twice the size of Alexander the Great's.

The new order established by the victor held forth clemency to the opposition, protection of life and property, assurance of order and security throughout the empire, and restoration of traditional institutions. Octavian hoped to unite the Romans through an ideological program of legitimacy, constitutionalism, and Romanism. Hence at a famous meeting of the Senate in January, 27 BC, which Octavian himself chaired, he renounced his *de facto* dictatorship, and reestablished legitimate government by proclaiming the "restoration of the Republic." The Senate was, however, to remain as junior "partner in government," and the people were to retain their traditional role in the republican constitution whose symbol was *S.P.Q.R.* ("The Senate and the Roman People"). But, in fact, through a series of pragmatic constitutional expedients, Octavian succeeded in establishing a veiled monarchy, with his authority as *princeps* ("first citizen," an informal title he preferred) overarching both Senate and people. As "patron" of numerous senators, of the Roman people, of countless peoples throughout the empire, and of client kings on the borders, he was the undisputed focus of power in the empire.

The name Augustus, bestowed upon him in 27 BC, surrounded him with an aura of religious sanctity and moral authority. From 23 BC on, though in fact a private citizen and not a magistrate (except for two special occasions), Augustus gathered into his hands more power than any Roman had ever had.

2

ESTABLISHMENT OF
THE PRINCIPATE

Tacitus, *Annals* Book 1

(Chapters 2 – 4.) After Brutus and Cassius were killed, the Republic was left with no army; Pompey was crushed off Sicily; Lepidus was stripped of power; Antony was slain. Not even the Julian party had a leader left except for Caesar [i.e., Octavian], who, dropping the title of triumvir, conducted himself as consul, and declared he was content with the tribunician power for the protection of the people. He then enticed the soldiers with gifts, the people with grain, and all men with the enchantment of peace, and by gradual degrees increased his powers, drawing to himself the functions of the Senate, magistrates and laws. He had no opposition since his most bitter adversaries had met death in battle or the proscriptions; with regard to the remaining nobles, the readier each was for servitude, the higher was he promoted by wealth and public offices, so that, aggrandized by revolution, they preferred the safety of the present to the dangers of the past. The provinces were not at all antipathetic to this state of affairs, for they distrusted the government of the Senate and the people because of the numerous power struggles and the rapacious greed of public officials, protection under the laws being ineffective, as they were in a constant state of turmoil from violence, intrigue and finally bribery....

The state of affairs at home was peaceful; public officials had the same titles; a younger generation was born after the victory of Actium, and even many of the older men had been born during the civil wars. How very few were left who had ever seen the Republic!

Thus the constitution of the state had been transformed, and there was nothing left of the old virtuous way of life. Deprived of equality all awaited the direct commands of the *princeps,* with no fear for the present, while Augustus in the prime of his life maintained his hold, his household and the peace....

In reporting popular assessment of Augustus at the time of his death in 14 AD, Tacitus includes some observations on his assumption of power and his administration.

(Chapters 9–10.) But among knowledgeable men his life was variously commented upon, extolled by some, blamed by others. Some said that it was out of duty toward his father and because of the crisis of the state — in which there was no place then for legal action — that he was driven to civil war, which could not be planned or conducted by gentle means. He deferred to Antony many times while he was exacting vengeance on his father's murderers, and many times also to Lepidus. After the latter grew old and feeble-minded, and the former was destroyed by his lust, no other remedy for the country in discord was possible except to be ruled by a single man. The government, however, was reconstituted not as a monarchy nor as a dictatorship but under the title of Principate. The ocean and remote rivers formed the empire's boundaries; the legions, provinces, fleets, all things were interconnected. There was law for citizens, and for the allies a moderate policy; the city was magnificently adorned. Only few occasions were handled by force — to maintain peace for the rest.

On the other hand it was argued that his duty toward his father and crises of state were assumed as a pretense, and it was in reality because of his desire for supreme power that he stirred up the veterans by bribery, raised an army as a young man and private citizen, corrupted the consul's legions, and pretended support of the Pompeian party....

Suetonius, *Life of Augustus* chapters 27–28, 46

He served as triumvir for regulating the government for ten years; in this office for some time he opposed his colleagues in an effort to prevent a proscription, but once it had begun he implemented it more severely than either of the other two. For although they were often approachable in many instances by personal influence and appeals, he alone insisted vigorously that no one be spared.... After the proscription was over, Marcus Lepidus acknowledged his regret in the Senate for the past and expressed the hope for clemency in the future, since enough punishment had been exacted; but Augustus on the contrary asserted he had granted an end to the proscriptions on the condition that he be left a free hand in everything....

He twice considered restoring the Republic, the first time immediately after crushing Antony, recalling that Antony often brought the accusation that it was because of him that it had not been restored; a second time in the depression of a long illness, when he even summoned the magistrates and Senate to his home and submitted an accounting of the empire. Reflecting, however, that he would not be free from danger as a private citizen, and that it would be risky to entrust the state to the discretion of the masses, he continued to keep control — it is hard to say whether the result or his intent was the better. This intent... was expressed in an edict as follows: "May I be able to set the government on a safe and secure basis, and to receive the benefit I seek from this, namely, that I may be known as the author of the very best type of government, and at my death I may take with me the hope that the foundations of the government which I have laid will remain in their original form." He succeeded in his hope by making every effort to prevent dissatisfaction with the new regime....

When he had thus regulated the city and urban affairs, he established twenty-eight colonies to increase Italy's population, and provided many parts of it with public works and revenues. After a fashion, at least partially, he made Italy equal to the city in status, by devising a method of voting whereby council members in each colony might vote for city magistrates and send the sealed ballots to Rome for the day of elections. And to prevent the supply of men of rank or the offspring of the masses from declining, he arranged for admission to an equestrian military career also those publicly recommended by any town; and to plebeians, when he approved their sons or daughters as he visited the regions of the city, he distributed 1,000 sesterces for each child.

3

POWERS, TITLES, HONORS OF AUGUSTUS

The restoration of traditional republican institutions subjected Augustus to the process of annual reelection to office and to the constitutional checks and balances of collegiality. Augustus found a solution for this "indignity" in the unrepublican concept of the separation of the powers of an office from the office itself. Thus from 23 BC, though he was in reality a private individual (yet a member of the Senate and exerting great power through his *auctoritas* ["authority"] and his role as *princeps*), Augustus based his rule upon two legal sources of power: *imperium proconsulare* ("proconsular power") and *tribunicia potestas* ("tribunician power"). Indeed, the official beginning of his sole rule was July 1, 23 BC, from which date the years of his regime were counted. The Principate, as his regime is called, was thus a practical constitutional facade for the administration of a monarchy in all but name.

A
The Trappings of Power

Dio Cassius, *History of Rome* Book 53

(Chapter 16.) In fact Caesar [Octavian] himself was on the road to having absolute power over all matters for life, since he was in control of the funds (for though he had nominally sequestered the public funds from his own, in actuality he spent these, too, at his own judgment), and was in control of the army. At any rate, when the ten-year period [of his proconsular power] ran out, there was voted to him another five years, then five again, and after that ten, and then another ten, and another ten for the fifth time, so that by this succession of ten-year terms, he was sole ruler for life....

Now Caesar had received many honors previously, when the

matter of forswearing the monarchy and the matter of the division of the provinces were discussed. Indeed, the placing of laurel trees in front of the imperial residence, and the hanging of the civic crown over the doors were then (27 BC) voted to him, to symbolize that he was ever conqueror of enemies and savior of citizens. The imperial residence is called the Palatium, not because it was ever decreed that it be thus named, but because Caesar lived on the Palatine Hill, and had his military headquarters there....

And when he had actually completed the reorganization, the name Augustus was bestowed upon him for this, by the Senate and the people. Indeed, when they wished to give him some special appellation, and various ones were proposed and urged, Caesar himself was very eager to be named Romulus, but perceiving that he would as a result be suspected of aiming at monarchy, he gave up this effort, and was called "Augustus," as being something more than human....

(Chapters 17–18, 21.) Thus the power of both the people and the Senate was transferred entirely into Augustus' hands, and from this time [27 BC], there was established strictly speaking a monarchy.... Now the title "monarch" was so hated by the Romans that they did not name their emperors either dictators or kings or anything of this sort.... The constitutional offices are in existence even now for the most part, except for the office of censors, but everything is conducted and administered entirely as the one in power desires. And yet, in order to give the appearance of having this not through their power but under the laws, the emperors have taken to themselves everything, including the titles, which in the Republic was a source of power with the consent of the people, except the dictatorship. They very often became consuls, and are always called proconsuls,[1] whenever they are outside the *pomerium.*[2] The title *imperator*[3] they hold for life, not only those who have won some victories, but all the others, to indicate their absolute power, instead of the title "king" or "dictator"....

Through these titles they have the right to raise troops, collect funds, declare war, make peace treaties, rule over both foreigners and citizens alike, always and everywhere, and even have the power to put to death both Equestrians and Senators within the *pomerium*,[4] and all the powers that used to be in the hands of consuls and magistrates with *imperium*. And by virtue of the censorship they investigate our lives and characters, and they take the census, and enrol some in the Equestrian and Senatorial Orders, and remove others from these orders, as they deem fit. By virtue of being consecrated in all the priesthoods, and in addition having the power to grant most of these to others (and even if two or three persons are co-emperors, one of these is *pontifex maximus*), they are masters of everything both sacred and profane.

The tribunician power, as it is called, which once those who were the most influential possessed, gives them the power to nullify the measures taken by any other official, if they do not approve, and protects them from injury;[5] and if they think they are wronged even in the slightest, not merely by deeds but even by words, they have the power to destroy the culprit without a trial as one accursed[6].... And it is by the tribunician power that they number the years of their rule....

Thus through these republican titles they have invested themselves with all the power of the state, so that they have the powers of kings without the usual title of king. The appellation "Caesar" or "Augustus" gives them no additional actual power but rather shows succession in the family line, and the splendor of their status. And the title "Father" [of his Country][7] perhaps gives them some authority over all of us, such as the authority which fathers once had over their children....

Augustus did not enact all laws on his own authority, but some he brought before the people, so that if anything was not suitable, he might correct it by foreknowledge. And he encouraged everyone whatsoever to give him counsel, if anyone of them thought of anything better, and he accorded them great freedom of speech, and he even changed some provisions. But most importantly, he joined to himself as advisors for periods of six months[8] the consuls, or the consul whenever he himself was consul, and from the other magistrates one from each office, and from the body of the senators fifteen chosen by lot, so that through them all legislation was customarily communicated in some manner to all the others.... And sometimes he sat in trials with them.

Indeed, the entire Senate — as previously — also sat in trials, and in certain matters dealt with embassies and messengers from both peoples and kings. The people and the plebs still met for elections; however, nothing was done which did not please him. At any rate, in the case of magistrates he himself selected and nominated some,[9] and though in the case of others he followed the age-old practice by leaving these to the people and the plebs, he took care that none who were unsuitable should be elected, or chosen as the result of partisan cliques or bribery.

B
Honors to Augustus

The myth of the virtues inherent in the Roman emperor begins with Augustus. The honors accorded the cardinal virtues of Augustus were intended to create the image of a leader equal to his goal of laying the moral foundations of a new society, but also to raise him above other mortals. On the virtues of Augustus, see also the *Res Gestae Divi Augustis* (no. 18 below).

Ehrenberg-Jones no. 22

This Latin inscription below, found in 1951 at Arles in southern France in the ruins of a temple of Augustus, was on a replica of the golden shield awarded to Augustus. The date is 26 BC.

The Senate and the Roman people gave the shield of virtue to Imperator Caesar Augustus, son of a god, consul eight times, on account of his virtue, clemency, justice, and devotion to gods and country.

Suetonius, *Life of Augustus* chapter 58

The title *pater patriae* (or *parens patriae*), which had often been accorded to Romans in the republican period (e.g., to Cicero and Caesar), was bestowed on Augustus in 2 BC. The extension to "Father of the World" was made during his lifetime (cf. Ovid, *Fasti* Book 2 verse 130).

The title "Father of his Country" was proffered to him by everybody, with a sudden and universal consensus, first by the plebs in a delegation sent to Antium; then, because he kept refusing it, at Rome as he was entering to view the games, in throngs wearing laurel wreaths; soon after in the senate house by the Senate, not by a decree nor by acclamation, but through Valerius Messala who with unanimous consent declared: "Good fortune and divine favor be yours and that of your house, Caesar Augustus! For it is thus we deem we are praying for everlasting prosperity for our country and for happiness for this city; the Senate, in accord with the Roman people, hails you 'Father of Our Country.' " Augustus in tears answered him as follows (I have recorded his words verbatim, as I have Messala's): "Having achieved my highest hopes, Senators, what more do I have to pray for to the immortal gods but that I may retain this consensus of yours to the very end of my life."

Macrobius, *Saturnalia* Book 1 chapter 12.35

By an earlier decree of the Senate, in 8 BC, the name of the month August was formalized in the calendar. The Senate may have acted in order not to be outdone by the calendar revision in the Province of Asia in 9 BC (see below no. 34). The *Saturnalia* of Macrobius (early fourth century AD) is a compendium of information on a great variety of topics.

Whereas Imperator Caesar Augustus entered upon his first consulship in the month Sextilis, and conducted three triumphs into the city, and the legions were brought down from the Janiculum Hill and accepted his auspices and oath, and also Egypt was subjected to the power of the Roman people in this month, and in this month an end was put to the civil wars;

And whereas for these reasons this month is and has been most fortunate for this empire, the Senate decreed that this month should be named Augustus.

C
Typical Inscriptions concerning Augustus

American Journal of Philology
Vol. xc (1969), pp. 178–182 = Ehrenberg-Jones no. 12.

Set up after Actium, at the site of the city Nicopolis founded there in 29 BC.

Dedicated to Neptune and Mars: Imperator Caesar, son of deified Julius, having attained victory in the war which he waged for the Republic in this region, when he was consul for the fifth time and imperator for the seventh time, when peace was won on land and sea, adorned with spoils the camp from which he had set out and dedicated this.

Ehrenberg-Jones no. 14 = Dessau, *ILS* no. 91

On an obelisk in Rome brought from Egypt; the date of the inscription is 10/9 BC.

Imperator Caesar Augustus, son of a god, *pontifex maximus,* hailed imperator twelve times, consul eleven times, holding the tribunician power for the fourteenth year, having reduced Egypt to the power of the Roman people, gave this as a gift to the Sun.

Ehrenberg-Jones no. 40

On the trophy of Augustus at La Turbie, in the Maritime, Alps, near Monaco, set up 7/6 BC.

To Imperator Caesar Augustus, son of a god, *pontifex maximus,* hailed imperator fourteen times, holding the tribunician power for the seventeenth year, the Senate and the Roman people set this up because under his leadership and auspices all the Alpine tribes from the Adriatic to the Tyrrhenian Sea were subjected to the empire of the Roman people. The conquered Alpine tribes: [a list of forty-five tribes follows, in geographical order from east to west].

Agrippa, veiled, in a procession of priests and members of the imperial family, from the Altar of the Augustan Peace.
Courtesy of Fratelli Alinari, Rome

4

THE HELPERS OF
AUGUSTUS

A
Agrippa

For three decades, until his sudden death at the age of fifty-one, Marcus Agrippa was the closest friend and associate of Augustus. A "new man," like many others in Augustus' entourage, he distinguished himself as a famed general and Rome's greatest admiral, as a provincial administrator and imperial geographer, as a city-planner and builder. In 21 BC he became the son-in-law of the *princeps* and presumptive successor, occupying the position of "vice-emperor." His great fortune (see no. 22 B below) was expended largely on adorning and building up the capital city and on benefactions to many other cities in Italy and the empire. At his death in 12 BC the buoyancy and dynamism of the new order began to fade away. It was said of Agrippa later that he "was the only one of all whom the civil wars had made famous and powerful who was felicitous for the public good." (Seneca, *Moral Epistles* no. 94 chapter 46).

Dio Cassius, *History of Rome* Book 49 chapter 43

The next year [33 BC] Agrippa volunteered to become aedile.[10] Without receiving anything from the public treasury he repaired all the public buildings, and all the streets and the sewers, and sailed through them into the Tiber. And seeing that people in the circus made mistakes regarding the number of laps, he set up the dolphins and the egg-shaped devices, so that with them the laps of the races might be indicated. And in addition he distributed olive oil and salt to all, and provided baths free all year to both men and women. And in connection with the festivals which he provided in great number and of all kinds (even the game of Troy, performed by the sons of senators), he hired barbers, so that no one should have to pay anything to them. And finally he scattered tickets in the theater over their heads, some of them providing money, some clothing, or something else; and placing all sorts of other wares in their midst, he allowed them to scramble for them. Besides doing these things, Agrippa also drove out the astrologers and magicians from the city....

Pliny, *Natural History* Book 36 chapter 121

Agrippa in his aedileship added the Aqua Virgo,[11] and joined other aqueducts together and repaired them, and constructed 700 basins, and in addition 500 water fountains and 130 catchbasins, many of them magnificently adorned. And on these works he placed 300 bronze or marble statues, and 400 marble pillars, and all this in one year's time. He himself adds in the memoirs of his aedileship that games were held for a full fifty-nine days, and that baths to the number of 170 were provided free of charge....

Frontinus, *Aqueducts of Rome* Book 2 chapter 98

Marcus Agrippa, after the aedileship which he held as ex-consul, was the first to be a sort of permanent curator of his works and services. Since the water supply now permitted it, he assigned what water should be allotted to public works, how much to the basins, and how much to private persons. He also had a slave gang of his own for the aqueducts, which maintained the aqueducts and the reservoirs and basins. This slave gang was made public property by Augustus, who had received it as an inheritance from Agrippa.

Dio Cassius, *History of Rome* (Cf. no 22 B below.)

(Book 53 chapter 27) Meanwhile, Agrippa adorned the city at his own expense. For one thing he completed the building of the Portico of Neptune, in honor of his naval victories, and added brilliance to it with the painting of the Argonauts. Then he constructed the Laconian hot bath.... And he completed the so-called Pantheon[12].... Agrippa wished to set up a statue of Augustus there, and to name the structure after him, but when Augustus would not accept either he placed in the temple itself a statue of the former Caesar, and in the vestibule a statue of Augustus and one of himself. And this was done not out of rivalry on Agrippa's part, so as to compete with Augustus, but out of his unswerving loyalty to him and out of constant zeal for the public interest....

(Book 52 Chapter 12.2 – 5.) Agrippa was advanced by Augustus to supreme power, after a fashion. For Augustus, seeing that public affairs required unrelenting attention, feared that, as tends to happen to such men, he would be conspired against.... He first added five years to his own Principate, since his ten-year term was expiring (this took place in the consulship of Publius and Gnaeus Lentulus [18 BC]); then he granted to Agrippa also other powers about equal to his own, especially the tribunician power for the same length of time....

(Book 54 Chapter 28.1 – 29.2) Meanwhile [12 BC] Augustus enhanced the status of Agrippa, who had come back from Syria, by giving him the tribunician power again for another five years, and sent him out to Pannonia, which was on the verge of war, granting him *imperium* greater than that of officials everywhere outside of Italy.... Agrippa returned [from Pannonia], and when he was in Campania, he fell ill. Learning of this, Augustus ... set out, and finding him already dead, he had his body carried to the city, and caused it to lie in state in the Forum. He spoke the eulogy over him, with a curtain hanging in front of the corpse.... [13] And he conducted his funeral in the same manner in which his own was later conducted, and he buried him in his own mausoleum, even though Agrippa had provided his own in the Campus Martius.

Such was the end of Agrippa, who had become clearly in every way the noblest man of his time, and used the friendship of Augustus for the greatest advantage to Augustus himself and to the country. For the more he surpassed others in virtue, the more he voluntarily kept himself below Augustus, and, devoting all his wisdom and valor to the highest advantages of Augustus, he expended all the honor and power he received from him upon benefactions to others.

Zeitschrift für Papyrologie und Epigraphik Vol. 5 (1970), pp. 217–283; Vol. 6 (1970), pp. 227–243

This is a papyrus fragment of the funeral oration of Augustus over Agrippa, in a Greek translation.

The tribunician power was given to you for five years, in accordance with a decree of the Senate in the consulship of the Lentuli [18 BC]. And again the same power was granted for another five-year term in the consulship of Tiberius Nero and Quinctilius Varus [13 BC], your sons-in-law.[14] And it was confirmed by a law that into whatever provinces the affairs of the Roman people might take you no one in those provinces should have greater power than you.... [The rest is fragmentary.]

Babylonian Talmud, Tractate Abuda Zara Book 4 chapter 7

Agrippa, the Roman general, asked the great rabbi Gamaliel:[15] It states in your law: "The Lord thy god is a consuming fire, a jealous god." In our everyday life we find it to be the rule that a man of power is jealous of his equal, a wise man of another wise man, a hero of another hero, a rich man of another rich man. Now if your god is jealous of an idol, the idol must have some power."

Bulletin de Correspondance Hellénique Vol. L (1926), pp. 447–448, nos. 88–89=Ehrenberg-Jones no. 76; Thespiae, Greece, ca. 13 BC

The people [honor] Agrippina, daughter of Marcus Agrippa.
The people [honor] Marcus Agrippa, son of Lucius, dedicated to the Muses.
The people, Lucius Caesar.
The people, Gaius Caesar.
The people, Julia, daughter of Imperator Caesar Augustus, wife of Marcus Agrippa, dedicated to the Muses.
The people, Livia, wife of Imperator Caesar Augustus, dedicated to the Muses.

Dessau, *ILS* no. 8897 = Ehrenberg-Jones no. 71; Ephesus, (Province of Asia), 4/3 BC

To Imperator Caesar Augustus, son of a god, *pontifex maximus*, consul twelve times, holding the tribunician power for the twentieth year, and to Livia, wife of Caesar Augustus.

To Marcus Agrippa, son of Lucius, consul three times, hailed imperator, tribunician power six years, and to Julia, daughter of Caesar Augustus.

Mazaeus and Mithridates to their patrons....

B
Maecenas

Trusted friend and counselor of Augustus, representative of the *princeps* in negotiations involving various political and personal disputes, Maecenas was also the leading patron of letters during the age; Vergil, Horace, Propertius, and several other major and minor figures of the period were members of his literary circle. An indiscretion on Maecenas's part in 23 BC. caused Augustus to drop him from the inner counsels of the Principate. (See no. 37 below.)

Dio Cassius, *History of Rome*

(Book 51 Chapter 3, 5–6.) Caesar, however, was suspicious of them,[16] and fearing that Maecenas, to whom he had entrusted at that time Rome and the rest of Italy, would be looked down upon by them since he was only of equestrian rank, he sent Agrippa to Italy ostensibly for some other purpose. He also gave Agrippa and Maecenas so much power in all matters that they might read beforehand the letters that he had written to the Senate and to others, and thus change whatever they wanted. For this reason they also received from him a seal-ring with which they could reseal the letters.

(Book 55 chapter 7.1–5) Augustus lamented the passing of Maecenas [8 BC], for he had received many benefits from him, and for this reason he had entrusted to him (although he was a member of the Equestrian Order) the city's administration for an extended period. Maecenas was particularly serviceable to him at times in view of his own rather uncontrollable temper. For he always was able to dispel his anger and turn him to a gentler mood. For example, once, coming upon him as he was holding court and seeing that he was about to pass the death sentence upon many men, Maecenas attempted to push his way through the bystanders and come near him. Being unable to do so, he wrote the following on a tablet, "Rise at last, O public executioner." He then threw it in his lap (as if it contained some other matter), with the result that Augustus had no one put to death, and immediately got up and left. In fact, he was not at all annoyed at such actions, but was actually happy, because, whenever he become unduly angered because of his nature or the stress of affairs, these were corrected by the freedom of speech of his friends. This was the supreme proof of Maecenas's excellence, that he ingratiated himself with Augustus although he countered his impulsive actions and pleased all the others. Maecenas was particularly influential with him, so that he was able to obtain for many men offices and political power, yet he was not pretentious, but remained to the end of his life in the Equestrian Order. For these reasons Augustus missed him very much, and also because Maecenas, although he was annoyed at his wife's affair with Augustus, left his entire estate to him and empowered him (with few exceptions) to give something to any of his friends, or nothing, if he should so desire.

5
THE SENATORIAL ORDER

A
The Role of The Senate

The centuries-old traditional role of the Senate as governing body of the Roman Empire was ended by the Augustan Principate. This controlling force was removed from the center of power and transformed by Augustus into a semi-hereditary new form of aristocracy, a fusion of the older nobility with many "new men" from less prestigious families that had supported the *princeps* in his rise to power. The Senatorial Order served the empire and the emperor in the highest administrative and military posts, and the Senate as a body was the principal legislative arm of the *princeps*, even serving as a court of justice in important criminal cases. Members of the Senatorial Order stood at the apex of the empire's hierarchical structure, forming the social and economic elite. A property qualification of 1,000,000 sesterces was required, and Augustus was frequently called upon to help out of his own purse to maintain this sum for certain families. It was Augustus's policy also to tie these powerful families to himself by a network of marriage alliances. "The schemes devised by Augustus in the ramification of family alliances were formidable and fantastic. He neglected no relative, however obscure, however distant, no tie whatever of marriage...." (R. Syme, *The Roman Revolution* [Oxford, 1939], p. 387.)

Dio Cassius, *History of Rome* Book 52 chapter 42, 1–8

Augustus ... purged the Senate. For many Equestrians and those of lower rank were in the Senate without merit on account of the civil wars, so that the complement of the Senate had grown to 1,000... And he made some others senators; he enrolled among those of consular rank two men of the Senatorial Order, a certain

Gaius Cluvius and a certain Gaius Furnius, because, although previously elected, they were not able to hold the consulship because others had usurped their office. And he increased the patrician families, presumably so authorized by a decree of the Senate, because most of them had perished (indeed no group is so wasted in our civil wars as the nobility), and because they are considered to be necessary for the performance of ancient institutions. In addition to these measures, he also forbade all the senators to leave Italy unless he personally ordered or permitted them to do so. And this is still preserved down to the present, for it is not permitted to a senator to leave the country anywhere at all except to Sicily and Narbonese Gaul. Because of the closeness of these provinces and because the inhabitants are unarmed and peaceful, it has been granted to those senators who have property there to go there without requesting permission, whenever they wish. And since he saw that many of the senators and others who had been adherents of Antony were still suspiciously disposed to him, and he feared they might cause a revolution, he announced that all the letters found in Antony's archives had been burned....

Suetonius, *Life of Augustus* chapters 35–37

Augustus provided that stated meetings of the Senate be held not more than twice a month, on the Kalends and Ides, and that in the months of September and October only those chosen by lot should be obligated to be present, to provide a quorum sufficient for making decrees. He also established for himself advisory councils chosen by lot, for six-month terms, with whom he might handle in advance business to be referred to the full Senate....

He was also the initiator of other matters, among them the following: that proceedings of the Senate should not be made public; that magistrates should not be sent to the provinces directly upon laying down their office; that fixed sums be determined for proconsuls for mules and tents, which used to be contracted for at public expense; that control of the treasury should be transferred from the urban quaestors to ex-praetors or praetors....

In order that more persons might have a role in administering the state, he devised new offices: the curatorships of public building, of roads, of aqueducts, of the channel of the Tiber, of distribution of grain to the people; the prefecture of the city; a board of three for organizing the Senate; and another for reviewing the companies of equestrians, whenever necessary. He arranged for censors to be chosen, an office which had lapsed for a long time. He increased the number of praetors....

B
Senatorial Careers

Next to those given the emperor, the most grandiose titles in Roman inscriptions appear in the commemorative records of Roman senators.

Dessau, *ILS* no. 886 = Ehrenberg-Jones no. 187; Gaeta, Italy; after 22 BC

Lucius Munatius Plancus, son of Lucius, grandson of Lucius, great-grandson of Lucius, consul, censor, hailed imperator twice, member of the Board of Seven for Sacrificial Feasts, having triumphed over the Rhaetians, he built the temple of Saturn from the booty. He assigned land in Italy, at Beneventum, and in Gaul he established colonies at Lugdunum and Raurica.

Dessau, *ILS* no. 915 = Ehrenberg-Jones no. 197; Histonium, Italy

Publius Paquius Scaeva, son of Scaeva and Flavia, grandson of Consus and Didia, great-grandson of Barbus and Dirutia, quaestor, in accordance with a decree of the Senate made member of the Board of Ten for Judging Cases after his quaestorship, member of the Board of Four for Judging Capital Cases (in accordance with a decree of the Senate after the quaestorship and membership in the Board of Ten for Judging Cases), tribune of the plebs, curule aedile, judge of the criminal court, praetor of the treasury, proconsul of the Province of Cyprus, curator of roads outside the city of Rome in accordance with a decree of the Senate for five years, proconsul second time (extraordinary, by authority of Augustus Caesar and a decree of the Senate), sent to settle affairs in the rest of the Province of Cyprus, fetial. Cousin and also husband of Flavia, daughter of Consus, granddaughter of Scapula, great-granddaughter of Barbus, buried here with her....

Dessau, *ILS* no. 928 = Ehrenberg-Jones no. 202; Athens.

To Lucius Aquillius Florus Tircianus Gallus, son of Gaius, of the Pomptine tribe, member of the Board of Ten for Judging Cases, tribune of the soldiers of Legion VIII Macedonica, quaestor of Imperator Caesar Augustus, proquaestor of the Province of Cyprus, tribune of the plebs, praetor, proconsul of Achaea....

Dessau, *ILS* no. 932 = Ehrenberg-Jones no. 205; Superaequum, in the Paelignian region of Italy.

To Quintus Varius Geminus, son of Quintus, legate of the deified Augustus twice, proconsul, praetor, tribune of the plebs, quaestor in charge of criminal investigations, prefect for distribution of grain, member of the Board of Ten for Judging Cases, curator for the protection of sacred shrines and public monuments. He was the first of all the Paelignians to become a senator and to hold these offices. The Superaequanians to their patron, at public expense.

6

CAREERS IN THE EQUESTRIAN ORDER

Augustus, with his predilection for hierarchy, transformed the Roman middle class, known as equestrians, into a distinctive elite social order. Previously a financial and business class, it was absorbed into the imperial service, directly responsible to the *princeps*. The property qualification was a minimum worth of 400,000 sesterces, but official public careers for these men were available to talent. They were given access to middle-grade administrative and military posts (as junior officers in the legions); in the imperial provinces they were appointed as procurators, serving as imperial financial agents or administrators of small provinces or of provincial districts. At the apex of the equestrian career were the prefectures of high government bureaus in Rome, such as the night patrol, grain supply, and of the imperial Praetorian Guard. Highest of all these was the post of Prefect of Egypt, a governorship open only to equestrians. They were also called upon to serve as select jurors in cases involving public law. The members of the order, like the senators, wore distinctive garb and status symbols and proudly displayed their careers on their monuments.

Dessau, *ILS* no. 9007 = Ehrenberg-Jones no. 224; Superaequum, in the Paelignian region of Italy.

Quintus Octavius Sagitta, son of Lucius, grandson of Gaius, great-grandson of Lucius, of the Sergian tribe, fifth-year duovir for the third time, prefect of the construction corps, praetor of the cavalry, people's tribune of the soldiers, procurator of Caesar Augustus in the territory of the Vindelicians and the Rhaetians and in the Poenine Valley for four years, and in the Province of Spain for ten years, and in Syria for two years.

Dessau, *ILS* no. 2683; = Ehrenberg-Jones no. 231; origin unknown.

Quintus Aemilius Secundus, son of Quintus, of the Palatine tribe, decorated with insignia in the camp of the deified Augustus under Publius Sulpicius Quirinius, legate of Caesar, prefect of a cohort of the Legion I Augusta, prefect of the naval cohort II. Likewise, by order of Quirinius, I conducted the census of 117,000 citizens of the city of Apamea. Likewise, I was sent by Quirinius against the Ituraeans in Mount Lebanon, and I captured their fort. And before my military career I was prefect of the construction corps, and was recommended by two consuls for financial reward. And in the colony I was quaestor, twice aedile, twice duumvir, *pontifex*. Here are buried Quintus Aemilius Secundus, son of Quintus, of the Palatine tribe, and Aemilia Chia, his freedwoman....

Dessau, *ILS* no. 8995 = Ehrenberg-Jones no. 21

Augustus in 30 BC appointed as the first governor of the newly annexed province of Egypt his friend Cornelius Gallus, poet, soldier, friend of Vergil. While establishing the Roman administrative and taxation system in the province, Gallus had to deal with a rebellion in the Thebaïd, and in the course of those military activities he advanced to the First Cataract of the Nile, where in 29 BC he set up at Philae the boastful inscription given below. (It was inscribed in Latin, Greek, and Egyptian hieroglyphics.) Before long he was recalled by the *princeps*, perhaps because of his bid for independent fame; all his political power was curtailed, and he was accused before Augustus of charges whose nature we no longer can discern. After a trial before the Senate in 26 BC he was condemned to exile and confiscation of his property, but committed suicide.

Gaius Cornelius Gallus, son of Gnaeus, Roman equestrian, as first prefect of Alexandria and Egypt after the victory of Caesar, son of a god, over the kings,[17] during the revolt of the Thebaïd in which he conquered the enemy within fifteen days, he was twice victor on the battlefield; he took by storm five cities, Boresis, Coptus, Ceramice, Diospolis Magna, Ophieus, capturing the leaders of this revolt. He led an army beyond the cataract of the Nile, where previously no armed forces, neither of the Roman people nor of the kings of Egypt had penetrated. He subdued the Thebaid, the continuing threat to all the kings. He gave audience to the envoys of the king of the Ethiopians at Philae, and received that king under his protection, and appointed him ruler of the "Thirty-schoenium Land"[18] of Ethiopia. Dedicated to his ancestral gods and to the Nile his helper.

7
ARMED FORCES

After the demobilization of the huge armies of the last decade of the Republic and the early Principate, Augustus stabilized the armed forces of the empire at about 300,000 men. These constituted a standing army of professional soldiers under personal oath to him, who defended the frontiers, policed the provinces, and fought his wars. In and near Rome were stationed the elite bodyguard of the *princeps*, the Praetorian Guard of about 9,000. The outlay for the military was the largest item in the imperial budget. After 6 AD, through the newly organized Military Treasury, veterans received their bonuses in cash, rather than in land grants in military colonies as they had previously.

Suetonius, *Life of Augustus* chapter 49.1–2

Of his military forces Augustus assigned the legions and auxiliary troops province by province and stationed a fleet at Misenum and a second at Ravenna to guard the Adriatic and Tyrrhenian Seas; and in addition there was a detachment partly for the defense of the city and partly for his own protection.... However, he never permitted more than three cohorts in the city, and these without a camp; the others he used to send to winter and summer quarters in the neighboring towns. Moreover, all the soldiers everywhere were held to a fixed scale of pay and bonuses, determined for each rank by length of military service and the advantageous terms of discharge, to prevent them after discharge from being stirred up to revolution by either age or poverty.

Dio Cassius, *History of Rome* Book 55 chapters 23–25

The soldiers were very much dissatisfied with the small size of the rewards for the wars then [5 AD] waged, and none was willing to stay in service beyond his regular term of enlistment. It was therefore voted to give members of the Praetorian Guard 20,000 sesterces when they had served sixteen years, and 12,000 sesterces to the others after twenty years of service. Twenty-three legions of citizen soldiers (or twenty-five, as others say)[19] were then being maintained.... There were also allied troops — infantry, cavalry, naval, whatever their number was, for I cannot give the exact figure.[20] There were also the bodyguards, 10,000 in number, organized in ten cohorts, and the urban cohorts, 6,000 in number, organized in four units....

Lacking funds, Augustus introduced a motion into the Senate that revenue in sufficient amount and of a permanent nature be sequestered, so that the soldiers might methodically receive their maintenance and bonuses from taxes, without any external source being put under strain. The means were being sought.... In the consulship of Aemilius Lepidus and Lucius Arruntius [6 AD], when no revenues [for the military fund] were found that satisfied anyone, but everybody indeed was annoyed that this was being sought. Augustus deposited, in his own name and that of Tiberius, moneys into the treasury which he called the Military Treasury, and assigned the administration of it to three ex-praetors, chosen by lot for three years, each employing two lictors and other appropriate assistance.... Now Augustus contributed to this treasury, and promised that he would do so annually, and accepted pledges toward it from kings and some communities. But he accepted nothing from private persons, though quite a large number made offers voluntarily, at least so they said. But since the sums were small in relation to the size of what was being spent, and a permanent source was needed, he ordered the senators, each privately and by himself, to seek out revenues, and to set down their plans in writing and submit them to him for his consideration. He did this not because he had no plan of his own, but so that he might persuade them to choose his particular plan. At any rate, after various plans had been proposed, he approved none of them, but established the five-percent tax on inheritances and gifts which people at their death left to any except their closest relatives and to the poor....

35

8

PROPAGANDA ON COINS

From the beginning of his career Augustus worked tirelessly to win over men's minds. During his long tenure of power Augustus left no available propaganda medium untapped: literature (which reached only a tiny elite); monuments (each unique and therefore effective only locally); sculpture and inscriptions (of wider impact because they could be multiplied); and coins (which, of course, had enormously wide distribution).

The use of coins as propaganda vehicles by Augustus constituted the greatest exploitation of coinage for this purpose in world history. Beginning in 31 BC Augustus began to employ coinage for this new purpose: to mould public opinion throughout the empire now under his command, thus establishing a policy followed by all Roman emperors thereafter. The messages (and the pictorial symbols) used by Augustus on coins were carefully controlled; they were intended to announce the achievements, political manifestoes, and promises of his Principate and to make familiar the political vocabulary of the new order. "The imperial coinage furnishes what is at once the most voluminous, most constant, the most official and most accurate series of documents which have come down to us. It was planned for an audience of countless thousands, all of whom ... looked to the *princeps* as the apex of a political system on which depended the stability of the civilized world...."(C.H.V. Sutherland, *Coinage in Roman Imperial Policy,* 31 BC–AD 68 [London, 1951], p.184.)

The small selection from Augustus's coinage that follows has been excerpted from Harold Mattingly, *Coins of the Roman Empire in the British Museum. Vol I: Augustus to Vitellius* (London, 1923). Generalized obverses or reverses have been omitted.

Mattingly, no. 691; mint of Ephesus, 28 BC.
Obverse: Head of Augustus. IMPERATOR CAESAR, SON OF A GOD, CONSUL VI, CHAMPION OF THE LIBERTY OF THE ROMAN PEOPLE.
Reverse: Goddess of Peace, with caduceus, snake in mystic box. PEACE.

36

No. 647; Eastern mints, 29–27 BC.
Obverse: Head of Augustus. CAESAR, IMPERATOR VII. *Reverse: Goddess of Victory with wreath and palm, mystic box, two snakes.* ASIA RECOVERED.

No. 650; Eastern mints, 28 BC.
Obverse: Head of Augustus. CAESAR, CONSUL VI. *Obverse: Crocodile.* EGYPT CAPTURED.

No. 737; Mint of Pergamum, 23 BC.
Obverse: Head of Augustus. IMPERATOR AUGUSTUS, TRIBUNICIAN POWER. *Reverse: Oak wreath, two laurel branches.* FOR SAVING CITIZENS.

No. 696; mint of Ephesus, 27–26 BC.
Obverse: Head of Augustus. IMPERATOR CAESAR. *Reverse: Capricorn, cornucopia, laurel wreath.* AUGUSTUS.

No. 703; Mint of Ephesus, 19–8 BC.
Obverse: Head of Augustus. IMPERATOR IX, TRIBUNICIAN POWER V. *Reverse: Triumphal arch with chariot on top, eagle.* IMPERATOR IX, TRIBUNICIAN POWER V. THE SENATE AND ROMAN PEOPLE. THE STANDARDS RECOVERED.

No. 676; Eastern mints, 20–18 BC.
Obverse: Head of Augustus. AUGUSTUS. *Reverse: Armenian with bow and spear.* CAESAR, SON OF A GOD, IMPERATOR VIIII. ARMENIA CAPTURED.

No. 10; Senatorial mint of Rome, 18 BC.
Reverse: Parthian kneeling, extending a standard. CAESAR AUGUSTUS. THE STANDARDS RECOVERED.

No. 427; Spanish mint 18/17 BC.
Obverse: Head of Augustus. S.P.Q.R. IMPERATOR CAESAR AUGUSTUS, CONSUL XI, TRIBUNICIAN POWER VI. *Reverse: Triumphal arch with chariot on top.* CITIZENS AND MILITARY STANDARDS RECOVERED FROM THE PARTHIANS.

No. 69; mint of Rome, 17 BC.
Obverse: Herald with caduceus and round shield. AUGUSTUS, SON OF A GOD, THE SECULAR GAMES.

No. 498; imperial mint of Lugdunum, 8(?) BC.
Obverse: Head of Augustus. AUGUSTUS, SON OF A GOD. *Reverse: Gaius Caesar on horse, with sword and shield, eagle between two standards.* GAIUS CAESAR, SON OF AUGUSTUS.

No. 513; mint of Lugdunum, 2 BC—11 AD.
Obverse: Head of Augustus. CAESAR AUGUSTUS, SON OF A GOD, FATHER OF HIS COUNTRY. *Reverse: Gaius and Lucius Caesar, with shields and spears.* GAIUS AND LUCIUS CAESAR, SONS OF AUGUSTUS, CONSULS DESIGNATE, LEADERS OF THE YOUTH.

No. 508; mint of Lugdunum, 13—14 AD.
Obverse: Head of Augustus. CAESAR AUGUSTUS, SON OF A GOD, FATHER OF HIS COUNTRY. *Reverse: Tiberius on triumphal chariot, with laurel branch and scepter surmounted by eagle.* TIBERIUS CAESAR, SON OF AUGUSTUS, TRIBUNICIAN POWER XV.

Coins of the Augustan Age: A = Mattingly, No. 612 (see no. 8) Obverse: Goddess Peace. Reverse: Octavian   B = Mattingly, 6/7 Obverse: Winged Victory. Reverse: Augustus on chariot   C = Mattingly, No. 650
D = Mattingly, No. 691
Courtesy of The American Numismatic Society, New York

9
REVIVAL OF ROMAN RELIGION

The Augustan regime is a classic example of the alliance of "throne and altar." The disasters at the end of the Republic were viewed by many Romans as divine punishment for national sin, and they were receptive to a cleansing of guilt. As an important aspect of the reconstruction of orderly society, Augustus vigorously promoted the restoration of the decaying Roman state religion. Obsolete religious institutions — rituals, priesthoods, festivals — were methodically revived as a matter of public policy. Visible proof was a wave of temple repairing and new temple building. Two significant innovations emerged: Augustus's special favor to his personal god Apollo (together with his sister and mother, Diana and Latona) with its cult center on the Palatine Hill, forming a sort of imperial cult rivaling the center of the state religion on the Capitoline Hill; and the irresistible spread of the worship of the living emperor, despite official deprecation.

A
The Ancestral State Cult

Suetonius, *Life of Augustus* chapter 31

The office of *pontifex maximus* he finally assumed after Lepidus'[21] death (he had not undertaken to deprive him of this in his lifetime). He then collected from all places whatever prophetic books of Greek or Latin type were in circulation either anonymously or under the names of unqualified authors, and burned more than 2,000 of them, preserving only the Sibylline Books, and even from these he made a selection. These he deposited in two gilded bookshelves in the basement of the temple of the Palatine Apollo.... He increased the number, the prestige, and the privileges of the priests, particularly of the Vestal Virgins. When it was necessary to appoint another Vestal in place of one who had died, and many men used their influence to prevent their daughters from being included in the selection by lot, he swore that if any of his grand-daughters had the age requirement, he would have offered her. He also revived some of the ancient religious ceremonies that had gradually become obsolete, such as the augury of Safety,[22] the office of the *flamen dialis*,[23] the festival of the Lupercalia,[24] the Secular Games, and the festival of the Compitalia.[25] At the Lupercalia he forbade beardless young men to make the run, and likewise at the Secular Games he prohibited the young of either sex to attend any night spectacle unless accompanied by an older relative. He began the practice of having the protecting gods of the crossroads decorated with flowers twice a year, in spring and in summer.

B
The Secular Games

In the spring of 17 BC Augustus celebrated spectacular, traditional Secular Games, last held in 146 BC. Since a *saeculum* was a period of about 100 years, the celebration should have been held in 46 BC, but the civil wars had prevented this. To justify the choice of 17 BC for ushering in a new century, Augustus arranged for a new definition of a *saeculum* as a of 110 years, and a revised secular series was promulgated for this purpose. The year 17 BC was a propitious time for Augustus: he had just adopted Gaius and Lucius Caesar; the war in Spain had finally ended; his moral legislation was on the books; and it was the tenth anniversary of the establishemnt of the Principate. To legitimate the celebration, a Sibylline oracle was "found" (the text is in Zosimus, *New History Book* 37 chapter 5.4) which spelled out in detail guidelines for the event. The proceedings were recorded for posterity on a huge marble inscription, part of which is given below.

CIL, Vol. VI no. 32,323 = Dessau, *ILS* no. 5050=*FIRA*, Vol. I, no. 40

May 25 in the Julian Voting Enclosure..., present at the writing were....Aemilius Lepidus, Lucius Cestius, Lucius Petronius Rufus....

Whereas the consul Gaius Silanus stated that after many years the Secular Games would take place this year, conducted by Imperator Caesar Augustus and Marcus Agrippa, holders of the tribunician power, and because it is proper that as many as possible view these games both out of religious duty and because no one will be present again at such a spectacle, it was deemed proper that those who were not yet married be present with impunity on the days of those games; and,

Whereas he asked the senators what was their pleasure regarding this matter, they decreed as follows: Since these games were established for religious reasons, and it is not granted to any mortal to view them more than once, it shall be permitted to those who are liable in accordance with the Law on Classes Permitted to Marry to view with impunity the games which the masters of the Board of Fifteen for Performing Sacrifices will present....

[Other decrees of the Senate and an edict of the Board of Fifteen, together with a description of the preparations for the festival follow, covering the period from May 25 to 31.]

On the following night [May 31] in the Campus Martius near the Tiber Imperator Caesar Augustus sacrificed as whole offering to the Fates, according to the Greek rite, nine ewes, and, according to the same rite, nine female goats, and he prayed as follows:

"O Fates! as it was written in those books,[26] and with regard to these matters may every good fortune come to the Roman people, the Quirites, let sacrifice be made to you of nine ewes and nine female goats. I ask and pray you, just as you increase the empire and majesty of the Roman people in war and peace, so may you always guard the Latin name, grant eternal safety, victory, health to the Roman people, the Quirites, and protect the Roman people, the Quirites, and the legions of the Roman people. And may you preserve the state of the Roman people, the Quirites, safe and sound; and may you be benevolent and propitious to the Roman people, the Quirites, to the Board of Fifteen, to me, my house and household. And deign to accept this sacrifice of nine ewes and nine female goats appropriate for sacrifice. With regard to this matter, be honored with the sacrifice of this ewe, and be and become benevolent and propitious to the Roman people, the

Quirites, to the Board of Fifteen, to me, my house and household."

After the completion of the sacrifice, plays were presented at night on a stage without the setting up of a theatre and without seats, and 110 matrons, who had been designated by the Board of Fifteen, held sacred banquets for the gods, setting up two seats for Juno and Diana.

On June 1 on the Capitoline Imperator Caesar Augustus sacrificed in whole offering a perfect bull to Jupiter Best and Greatest, and likewise Marcus Agrippa sacrificed a second bull, and they prayed as follows:

"O Jupiter Best and Greatest! As it was written for you in those books, and with regard to these matters may every good fortune come to the Roman people, the Quirites. Let a sacrifice be made to you with this beautiful bull. I ask and pray you." The rest as above.

At the sacred vessel were Caesar, Agrippa, Scaevola, Sentius, Lollius, Asinius Gallus, Rebilus.[27]

Then Latin games were presented on a wooden theater, which had been set up in the Campus Martius alongside the Tiber, and, in the same manner, matrons conducted sacred banquets for the gods, and the theatrical events which had been begun that night were not interrupted....

At night, moreover, near the Tiber Imperator Augustus Caesar made a sacrifice to the Ilithyiae[28] of nine sacrificial cakes, nine *popana* and nine *phthoes*,[29] and prayed as follows:

"O Ilithyia, as it was written in those books for you, and with regard to these matters may every good fortune come to the Roman people, the Quirites, let a sacrifice be made to you with nine *popana,* nine sacrificial cakes, and nine *phthoes.* I ask and pray you." The rest as above.

On June 2 on the Capitoline Imperator Caesar Augustus made a whole sacrifice of a cow to Queen Juno, likewise Marcus Agrippa a second one, and he prayed as follows:

"O Queen Juno! As it was written in those books for you, and with regard to these matters may every good fortune come to the Roman people, the Quirites, let a sacrifice be made to you with a beautiful cow. I ask and pray you." The rest as above.

Next Marcus Agrippa(?) led 110 married matrons, who had been designated ... in the following prayer:

"O Queen Juno! If there may be any better fortune for the Roman people, the Quirites..., we married matrons, kneeling, [ask and pray] you..., just as you have increased the empire and majesty of the Roman people, the Quirites, in war and peace, so may you ever protect the Latin name and grant eternal safety, victory, and health to the Roman people, the Quirites, and protect the Roman people, the Quirites, and the legions of the Roman people, the Quirites, and keep the state of the Roman people, the Quirites, safe and sound, that you be benevolent and propitious to the Roman people, the Quirites, to the Board of Fifteen for Making Sacrifices, to us.... These things we 110 married matrons of the Roman people, the Quirites, kneeling, ask and pray you."...

Further, at night near the Tiber Imperator Caesar Augustus made a whole sacrifice of a pregnant sow.... to Mother Earth, and prayed as follows:

"O Mother Earth! As it was written in those books for you, and with regard to these matters may every good fortune come to the Roman people, the Quirites, let a sacrifice be made to you with a proper pregnant sow ... I ask and pray you." The rest as above.

The matrons offered sacred banquets to the gods on this day in the same manner as on the preceding day.

On June 3 on the Palatine Imperator Caesar Augustus and Marcus Agrippa made a sacrifice to Apollo and Diana with nine sacrificial cakes, nine *popana* and nine *phthoes,* and prayed as follows:

"O Apollo! As it was written for you in those books, and with regard to this matter may every good fortune come to the Roman people, the Quirites, let a sacrifice be made to you with nine *popana,* nine sacrificial cakes, and nine *phthoes.* I ask and pray you." The rest as above.

"O Apollo! Just as I have prayed to you with a good prayer, offering sacrificial cakes, with regard to this same matter, be honored by the offering of these sacrificial cakes, and become benevolent and propitious."

Likewise with the *phthoes.*

43

To Diana with the same words.

And when the sacrifice was completed twenty-seven boys previously designated, with both parents alive, and the same number of girls, sang a hymn, and in the same manner on the Capitoline. Quintus Horatius Flaccus composed the hymn.

[The rest of the inscription deals with theatrical performances, chariot races, animal hunts and other events, lasting until June 12.]

C
The Centennial Hymn

Horace, *Carmen Saeculare*

Phoebus, and Diana, ruler over forests, radiant glory of heaven, both of you worshipped and to be worshipped forever, grant what we pray in a period of reverence, when the Sibylline verses have ordered selected virgins and chaste boys to sing a song to the gods who have favored the seven hills. Fostering Sun, you who introduce the day with your shining chariot and then conceal it, and who are reborn anew and are yet still the same, may you gaze upon nothing greater than the city Rome. Be gracious, Ilithyia, duly protect mothers to bear children in due season, whether you prefer to be called Lucina or Genitalis: goddess, rear our descendants and prosper the decrees of the fathers concerning marriages and the law of marriage for proliferation of new offspring, so that the determined cycle of ten times eleven years may bring again singing and games celebrated in throngs for three times in bright daylight and as many joyful nights. May you, too, O Fates, truthful in past predictions (may the fixed course of events preserve that which has been once ordained), now add favorable destinies to those already fulfilled. May the earth, fertile in fruits and rich in cattle, present to Ceres a garland of wheat-spikes; may both the healthful rains and breezes of Jove nourish the crops. Concealing your weapon, O Apollo, be kind and gracious, and hear the boys in supplications; and you, O Moon, crescent queen of the stars, listen to the virgins. O gods, if Rome is your making, and bands from Troy occupied the Etruscan coast, and the remnant ordered to change their homes and city in a savior journey, for whom through Troy ablaze righteous Aeneas, surviving his fatherland with integrity, paved a liberating road destined to give more than that left behind; O gods, make the youth teachable and grant them virtuous habits; O gods, grant peace and quiet to the aged, and to the Roman people bring prosperity, children and all glory. May the distinguished descendant of Anchises' and Venus' blood, victorious over the belligerent, but lenient to the prostrate enemy, win whatever he asks in reverent sacrifice of white bulls. The Parthian now fears the forces powerful on sea and land and the Italian weapons, and now Scythians and Indians, not long ago proud, seek out our responses. Now Faith and Peace and Honor and old-fashioned Modesty and neglected Virtue dare to return, and blessed Prosperity with full horn is here. Phoebus, the prophet, illustrious with the gleaming bow, dear to the nine Muses, who with his healing art relieves the weary limbs of the body, if he looks with favor on the altars of the Palatine, he keeps the Roman state and Latium prosperous for another century and an always better future; and Diana, who holds the Aventine and Mt. Algidus, heeds the prayers of the Board of Fifteen, and directs friendly ears to the devout entreaties of the children. I bring back home the good and steadfast hope that Jupiter and all the other gods are hearing these prayers, yes, I, a chorus trained to hymn the praises of Phoebus and Diana.

10
MORAL AND SOCIAL REFORMS

Augustus persistently sought to reverse the moral decay in Roman society by a legislative program designed to encourage marriage, increase the birth rate of the upper classes, and curb the massive influx of aliens into the Roman civic body (through manumissions of slaves). It was a bold attempt to reform society by placing the family as an institution under public supervision, and by enhancing the prestige of marriage and the begetting of children as a civic duty. After an abortive attempt in 28 BC — withdrawn after stiff opposition — Augustus launched his moral and social program in 18 BC with two formidable pieces of legislation: the Julian Law on Adultery (which defined adultery as essentially an offense of women, subject to criminal prosecution), and the Julian Law on Classes Permitted to Marry (moderated by the Papian-Poppaean Law of 9 AD). The laws were futile; vigorous opposition ensued and there were numerous evasions of and dispensations from the rigors of the laws. "Augustus reformed the state: he could not reform society. Public morality remained what it had been under the Republic." (P.A. Brunt, *Historia* Vol. 10 [1961], p. 221.)

A
Legislating Morality

Suetonius, *Life of Augustus* chapter 34

He revised the laws and promulgated some new ones, such as on extravagance, on adultery, on chastity, on bribery, and on marriages between the various classes. After he had amended the latter law with somewhat more severe provisions than the others, in the face of tumultuous demonstrations from opponents he was unable to enforce it until at length he had abrogated or mitigated a part of the penalties and had granted an exemption of three years before remarriage and had increased its rewards. And when even then the Equestrian Order stubbornly demanded its repeal at a public show, he had the children of Germanicus summoned and he exhibited them, some at his side, others in the lap of their father, indicating by his gesture and expression that they should not hesitate to imitate the example of the young father. And when he noticed that the effect of the law was being circumvented both by engagements to pre-puberty girls and by frequent changes in marriage partners, he curtailed long engagements and set a limit upon divorces.

B
Julian Law on Curbing Adultery

ADA, pp. 112–128

These words of the law, "No one hereafter shall knowingly and with malice aforethought commit debauchery or adultery," pertain to him who has encouraged or to him who has committed debauchery or adultery.

The Julian Law on Curbing Adultery punishes not only those violating the wives of others but also punishes the criminal offense of debauchery, namely, when anyone without recourse to force violates either a virgin or a widow leading a respectable and decent life.

By the second section of the law, 'a father, if he catches an adulterer of his daughter ... in his own home or the home of his son-in-law, or if the son-in-law summons his father-in-law in this matter, is allowed to kill not only this adulterer without legal risk but also may kill his daughter on the spot.

The husband also is permitted to kill an adulterer of his wife, but not anyone at all, as is the case with a father. For the law provides that a husband may kill a procurer, [actor, gladiator, convicted felon], freedman [of the immediate family], or a slave caught in the act of adultery with his wife in his own home [but not in the home of his father-in-law].

But it provides that a husband who has killed any of these is to divorce his wife without delay. He must make declaration to the person who has jurisdiction in the area where the killing took place, and he must divorce his wife; if he fails to do this, he does not kill with impunity.

The fifth section of the Julian Law provides for the husband the right without legal risk to detain an adulterer of his wife caught in the act, whom he is either unwilling to or may not kill, for no more than twenty consecutive hours of the day and night for the purpose of obtaining witnesses in this case.

The Julian Law on Adultery specifically prohibits accusations of adultery against certain persons, such as a person under twenty-five.

The law provides that no one may cite a person as a defendant who at the time was absent on public business without being excused.

According to a provision of the law, women also are to be arrested who furnished their home or received anything in return for debauchery that was detected.

The law punishes as a procurer a husband who retains his wife although she has been caught in adultery and lets the adulterer go (for he ought to be enraged at his wife, too, who violated his marriage). In such a case the husband is to be punished, for he cannot use ignorance as an excuse or pretend patience on the pretext of not believing [that adultery was committed].

He who makes a profit from the adultery of his wife is flogged.

If a wife receives payment from the adultery of her husband, under the Julian Law she is held liable as if she herself were an adulteress.

As the law states, if any man takes as wife a woman convicted of adultery, he is held liable under this law.

The charge of procuring is specified by the Julian Law on Adultery, as the penalty has been fixed by statute in the case of the husband who had made any profit from the adultery of his wife, and likewise in the case of the husband who retains a wife caught in adultery.

A person by whose assistance and advice with malice aforethought it happens that a man or woman caught in adultery escapes justice, through a bribe or some other collusion, is condemned to the same penalty which is specified for those who are convicted of the crime of procuring.

The Julian Law on Curbing Adultery also punishes those who dare to practice unspeakable lust with males. Whoever debauches a freeborn male against his will is liable to capital punishment. According to civil law, marriages between parents and children cannot be contracted.... It is not permitted a man to take as wife his mother-in-law, or daughter-in-law, or step-daughter, or step-mother at any time without the punishment [of the crime] of incest, just as [it is illegal to marry] one's aunt, paternal or maternal. Moreover, he who marries a cousin against the prohibition ... suffers the penalty of adultery according to the Julian Law.

It was enacted that women convicted of adultery be punished by confiscation of one-half of their dowry and one-third of their property, and by banishment to an island. For male adulterers, on the other hand, the punishment is a like banishment to an island (provided that they [i.e., adulterer and adulteress] be relegated to separate islands), and confiscation of half of their property.

The framers of the laws prescribe that, after a notice of divorce has been sent on suspicion of the crime of adultery, emancipation of slaves belonging to the wife or husband or their parents is to be delayed for a space of two months, counted from the date of notice of divorce, in order to set up an examination [of the slaves] under torture if the need should arise.

C
Julian Law on Marriage and Papian-Poppaean Law

ADA, pp. 166−198

In the Papian Law there is a provision that it is permissible to all freeborn except senators and their children to have a freed woman as wife.

The Julian Law provides as follows: no one who is a senator, or is or will be a son, or grandson of a son, or great-grandson born of a son's son of any one of these, shall knowingly and with malice aforethought take as betrothed or wife a freedwoman or a woman

49

who herself or whose father or mother engages or has engaged in acting. And no daughter of a senator, or granddaughter born of a son, or great-granddaughter born of a grandson (a son's son), shall knowingly and with malice aforethought be engaged or married to a freedman or to a man who himself or whose father or mother engages or has engaged in acting, and none of these men shall knowingly and with malice aforethought take her as betrothed or wife.

Freeborn men are prohibited from marrying a prostitute, or procuress, or a woman manumitted by a procurer or procuress, or a woman caught in adultery, or one convicted at a public trial, or a woman who has engaged in acting.

It must be observed that men of a lower rank may marry those women whom those of higher rank are, on account of their status, prohibited by law from marrying; but on the other hand men of the next highest rank may not marry those women whom those of a lower rank are forbidden to marry.

Conditions contrary to the laws and to the decrees of the emperors or to sound morality that are added — such as, "If you do not take a wife," or "If you have no children" — are of no consequence.

In the seventh section of the Julian Law the right of priority in assuming the *fasces* lies not with the consul who is older but with the one who has more children than his colleague, either living under his control or lost in war. But if each has the same number of children, the married man or the one who is included among the husbands is preferred. But if both are married and fathers of the same number of children, then the time-honored tradition is reinstituted, and he who is older assumes the *fasces* first. In addition to this, if both are bachelors, or both married with the same number of children, or both have no children, the law does not state anything concerning [the honor] of age. Nevertheless ... it is customary to grant the *fasces* of the first month to colleagues who are either very much older or much more noble, or are entering upon their second consulship.

Persons are excused from serving as guardians or trustees for various reasons, but for the most part because of their children, whether they are in the power [of their father] or have been freed [from his power]. For anyone who has three children alive in Rome, or four in Italy, or five in the provinces, may be excused from guardianship or trusteeship in accordance with the example of other public services.

No freedman who has two or more sons or daughters of his own in his power (with the exception of one who has engaged in acting, or one who has hired out his services to fight with animals) shall be obligated to give, perform, or offer to his patron, patroness or their children his services or anything else as gift or duty to which he may have sworn or promised or obligated himself for the sake of his freedom.

A freedwoman who is married to her patron shall not have the right to divorce ... as long as the patron wants her to be his wife.

If a man provides in his will for a guardian over his son or daughter and both have reached puberty, the son ceases to keep the guardian, but the daughter nonetheless remains under guardianship. For in accordance with the Julian Law and the Papian-Poppaean Law women are released from guardianship only by the "privilege of [three] children."

A man or wife can by virtue of marriage inherit a tenth of the other's estate. But if they have living children from a previous marriage, in addition to the tenth which they receive by virtue of marriage they are entitled to as many tenths as the number of children. Likewise, a common son or daughter lost after the day of naming adds a tenth of the estate; two children lost after the ninth day [of naming] add two-tenths. In addition to the tenth they can receive also the usufruct of one-third of the estate, and whenever they have children receive ownership of the same part.

Sometimes a man and woman can inherit the other's total estate, for example, if both or either are not yet of that age at which the law requires children — that is, if the husband is under twenty-five or the wife less than twenty; or if both during their marriage have passed the age established by the Papian Law, that is, sixty for the man, fifty for the woman.... They have the right of making a will for each other's advantage if they have obtained the "privilege of [three] children" from the emperor, if they have a common son or daughter, or if they have lost a fourteen-year-old son or twelve-year-old daughter or two three-year-olds after the

51

day of naming, so that within one year and six months the loss of even a single minor of any age whatsoever accords the right of inheriting a total estate; likewise, if the wife gives birth to a child by her husband within ten months after his death she receives the whole of his estate.

Sometimes they inherit nothing from each other's estate, that is, if they contracted a marriage contrary to the Julian Law and Papian-Poppaean Law, for example, if anyone marries a woman of ill repute, or a senator marries a freedwoman.

Bachelors also are forbidden by the Julian Law to receive inheritances or legacies.... Likewise childless persons, for the very fact that they do not have children, by the Julian Law lose one-half of inheritances and legacies.

The Julian Law granted women an exemption from marriage of one year after the death of a husband and of six months after a divorce; the Papian Law, however, [allows an exemption of] two years after the death of a husband and a year and six months after divorce.

The thirty-fifth section of the Julian Law states: Those who unjustly prevent children under their power from marrying, or who refuse to give a dowry ... are forced to arrange marriage and give a dowry.

Since the time of the Papian Law the portion of one who is ineligible lapses and belongs to those named in the will who have children.

If there is no one to whom the possession of an estate can belong, of if there is someone but he has failed to exercise his right, the estate passes to the public treasury according to the Julian Law concerning lapses in estates.

Tacitus, *Annals* Book 3 chapter 25

Augustus in his old age had enacted the Papian-Poppaean Law, to supplement the Julian measures, in order to increase the penalties for celibates and enrich the treasury. But this did not result in a great increase in marriages and the rearing of children, for childlessness remained the prevailing practice. But the number of those placed in jeopardy grew apace, with every household being undermined by the denunciations of informers. As a result, the people suffered now from its laws, as it previously had from its vices.

D
Controls on Freeing Slaves

Augustus took many measures to preserve the priority of the Italian stock and to increase its numbers. A negative measure was the limitation on the number of freedmen. The liberation of slaves was controlled in various ways: the Junian Law (probably 17 BC) limited the rights of freedmen as citizens; the Fufian-Caninian Law restricted wholesale manumission by wills; and the Aelian-Sentian Law imposed limits on the manumission of slaves while their masters were alive.

THE PROBLEM

Dionysius of Halicarnassus, *Roman Antiquities* Book 4 chapter 24.4−6

Dionysius of Halicarnassus (ca. 60/55 BC to after 7 BC) was a Greek teacher of rhetoric and literary critic, as well as historian. His *Roman Antiquities*, in twenty books, covers the first half of the Republic.

In our times [ca. 7 BC] matters have come to such a state of confusion, and the ideals of the Roman state have become so without honor and so demeaned that some who have made money by robbery, housebreaking, prostitution, and in every other base manner, buy their freedom with this money and at once become Romans. Others who have become privy to and accomplices of their masters in poisonings and murders and crimes against the gods or the community receive this reward from them. Others are freed in order that when they receive the monthly allotment of wheat given at public expense, or if there is some other largess given by the leaders among the citizens, they

53

may bring it to those who have given them freedom. Others are freed through the levity of their masters and their idle striving for glory. I myself know of some who have granted freedom to all their slaves after their death so that they might be called excellent men when they are dead, and so that many might attend their funeral processions wearing liberty caps on their heads. Some of those taking part in such processions ... were criminals just released from jail, men who had committed crimes worthy of a thousand deaths. Most people, however, when they observe these stains that are difficult to cleanse away from the city, are grieved and cite this practice as evidence, considering it improper that an imperial city aspiring to world rule should make such men citizens.

FUFIAN-CANINIAN LAW (2 BC)

ADA, pp. 202–205

The Fufian-Caninian Law established a limit on testamentary manumissions of slaves. A person who has more than two but not more than ten slaves is permitted to manumit up to one-half of this number; a person who has more than ten but not more than thirty slaves is permitted to manumit up to one-third of that number; a person who has more than thirty but not more than one hundred is given the right to manumit up to one-quarter; lastly, a person who has more than 100 but not more than 500 is permitted to manumit not more than one-fifth....

If anyone desires to manumit by his will more than the number indicated above, the order of listing is to be followed, so that freedom is valid only for those listed first, up the number that the explanation previously outlined provides.

If in a will the names of slaves given freedom have been written in a circle, because no order of manumission is found none are to be free, because the Fufian-Caninian Law revokes what has been done to evade it.

AELIAN-SENTIAN LAW (2 AD)

ADA, pp. 205-219

Under this law an owner under twenty years of age is not permitted to manumit except by the rod, after adequate cause for manumission has been proven before a council.[30]

Moreover, an age requirement for freeing a slave was introduced by the Aelian-Sentian Law. This law did not allow slaves under thirty years of age to become Roman citizens upon manumission unless they were freed after adequate cause for manumission was proved before a council.

The law stipulates that a person manumitted by a will continues to be in the status he would be if he were free with the consent of the owner, and therefore became a Latin.

By the Aelian-Sentian Law persons under thirty years of age who are manumitted become Latins, and if they marry either Roman citizens or Latin colonists, or persons of the same status as themselves, and have so declared in the presence of no less than seven witnesses who are adult Romans citizens, and they beget a child, when that child reaches the age of one, the right is given in accordance with this law to go before a praetor, or in the provinces before the governor of the province, and prove that in accordance with the Aelian-Sentian Law he has married, and has a one-year-old child from his wife. And if the person before whom the claim is validated declares this to be so, then the Latin himself and his wife, if she is of the same status, and the child, if it also is of the same status, shall be declared to be Roman citizens.

11

PANEGYRICS ON AUGUSTUS: HAIL TO THE CHIEF

Horace, *Odes*

(Book 1 no. 2.) The father [of the gods] has now sent enough portentous snow and hail on the earth, and by hurling thunderbolts with his glowing right hand against the sacred citadel has terrified the city; he has terrified the people of the world fearing that the grim age of Pyrrha[31] bewailing strange marvels would return, when Proteus drove his entire herd [of seals] to visit high mountains, and the species of fish clung to the tops of elms, the usual home of doves, and the trembling deer swam in the overwhelming sea. We have seen the yellow Tiber with its waves whirled violently from the Etruscan bank flowing on to overwhelm the Regia[32] and Vesta's shrine, as he boasts himself the over-zealous avenger of Ilia's complaint, and the uxurious river overflows the left bank without the approval of Jupiter. The younger generation, thinned out by the sins of their parents, will hear that citizens sharpened against citizens swords by which they might better kill the formidable Parthians, and it will hear of battles.

What god should the people invoke for the fortunes of a falling empire? With what prayers should the sacred virgins importune Vesta who does not listen to their chants? To whom shall Jupiter offer the role of expiating our crime? At length we pray that you, mantic Apollo, come, clothing your radiant shoulders in a cloud; or you come, smiling Venus, if you prefer, around whom flit Merriment and Cupid; or you, our founder, if you have any regard for your neglected people and descendants, glutted with an alas too-long sport, you who enjoy the shrill battle cry, the polished helmets, and the grim face of the Marsian foot-soldier against the bloodied enemy; or you, winged son of fostering

Maia, changing your form, assume the appearance of a youth on earth, allowing yourself to be called Caesar's avenger, late may you return to heaven, and long may you happily stay among Romulus' people, and may not an untimely breeze lift you off, turned hostile because of our sins. But here rather may you have great triumphs, here may you enjoy being called father and *princeps,* and may you not allow the Parthians to ride unpunished, while you are leader, O Caesar.

(Book 1 no. 12.) What man or hero do you, Clio, [33] choose to celebrate on the lyre or shrill flute? What god? Whose name will a playful echo resound, either on shady slopes of Mt. Helicon, or on Mt. Pindus,[34] or on icy Haemus?[35] There the woods spellbound followed the singing Orpheus, who by his mother's art restrained the rapid flow of rivers and the swift winds, charming enough to cause the oaks to be attentive to his melodious lyre. What shall I say first in the usual praises of the father [of the gods,], who controls the affairs of men and gods, and who rules the sea and lands and the universe with the changing seasons? From him nothing is produced greater than him, and nothing flourishes like him or even next to him. Yet Pallas aggressive in battle possesses honors nearest his. I shall not keep quiet in heralding you, Bacchus, and you, virgin goddess [Diana] hostile to savage beasts, or you, Phoebus, feared for your unerring arrows. I shall mention Hercules, too, and Leda's sons [Castor and Pollux], one famous for taming horses, the other for excellence in boxing. As soon as their constellation has shone bright for sailors, water churned up flows down from the rocks, winds subside, clouds scatter, and the menacing wave, as they will it, falls to rest on the sea.

After these I hesistate whether to recall Romulus first or the peaceful reign of Numa Pompilius,[36] or the proud *fasces* of Tarquin,[37] or the famed death of Cato. In ennobling poetry I shall herald in gratitude Regulus and Scaurus and Paulus who did not spare his great life while the Punic Hannibal was winning, and Fabricius. This man and Curius with unbarbered hair, fit for warfare, and Camillus, were reared by rugged poverty and an ancestral estate with an appropriate dwelling.[38] The reputation of Marcellus[39] is growing as a tree grows in time unnoticed. The star of Julius shines among all the constellations like the moon among the smaller stars. Father and guardian of the human race, son of Saturn, to you fate has granted the protection of mighty Caesar: may you rule with Caesar second to you. Whether he will lead the conquered Parthians, who threaten Latium, in justified triumph, or upon the Chinese or Indians who lie at the end of the East, let him rule the broad earth in justice as subordinate to you. You will shake Olympus with your mighty chariot, you will hurl hostile thunderbolts against polluted groves.

Written by Horace during the absence of Augustus in the western provinces, 16 to 13 BC

(Book 4 no. 5.) O best guardian of the Roman people, born when the gods were kindly, you have been away too long already. Since you promised an early return to the august council of senators, come back. Restore light to your country, O good leader. For when your countenance, like the spring, sheds its radiance upon the people, the day passes more pleasingly, and the sun shines better.

As a mother calls with all vows and prayers for her son, and does not take her eyes from the curved shore, her son whom the begrudging blast as he lingers across the waters of the Carpathian Sea keeps away from his sweet home beyond the time of the year for sailing, so our country, smitten with yearnings of loyalty, asks for Caesar. The ox grazes in the fields, and Ceres and kindly Fertility nourish the fields, sailors speed through the peaceful sea, good faith fears censure, the chaste home is defiled by no debauchery. Custom and law have conquered the defilement of sin, child-bearing women are praised because the children resemble them, and attendant punishment prevents faults.

Who would fear the Parthian, who the frigid Scythian, who the spawn which rude Germany breeds, so long as Caesar is safe? Who would look after war against savage Spain? Each one brings the day to a close in his own hills and conducts the vine to the unmarried trees; from here he returns joyfully to his wine, and at a second part of the meal invites you as a god.[40] You he hails with much prayer and, with the pouring out of wine from sacrificial bowls, mingles your genius with the Lares, as Greece does in commemoration of Castor and mighty Hercules....

(Book 4 no. 15.) Apollo, when I wished to write lyrics of battles and conquered cities, cried out to me not to entrust my small bark to the Tyrrhenian Sea. Your age, O Caesar, has brought back fertile crops to the fields, and has restored to our Jupiter the standards taken from the proud portals of the Parthians, and has closed the temple of Janus Quirinus free of wars, and has placed reins on license straying from the moral order, and has removed faults and restored the ancient virtues, through which the Latin name and the might of Italy grew and the glory and majesty of our empire extended from the West to the East. With Caesar as guardian of the world, no political madness or violence will drive out peace, no anger which forges swords and creates enmity among cities and makes them wretched. Not those who drink the deep Danube will violate the dictates of Augustus, nor the Getae, nor the Chinese, nor the perfidious Parthians, nor those who stem from the region near the Don River.

And we, both on business days and on holy days, with the gifts of mirthful Bacchus, together with our offspring and our matrons, first duly praying to the gods, shall sing, in song blended with Lydian pipes, of leaders whose virtuous work has been done after the fashion of our ancestors, shall sing of Troy and Anchises and the descendants of bountiful Venus.

12

THE OPPOSITION TO AUGUSTUS

It is an illusion to look upon the Augustan Age as a time of euphoric national harmony and consensus. In the first two decades of Augustus' Principate there was, indeed, a large measure of freedom of speech, as Augustus felt his way pragmatically through the maze of problems, conflicting ambitions, aspirations, and needs. Many of the older nobility in the Senatorial Order were not reconciled to the life-long domination of one man, especially an upstart who had been adopted into one noble family (the Julians) and had married into another (the Claudians). Even among Augustan writers, such adherents of the regime as Vergil and Horace permitted their reservations about the *princeps* to surface in their works. The literary circle of Messalla, next in importance to the pro-Augustan circle of Maecenas, showed its disdain of Augustus by fostering un−Augustan style and apolitical themes. Most important of all, in the years after he achieved sole power in 31 BC there were at least five plots against Augustus.

Suetonius, *Life of Augustus* chapter 19

At various times Augustus suppressed several disturbances, beginnings of revolutions, and conspiracies, which were detected by information received before they became serious: those of the young Lepidus; then of Varro Murena and Fannius Caepio; later of Marcus Egnatius; next of Plautius Rufus and Lucius Paulus, his granddaughter's husband; and, besides them, of Lucius Audasius, accused of forging documents, decrepit in age and body; likewise of Asinius Epicadius, a half-breed of Parthian origin; finally of Telephus, a woman's slave who was an announcer of names of callers. For Augustus was conspired against and endangered even by men of the lowest social rank....

Dio Cassius, *History of Rome* Book 54 chapter 3.4–6

Others formed a plot against Augustus [in 23 BC]; Fannius Caepio was the leader of it, and others participated. [Varro] Murena was also said to have joined the conspirators, whether actually or to slander him, since he used unrestrained and immoderate freedom of speech toward all alike. As a matter of fact, the conspirators did not undergo a trial, but the case was undefended, on the grounds that they were captured while planning to flee; and not much later they were put to death. Neither Proculeius, the brother of Murena, nor Maecenas, his brother-in-law, could help, even though they were among the most highly honored by Augustus.

Velleius, *Roman History* Book 2

(Chapter 88.) While Caesar was engaged in mopping-up operations in the war at Actium and Alexandria, Marcus [Aemilius] Lepidus, a youth whose handsomeness exceeded his intelligence, the son of the Lepidus who had been a triumvir for regulating the state, born from Junia, sister of Brutus, had formed a plot to assassinate Caesar as soon as he returned to the city. Gaius Maecenas was then [31/30 BC] in charge of guarding the city, a man of equestrian rank but a scion of illustrious family.... With the utmost caution and concealment he investigated this plot of the headstrong youth, crushing Lepidus with remarkable speed and, without causing a disturbance of affairs or men, he quelled the monstrous beginning of a new and reviving civil war. And Lepidus paid the penalty for his ill-conceived plot. Servilia, the wife of Lepidus..., by swallowing live coals, compensated for her early death by the undying memory of her name.

(Chapter 91.) There were some, however, who hated this very happy state of affairs. For example, Lucius Murena and Fannius Caepio ... entered into a plot to assassinate Caesar, but were suppressed by public authority; and what they had wished to accomplish by violence they themselves suffered by law. Not much later [19 BC], Rufus Egnatius, who was in all respects more like a gladiator than a senator, acquired the favor of the populace in his aedileship [21 BC] by putting out fires with a private gang of slaves; and he incurred more favor from day to day to such an extent that the people elected him to the praetorship without any interval, and presently he dared to seek the consulship.... He gathered about him men very much like himself, and decided to assassinate Caesar, with a view to dying himself when he had gotten rid of the man who prevented him from being safe so long as he was safe. But he was no more successful than the preceding men in concealing his plans, and was clapped into prison with the fellow-conspirators in his crime, and died a most deserving death.

Seneca

(*On Anger* Book 3 chapter 23, 4−8.) The historian Timagenes said some things against Augustus, his wife, and his whole family, and yet the words have not been utterly lost. For reckless witticisms are more widely circulated and on the lips of men. Caesar often warned him to use more moderation in his language; when he persisted, he excluded him from his home. Afterwards Timagenes lived to old age in the entourage of Asinius Pollio, and he was lionized in the whole city. Though he was excluded from Caesar's house, this did not close any doors to him. He gave recitations of histories that he wrote subsequently, and his books containing the deeds of Caesar he put into the fire and burned. Though he was hostile to Caesar, no one feared his friendship, no one fled from him as if he were a man struck by lightning. There were people who offered him shelter, though he had fallen from eminence. Caesar, as I said, endured this patiently, not even disturbed by the fact that he had sullied his renown and deeds. He never complained to the host of his enemy. He merely said this to Asinius Pollio: "You are keeping a wild beast;" and when Pollio tried to offer an excuse, he prevented him and said: "Enjoy it, my dear Pollio, enjoy it!" And when Pollio said: "If you order me, I shall at once exclude him from my home," he answered: "Do you think I would do this, after I brought you together?"

13

'TREASON' UPDATED

The peculiar Roman concept of *maiestas populi Romani* (the "majesty of the Roman people") embraced not only the claim of obedience and submission of all peoples to Rome, but acts on the part of Roman citizens that might reduce the *maiestas* ("greatness") of Rome. Such acts were severely punished as treason. Diminishment or injury to the "majesty" of the Roman people, the crime of *laesa maiestas*, was extended to magistrates and provincial governors as their representatives. Under the Principate the *princeps*, as chief authority of the state, was protected by the concept of *laesa maiestas (lèse majesté)*. Gradually treason was defined as acts that violated the majesty of the *princeps*, a concept that was subjected to ever wider extensions of interpretation. It is noteworthy that Horace *(Epistles* no. 1 verses 257–258) and Ovid *(Tristia* Book 2 verse 512) called Augustus *tua maiestas* ("your majesty"). The Julian Law on Treason, promulgated under Augustus, remained the norm throughout the imperial period. Under Augustus, treason trials were heard by the Senate or by the *princeps* himself. The penalty was permanent exile from Italy.

Dio Cassius, *History of Rome* Book 54 chapter 3.2–4

When a certain Marcus Primus was on trial [in 22 BC] for having made war on the Odrysians[41] while he was governor of Macedonia, and declared at one time that he had done this by authority of Augustus, at another by that of Marcellus,[42] Augustus came voluntarily to the courtroom, and when asked by him if he had authorized him to wage war, he denied it. And when Primus' advocate, Licinius Murena, after hurling some unpleasant remarks at Augustus, asked: "What are you doing here, and who summoned you?", Augustus answered only this: "The public interest." ... However, not a few senators voted for the acquittal of Primus....

The Julian Law on Treason

ADA, pp. 156–160

There is a charge of treason, to the Roman people and its security, against a person by whose agency a plot is entered upon with malice aforethought whereby without an order of the *princeps* hostages are killed; or whereby men armed with weapons or stones are present in the city or assemble against the state, or places or temples are seized; or whereby meetings or gatherings take place or men are assembled for sedition; or by whose agency with malice aforethought a plot is entered upon whereby any magistrate of the Roman people, or person who holds *imperium* or authority, is killed; or whereby anyone bears arms against the state; or if someone sends a messenger or letter to enemies of the Roman people, or gives a signal, or acts with malice aforethought so that enemies of the Roman people are aided by advice against the state; or if anyone stirs up or incites soldiers, whereby a sedition or disturbance is caused against the state; or anyone who has not left a province when he has been superseded; or anyone who deserts from the army, or as a civilian goes over to the enemy; or anyone who knowingly makes or cites a false entry in the public records....

Moreover, the Julian Law on Treason directs that a person who injures the majesty of the state is to be held — such as the person who retreats in war or does not hold a stronghold, or surrenders a camp. By the same law a person is held who, without an order of the *princeps,* wages war or holds a levy or mobilizes an army; or who when he has been superseded in a province does not hand over the army to his successsor; or who deserts his command or any army of the Roman people; or as a civilian knowingly and with malice aforethought does anything [that belongs] under the jurisdiction of an authority or magistrate; or who arranges for any of the aforementioned to be done, or by whom with malice aforethought anyone is compelled by oath to do anything against the state; or by whom with malice aforethought an army of the Roman people is led into ambush and betrayed to the enemy; or by whom with malice aforethought a fact is stated whereby the enemy is prevented from coming into the power of the Roman

64

people; or by whose agency with malice aforethought the enemies of the Roman people are aided with provisions, arms, weapons, horses, money, or anything else, or friends become enemies of the Roman people; or by whom with malice aforethought it comes about that a king of a foreign people is less obedient to the Roman people; or by whose agency with malice aforethought it comes about that it is facilitated that hostages, money, and pack animals are given to enemies of the Roman people against the state; likewise, one who releases a person who is a confessed defendant in a trial and on account of this was put into chains....

A charge is extinguished by death, unless by chance someone was a defendant in a case involving treason. For unless he is purged of this charge by his heirs, the inheritance is claimed by the privy purse. Clearly not everyone who is a defendant under the Julian Law of Treason is in this condition, but only a person who is accused of high treason, that is, a person motivated with hostile intent against the state or the *princeps*. But if someone is accused of treason under any other section of the Julian Law, his death extinguishes the charge.

14

FROM
FREEDOM OF SPEECH
TO CENSORSHIP

Outside the Senatorial Order, in practice few Romans had enjoyed freedom of speech during the Republic. The law of libel in Rome was an age-old deterrent, especially where the aristocracy and public officials were involved. In the case of magistrates, the laws on *maiestas* ("treason") were virtually indistinguishable from libel law.

Under Augustus the traditional "freedom of speech" was tolerated for four decades, but a few years before his death the aged Augustus began to resent criticism and defamatory writings. In the landmark cases of Titus Labienus (8–12 AD) and Cassius Severus (12 AD) repression of freedom of speech began, through extension of the Julian Law on Treason (see no. 13 above), to cover "defamatory writings," and anonymous publications, and the use of pseudonyms in such writings were outlawed. It was in this atmosphere that the poet Ovid was suddenly and permanently exiled by Augustus, in 8 AD, for an inexcusable indiscretion perhaps involving the emperor's granddaughter Julia, and for a poem he had written, the *Art of Love* (see no. 44 below). It is noteworthy that Augustus' successor Tiberius once said: "In a free state there ought to be free speech and free thought." (Suetonius, *Life of Tiberius* chapter 28.1).

Seneca the Elder, *Controversiae* Book 2 chapter 4.12 – 13

In this *controversia* [Porcius Latro] said something adverse, not to his declamation, but to himself. He was declaiming when Augustus and Marcus Agrippa were in the audience. Augustus seemed to be on the point of adopting Agrippa's sons, his own grandchildren [ca. 17 BC]. Marcus Agrippa was one of those who were not born of noble rank but made noble. When Latro was speaking the part of the youth and handling the topic of adoption, he said:

66

"Now he is being grafted, out of the depths, into the nobility by adoption;" and other observations in this tenor. Maecenas motioned to Latro that Caesar was in a hurry, and that he should finish the declamation at once. Some thought that this was malice on Maecenas' part. For he had brought it about not that Caesar should fail to hear what had been said, but that he actually noticed it. However, so much freedom existed under the deified Augustus that, though Marcus Agrippa was very powerful then, there were not lacking those who criticized his lack of nobility. He had been Vipsanius Agrippa, but he had suppressed the *nomen* Vipsanius as evidence of his father's low station, and was called Marcus Agrippa.... The deified Augustus seems to me worthy of admiration for the great licence permitted under him....

Suetonius, *Life of Augustus* chapter 43.2

Asinius Pollio, a survivor of the revolution and the civil wars, remained an outspoken, independent spirit throughout the Augustan Age, as a speech he gave in the Senate ca. 1 BC shows.

Augustus also very frequently exhibited the Game of Troy, performed by older and younger boys, deeming it a venerable and splendid custom for the native quality of the nobility to become known in this way. When Nonius Asprenas was lamed by a fall in this sport, he bestowed upon him a golden necklace and permitted him and his descendants to have the *cognomen* Torquatus. But soon after he stopped exhibiting this sport when Asinius Pollio, the orator, complained bitterly and angrily in the Senate of an accident to his grandson [Marcus Claudius Marcellus] Aeserninus, who had also broken his leg.

Seneca the Elder, *Controversiae* no. 10, *Preface* chapters 5−8

Titus Labienus's freedom of speech was so great that he exceeded the word "freedom"; and because he tore to pieces all classes and men he was called "Rabienus." Despite his fault he had great spirit, violent like his genius, and in the midst of all this peace he had not yet abandoned Pompeian[43] spirits.

In his case a new type of penalty was first devised: it was brought about through his enemies that all his books were burned — something new and previously unknown, that punishment should be exacted from literature.... How great is the savagery that puts the torch to literature and punishes monuments of learning!...

I remember once when he was reciting his history he rolled up a great part of the book and said: "I pass over these matters which will be read after my death." How great was the freedom these men had that even Labienus was frightened! A clever saying of Cassius Severus, a man who hated Labienus bitterly, was in circulation at the time when Labienus' books were burned by decree of the Senate. "Now," he said, "I ought to be burned, for I have learned these books by heart."

Tacitus, *Annals* Book 1 chapter 72

Augustus was the first [in 12 AD] to conduct a trial on libelous writings, under the guise of this law [on treason], because he was upset by the scurrility of Cassius Severus, who had defamed distinguished men and women with insolent writings.[44]

15
PERSONAL GLIMPSES OF AUGUSTUS

Augustus was one of the master toilers of the world. For about sixty years, from his entry on the political scene at the age of eighteen to his death in 14 AD, he was intensely absorbed in the multi-faceted affairs of the city of Rome and of the empire, absorbing, welcoming — even soliciting — ever more responsibilities. In all this time he rarely found time for a vacation from duties and decision-making. In the following vignettes of his private persona we can see how inextricably intermeshed were his private and his public life.

A
A Letter from Augustus to Livia

Suetonius, *Life of Claudius* chapter 3.1−4

I had a consultation with Tiberius, as you requested of me, my dear Livia, concerning what your grandson Tiberius [the future emperor Claudius] should do at the *Ludi Martiales*.[45] Now we both agreed that we should determine once and for all what course we are to follow in his case. For if he is sound and, so to say, in complete health, is there any doubt that he ought to be advanced through the same grades and steps as his brother[46] was? But if we find him to be wanting and defective in soundness of body and spirit, we should not provide the means of exposing both him and us to men accustomed to scoff and sneer at such things. For we shall always vacillate if we deliberate about each occasion separately and do not make up our minds in advance whether we deem him capable of holding office or not. For the present, however, on the matters about which you ask my advice, we do not object that at the *Ludi Martiales* he look after the banquet of the priests, provided he allow himself to be guided by Silvanus' son, his kinsman, so that he won't do something that might make him conspicuous and ridiculous. We do not approve his viewing the chariot races from the imperial box, for he would be conspicuous if he were exposed in the first row at the games. We do not approve his going to Mons Albanus,[47] or being in Rome on the days of the Latin Games. Why don't we make him prefect of the city, if he may accompany his brother to the Mons? You have, my dear Livia, our views, namely, that we agree to make a decision about the whole matter once and for all, so that we won't waver between hope and fear. You may, if you wish, give our Antonia[48] this part of my letter to read.

B
His Love of Gambling

Suetonius, *Life of Augustus* chapter 71.3

We had quite a pleasant time, my dear Tiberius, during the Quinquatria,[49] for every day we played all day and kept the dice-board warm. Your brother carried on with noisy shouts; in the end, however, he did not lose much, for, after heavy losses, little by little, beyond his expectations, he recouped them. I lost 20,000 sesterces on my own account, simply because I was lavishly generous in my play, as usual. For if I had collected from each one the stakes I let go, and kept what I gave away to each person, I would have won as much as 50,000. But I prefer this, for my generosity will elevate me to heavenly glory.

C
Letter to His Grandson, 1 AD

Aulus Gellius, *Attic Nights* Book 15 chapter 7.3

Aulus Gellius (ca. 123–169 AD), a Roman lawyer, wrote *Attic Nights*, a miscellany in twenty books on a wide variety of subjects.

Hello, my dear Gaius, my sweetest little donkey! I always miss you, it's a fact, when you're away from me. But especially on such days as today, my eyes look for my Gaius. Wherever you have been today, I hope you celebrated my sixty-fourth birthday in happiness and good health. As you see, I have passed the sixty-third year, the climacteric common to all old men. I pray the gods that, whatever time is left to me, I be permitted to spend it in good health, with the country highly prosperous and you[50] becoming fine men and succeeding to my position.

D
To Horace

Suetonius, *Life of Horace*

I want you to know that I am angry with you, because in several writings of this kind you don't converse with me especially. Are you afraid that you may get a bad reputation with posterity if you seem to be intimate with me?

E
"Make Haste Slowly"

Aulus Gellius, *Attic Nights* Book 10 chapter 11.5

The deified Augustus used to express this very elegantly in two Greek words. They say he was accustomed to say in conversations, and wrote in his letters, "Make haste slowly," by which he cautioned that in administration one must apply at the same time speed and energy, as well as slowness and carefulness. From these two opposites maturity emerges.

F
A Drunken Senator's Words

Seneca, *On Benefits* Book 3 chapter 27.1–3

Under the deified Augustus words were not yet dangerous to men, though they were troublesome. Rufus, a man of the Senatorial Order, had expressed a wish during a dinner that Caesar might not return safely from the journey he was then planning. And he had added that all the bulls and calves wished this too. Some of those present noted these words carefully. As soon as it was dawn, a slave, who had stood at his feet when he was dining, told him what he had said at dinner in a drunken state, and urged him to get hold of Caesar and denounce himself. Taking his advice, he met Caesar coming down to the Forum, and, when he had sworn that he had lost his head the day before, wished that this disaster should happen to himself and his children, and asked Caesar to pardon him and restore him to favor. When Caesar assented, Rufus said: "No one will believe that you restored me to favor unless you give me some gift." And he asked for and obtained a sum that would not be disdained even by one in favor. Caesar said: "In my own interest, I shall try never to be angry with you."

G
Augustus' Superstitions

Suetonius, *Life of Augustus* chapters 90–92

He was rather lacking in nerve in his fear of thunder and lightning, so that he always carried about with him everywhere a seal skin[51] as protection, and at every suspicion of a major storm he used to seek shelter in a secret, vaulted room...

He paid attention to both his own dreams and those of others about himself.... Throughout the entire spring his dreams were very frequent and very terrifying, but idle and unfulfilled; the rest of the time they were less frequent but less idle. He used constantly to visit the temple of Jupiter the Thunderer, which he had dedicated on the Capitoline Hill, and he once dreamed that Jupiter Capitolinus complained that his worshippers were being taken away from him, and that Augustus answered that he had placed the Thunderer next to him as his doorkeeper, and therefore soon after he adorned the gable of the temple with bells, because these commonly hang from doors....

Some auspices and omens he regarded as very certain: if his shoe was put on in the morning in the wrong way — the left for the right — he considered it a harmful sign; if by chance it drizzled on land or sea as he was embarking on a distant journey, he considered it a happy sign — of a speedy and prosperous return. But he was especially affected by prodigies. He had a palm tree which sprang up between the crevices of the pavement before his house transferred to the inner court belonging to the household gods and made careful provision for it to grow. At the island of Capri he was so delighted that the branches of a very old oak tree which had already drooped to the ground and were withering came back to life at his very arrival there that he exchanged the island for Aenaria with the people of Naples. He also observed certain days, and would not set out on a day after a market day, or begin any important matter on the Nones. In the latter, as he wrote Tiberius, he avoided nothing in this but the unlucky sound of the word.[52]

16
PROVISIONS FOR A DYNASTY

Less than a few years after the "restoration of the Republic" it was evident that Augustus was planning to pass on his position of authority to his own hand-picked designate — from among his own family. Since he had no sons of his own, Augustus first groomed his nephew Marcellus (as Caesar had groomed him), then his best friend and son-in-law Marcus Agrippa, then his grandsons Gaius and Lucius Caesar, and finally his stepson Tiberius Claudius Nero. The means that Augustus devised to provide for succession to his power were adoption of an heir- or heirs-apparent and sharing his extraordinary powers with his chosen successor. After the death of Agrippa, his widow, Augustus' daughter Julia, was married to Tiberius. Thereafter, the latter's mother Livia was at the center of the dynastic struggle that culminated, through the deaths of all possible successors, in the elevation of Tiberius to co-regent and designated heir. The transition at Augustus' death was peaceful, not only because Tiberius already held the powers of the *princeps,* but also because by 14 AD, as Tacitus wrote: "How few there were who had seen the Republic!" (*Annals* Book 1 chapter 3.) Augustus' blighted hope for a successor who was a lineal descendant is revealed in the words he used in his will to name Tiberius the principal heir to his estate: "Since cruel fate has snatched from me my sons Gaius and Lucius, Tiberius Caesar is to be heir to two-thirds of my estate." (Suetonius, *Life of Tiberius* chapter 23.)

A
Dynastic Policy

Tacitus, *Annals* Book 1 chapter 3.1−5

As supports for his power Augustus raised Claudius Marcellus, his sister's son, still a mere stripling, to the position of *pontifex* and curule aedile, and Marcus Agrippa, not of noble birth but a fine soldier and his associate in victory, to two consulships consecutively. Then when Marcellus died young, he took Agrippa as his son-in-law, Tiberius Nero and Claudius Drusus, his step-sons, were elevated by him with the title *imperator*, even though his own house was still at that time intact. For he had adopted Gaius and Lucius, sons of Agrippa [and Julia], into the house of the Caesars, and he was very eager — though he pretended to reject it — to have them named leaders of the youth even before they laid aside their boys' purple-bordered togas, and to have them made consuls designate. When Agrippa died, and the fate of premature death or the treachery of their step-mother Livia,[53] carried off Lucius Caesar en route to the Spanish legions and Gaius Caesar returning from Armenia and ill from a wound, since Drusus was already dead, [Tiberius] Nero was the sole one of his step-sons left, and so everything turned to him. He was adopted as son,[54] made colleague in the *imperium* and colleague in the tribunician power, and was paraded before all the armies, not as before through the devious plans of his mother, but openly now with her encouragement. For she had developed such a hold on the old man Augustus that he had relegated his only [surviving] grandson, Agrippa Postumus,[55] to the island of Planasia.... But, mind you, he had put Drusus' son Germanicus in charge of eight legions on the Rhine and ordered Tiberius to adopt him, even though Tiberius had a grown son in his own household. Augustus' purpose was to provide himself with additional safeguards.

B
Honors to the Imperial House

CIL, Vol. v no. 6411 = Dessau, *ILS* no. 107
= Ehrenberg-Jones, no. 61

Inscriptions from Pavia or Ticinum, in Italy, from bases of statues to members of Augustus' household set up 7/8 AD.

To Imperator Caesar Augustus, son of a god, *pontifex maximus*, father of our country, augur, member of the Board of Fifteen for Making Sacrifices, member of the Board of Seven for Sacrificial

Banquets, consul for the thirteenth time, hailed imperator seventeen times, holding the tribunician power for the thirtieth year.

To Livia, daughter of Drusus, wife of Caesar Augustus.

To Gaius Caesar, son of Augustus, grandson of a god, *pontifex*, consul, hailed imperator.

To Lucius Caesar, son of Augustus, grandson of a god, augur, consul designate, leader of the youth.

To Tiberius Caesar, son of Augustus, grandson of a god, *pontifex*, consul for the second time, hailed imperator three times, augur, holding the tribunician power for the ninth year.

To Germanicus Julius Caesar, son of Tiberius, grandson of Augustus, great-grandson of a god.

To Drusus Julius Caesar, son of Tiberius, grandson of Augustus, great-grandson of a god, *pontifex*.

To Nero Julius Caesar, son of Germanicus, great-grandson of Augustus.

To Drusus Julius Germanicus, son of Germanicus, great-grandson of Augustus.

To Tiberius Claudius Nero Germanicus, son of Drusus Germanicus.

Ehrenberg-Jones no. 62; Pelusium, Egypt, 4 BC

In honor of Imperator Caesar Augustus, son of a god, and Livia, wife of Augustus, and Gaius Caesar and Lucius Caesar, sons of the Imperator, and Julia, daughter of the Imperator, and Gaius Turranius, Prefect of Egypt, the chair of state and the altar were dedicated by Quintus Curvius Flaccus, son of Quintus, governor of the Thebaïd, administering justice at Pelusium, year 26 of Caesar, 13th day of Tybi.

Ehrenberg-Jones no. 65; Rome 3 BC

To Lucius Caesar, son of Augustus, grandson of a god, leader of the youth, consul designate when he was fourteen years of age, by the Senate.

Ehrenberg-Jones no. 72 = *IGRR*, Vol. 3 no. 719; Myra (in Lycia), after 14 AD

To the god Augustus Caesar, son of a god, imperator of land and sea, benefactor and savior of the whole world, by the people of Myra.

To Marcus Agrippa, benefactor and savior of our people, by the people of Myra.

Dessau, *ILS* no. 8784 = Ehrenberg-Jones no. 77; Thasos

The people to Livia Drusilla, wife of Caesar Augustus, divine benefactress.

The people to Julia, daughter of Caesar Augustus, ancestral benefactress.

The people to Julia, daughter of Marcus Agrippa.

C
Honors to Gaius Caesar

IGRR, Vol. IV no. 1756 = Ehrenberg-Jones no. 99

A decree of the council of the Province of Asia and by the city of Sardis in 5 BC in honor of the coming of age of Gaius Caesar, then fifteen, followed by Augustus' reply.

On motion of the chief magistrates, Metrodorus, son of Conon, and Cleinius, Musaeus, and Dionysius:

Whereas Gaius Julius Caesar, the eldest of the sons of Augustus assumed the fervently hoped-for white toga in all its splendor in place of the purple-bordered garb [of youth], and all men rejoiced witnessing the prayers for his son blossoming for Augustus;

And whereas our city on such a joyous occasion has decided that the day which brought him from boy to man be holy, a day on which annually all shall be in festal garb and wear wreaths, the annual chief magistrates shall make sacrifices to the gods and offer prayers for his safety through the sacred heralds, and consecrate jointly a statue of him, setting it up in his father's temple, and on the day on which the city received the good tidings and the decree was passed, on that day too wreaths shall be worn and sumptuous sacrifices made to the gods; and an embassy is to go to Rome and congratulate him and Augustus;

It was voted by the council and the people to send envoys chosen from the leading men to bring greetings from the city and to transmit to him a copy of this decree sealed with the official seal, and to discuss with Augustus matters of common interest for the Province of Asia and the city....

Imperator Caesar Augustus, son of a god, *pontifex maximus,* holding the tribunician power for the nineteenth year, to the magistrates and council of Sardis, greeting. Your envoys, Iollas, son of Metrodorus, and Menogenes, son of Isidorus and grandson of Menogenes, had an audience with me in Rome and transmitted to me your decree, through which you make known your decrees concerning us and show your joy at the coming to manhood of the elder of my sons. I commend your eagerness to express your thanks to me and all my house for the benefactions you receive from me. Farewell.

Année Epigraphique, 1967, no. 458 =*SEG* Vol. xxiii (1968) no. 206

Gaius Caesar, Augustus' grandson, was adopted by him, together with his brother Lucius, in 17 BC. At the age of fifteen he was designated consul for the year 1 AD, when he was to be twenty. In 1 BC, in connection with the troublesome problem of Armenia, a Roman protectorate and buffer state against the Parthians, he was put in charge of the eastern provinces with proconsular power. He died en route home in 4 AD. The following Greek inscription was set up at Messene, Province of Achaea, between 2 and 4 AD.

When Philoxenidas was secretary of the council and Theodorus magistrate, it was decreed:

Whereas Publius Cornelius Scipio, *quaestor pro praetore*,[56] with unbounded good will toward Augustus and his entire house, having made a magnificent and glorious vow to guard him from all possible harm (a vow which he has fulfilled by each and every one of his acts), conducted the Caesarian games, sparing neither expense nor zeal nor gratitude toward the gods in the sacrifices on behalf of Augustus, at the same time arranging for most of the cities throughout the province to join him in doing the same;

And whereas, when he learned that Gaius, son of Augustus, who was fighting the barbarians for the safety of all mankind, was in good health, had escaped danger, and had taken vengeance on the enemy, overjoyed at the splendid news he instructed all to be easy and calm, to put on wreaths and make sacrifices; and he himself made animal sacrifices for the safety of Gaius and was lavish with varied spectacles. In regard to these activities he was zealous that they should rival those that had gone before and at the same time that the solemnity of honors to Augustus should be equally preserved; accordingly, he left two days off the days for Augustus and began the sacrifices on behalf of Gaius from the day on which he was first designated consul;[57] and he instructed us to observe this day annually with sacrifices and the wearing of wreaths as joyfully and ... as possible....

Voted by the council on the fifteenth day before the kalends....

CIL, Vol. xi no. 1421 = Dessau, *ILS* no. 140 = Ehrenberg-Jones no. 69

The deaths of Augustus' grandsons and adopted sons, Lucius Caesar in 2 AD, and Gaius Caesar in 4 AD, who had been systematically groomed and displayed as putative successors of Augustus, evoked outpourings of grief throughout the empire. The council of Pisa in Italy erected a cenotaph for each of them. The following decree concerns that of Gaius Caesar; the briefer inscription for Lucius Caesar is also extant (*CIL*, Vol. xi no. 1420 = Dessau, *ILS* no. 139 = Ehrenberg-Jones no. 68).

Whereas on April 2 the news reached us that Gaius Caesar, son of Augustus, father of our country, *pontifex maximus*, guardian of the Roman Empire and protector of the whole world, grandson of a

79

god, after his consulship which he happily completed waging war beyond the frontiers of the Roman people, after conducting affairs of state well and conquering or receiving under our protection most warlike and mighty peoples, was wounded in the service of the country, and was snatched away from the Roman people by cruel fate because of that mischance, when he was already designated *princeps* most just and most like his father in virtues, only protector of our colony;

And whereas this event, at a time when the grief had not yet subsided which the whole colony had experienced at the demise of Lucius Caesar his brother, consul designate, augur, our patron, *princeps* of the youth, renewed and increased the grief of all of us, both as individuals and as community;

Now therefore, all the decurions and colonists ... unanimously agreed, in view of the magnitude of this great and unexpected calamity, that from that day on which news was brought of his demise up to the day on which his ashes are brought back and buried and the rites for his departed spirit have been performed, that all should put on mourning, that all the temples of the immortal gods, public baths and shops be closed, that all abstain from festivities, and that the matrons in our colony make lamentation; and that that day on which Gaius Caesar departed, the date of which is February 21, should be handed down to posterity as a day of mourning like that of the Allia,[58] and that it be observed at the present time by order and wish of all, and that it be forbidden to hold, plan, or announce hereafter on this day, that is, February 21, any public sacrifice, any thanksgivings, weddings, or public banquets, or to hold or be a spectator on that day of theatrical performances or events in the circus; and that on that day annually at public expense, through the magistrates or those who will be in charge of administration of justice at Pisa, sacrifices be offered to his departed spirit in the same place and in the same manner as such sacrifice was established for Lucius Caesar; and that there be set up in a very frequented place of our colony an arch adorned with the spoils of the peoples conquered by him or received under our protection by him, and that upon it there be placed a statue of him standing, adorned in his triumphal decorations, and next to it two gilded equestrian statues of Gaius and Lucius Caesar; and that as soon as we are able by law to elect and have duovirs of the colony, those duovirs who are first elected shall refer this decision of the decurions and all the colonists officially to the decurions, so that this may be legally enacted by virtue of their public authority, and, by their authorization, entered into the public records; and that meanwhile Titus Statulenus Iuncus, priest of Augustus, *pontifex minor* of the public worship of the Roman people, should be requested to go with envoys and beg indulgence for the present unavoidable circumstances of the colony, report this public action and will of all of us by presenting a document to Imperator Caesar Augustus, father of our country, *pontifex maximus,* holding the tribunican power for the twenty-sixth year. And this was done by Titus Statulenus Iuncus, *princeps* of our colony, priest of Augustus, *pontifex minor* of the public worship of the Roman people, by transmitting the document, as stated above, to Imperator Caesar Augustus, *pontifex maximus,* holder of the tribunician power for the twenty-sixth year, father of our country.... [The subsequent enabling decree of the decurions officially sanctioning the proposed actions is here omitted.]

CIL, Vol. xii no. 3156 = Ehrenberg-Jones no. 75

Inscription in Nemausus (Nîmes), in Narbonese Gaul, ca. 4 AD, on the temple now known as the Maison Carrée.

To Gaius Caesar, son of Augustus, consul, and to Lucius Caesar, son of Augustus, consul designate, leaders of the youth.[59]

D
Exploits of Drusus

After the first decade of the Principate, as materialism grew in Rome, Maecenas was dropped from Augustus' favor, and harsh realities of policy replaced the earlier wave of idealism, Horace no longer felt his previous deep commitment to the new order. His continuing praises of Augustus and the imperial family became conventional, bordering on Ovidian flattery. The following ode was written in 15 BC, after Drusus,

Augustus' stepson, decisively defeated Alpine tribes in the Tridentine Alps.

Horace, *Odes* Book 4 no. 4

Just like the eagle, minister of the thunderbolt, to whom the king of the gods granted dominion over the flying birds ..., so Drusus was seen by the Vindelici waging war in the Rhaetian Alps.... But their bands, victorious far and wide for a long time, beaten in their turn by the strategy of a youth, learned what a mind, what character properly nourished in an auspicious home could achieve, what the paternal spirit of Augustus toward the two Neros could accomplish. The brave are begotten by the brave and good. Bullocks and horses have the excellence of their sires, and fierce eagles do not beget the peaceful dove. But education develops inborn potentiality, and moral training strengthens the heart. Whenever discipline is lacking, sins disgrace a noble heart.

What you owe, O Rome, to the line of Nero the Metaurus River is witness, and conquered Hasdrubal, and the beautiful day when the darkness was dispelled from Latium[60] that first smiled with benevolent victory, as the dread African rode through the Italian cities like a flame through torches or the East Wind over Sicilian waters.

After this, increasingly the Roman people grew more determined with their favorable efforts, and the shrines devastated by the wicked riots of the Carthaginians had the gods made upright again, and finally perfidious Hannibal said: "Like deer, the prey of rapacious wolves, we actually pursue people whose greatest triumph it is when they deceive and elude. An heroic people, which from the ashes of Troy brought to Italian cities their sacred things tossed on the Tyrrhenian Sea, and their children and elderly parents... The hydra was not stronger when its body was severed and it grew back against Hercules, fearful of being overcome; and the Colchians did not provide a greater wonder, nor Echion's Thebes.[61] Plunge them in the depths, they come out brighter; struggle with them, they rush forth an unscathed victor, with great credit, and will wage battles talked about by their wives.

No longer shall I send proud messages to Carthage. All hope and the fortune of our name have fallen, have fallen, with the removal of Hasdrubal.

"There is nothing that the Claudian family cannot accomplish, that family which Jupiter with his benevolent divine will protects, and their wise counsels are beneficial through the crises of war."

17
WOMEN OF
THE IMPERIAL FAMILY

Augustus was indeed fortunate to have in his immediate family two women such as his wife Livia and his half-sister Octavia, exemplars of traditional Roman womanhood.

Livia was the first of the line of influential Roman women who, in the centuries following, came to dominate the royal court. Her influence on Augustus would appear to have been in the direction of clemency and moderation. As devoted mother of Tiberius, and step-mother to Augustus' adopted sons, she was subjected to much malicious gossip. But Augustus died with her name on his lips: "Livia, live mindful of our marriage, and farewell." (Suetonius, *Life of Augustus* chapter 99.1.) She died in 29 AD at the age of eighty-six, having been hailed in the empire as "Mother of Her Country," and "Progenitor of the World." "In spite of malignant tradition we may well believe that she well deserved the honorific titles that many provincial cities gratefully gave her, and she was fully worthy of the great age in which she lived." (M. P. Charlesworth, *Cambridge Ancient History,* Vol. x, p. 634.)

Octavia, on the other hand, was a retiring figure, devoted to her children and to her "only husband," Mark Antony.

To Augustus' shame and frustration, his only child, Julia, long the helpless pawn of his dynastic plans, in a mature display of independence turned out to be one of the most dissolute women of the times.

A
Livia

Velleius, *Roman History* Book 2 chapter 75.3

Livia, the daughter of the most noble and most brave man, Drusus Claudianus, was the most eminent of Roman women in birth, in character, and in beauty, whom we later saw as the wife of Augustus, and, after his deification, as his priestess and daughter.

Long before, she was in flight from the arms and troops of the same Caesar who was soon to be her husband, carrying in her bosom her two-year-old Tiberius Caesar, destined to become the defender of the Roman Empire and the son of this same Caesar....

Tacitus, *Annals* Book 1 chapter 5

Tiberius, just as he was entering Illyria, was summoned by hasty letters from his mother. Sufficient evidence is lacking whether at the city of Nola he found Augustus still breathing or already dead. For Livia had the house and the roads blockaded under heavy guard, and from time to time favourable reports were distributed until, after provisions were made as the situation demanded, the same bulletin announced that Augustus had died and that Nero [Tiberius] was in control of the state.

Dio Cassius, *History of Rome* Book 57 chapter 12.2−6

Livia was honored very greatly, far above all women of the past, so that she could at any time receive the Senate and those individuals of the people who desired to greet her at home; and this was entered in the public record. The rescripts of Tiberius for some time included her name also, and communications were addressed to both alike. She never ventured to enter the Senate House or the camps or the assemblies, but she undertook to administer everything as if she were the empress. For during Augustus' lifetime she had enormous influence, and she often claimed that she had made Tiberius the emperor. Therefore, she was unwilling to rule on an equal basis with him, but wanted to have priority over him. Consequently, various extraordinary propositions were introduced: many expressed the opinion that she be addressed as "Mother of Her Country," while many others proposed that she be called "Parent." And others propounded that Tiberius be named after her, so that, as Greeks were called by their father's name, he be called by the name of his mother. Piqued by these matters, he neither confirmed the decrees on her behalf, except for a few, nor did he permit her to do anything immoderate.... At length he removed her entirely from public affairs, but permitted her to manage affairs at home; as she was troublesome in that capacity, he absented himself from the city, and in every way kept away from her, and ultimately withdrew to Capri chiefly because of her.

Tacitus, *Annals* Book 5 chapter 1

During the consulship of Rubellius and Fufius [29 AD], both of whom had the surname Geminus, Julia Augusta [i.e., Livia] died in extreme old age, a woman of most eminent nobility through her birth in the Claudian family and by virtue of her adoption among the Livii and Julii. She had children by her first marriage to Tiberius Nero, who was an exile from the Perusine War but returned to the city when peace had been reached between Sextus Pompey and the triumvirs [39 BC]. Shortly after, Caesar, attracted by her beauty, took her from her husband (no one knows if she was unwilling) and was so hasty that he brought her pregnant into his home with no decent interval allowed for her labor. After this she produced no other offspring, but her connection with the Augustan blood-line increased with the marriage of Agrippina and Germanicus, by which she shared [with Augustus] great-grandchildren. In the purity of her household she used the ancient model, but she was more sophisticated than approved by women of old; headstrong as a mother and gracious as a wife, she complemented well the political skills of her husband and the deception of her son. Her funeral was ordinary, and her will was for a long time unexecuted. A eulogy was delivered from the Rostra by Gaius Caesar [Caligula], her great-grandson, who soon gained the imperial power.

B
Octavia

Plutarch, *Life of Antony* chapters 31.1−3 and 54.1−2

Octavia was an older sister of Caesar [Octavian], but not by the same mother, for she was born from Ancharia, while he, by a later marriage, was the child of Atia. He loved his sister very much, a wondrous thing of a woman, as the saying goes.... All encouraged this marriage [with Antony], hoping that Octavia, who had dignity and intelligence in addition to such great beauty, as soon as she became his and the object of his love — as is natural with such a woman — would be the source of agreement and complete salvation for them. Therefore, when both men [Antony and Octavian] came to an agreement, they went to Rome and there they celebrated the marriage of Octavia, although remarriage was not permitted by law until ten months after the death of the husband. However, by a special decree of the Senate the time restriction was remitted for them....

Octavia was deemed to have been insulted [by Antony's affair with Cleopatra], and so Caesar ordered her, when she returned from Athens, to live in her own house. However, she refused to leave her husband's home, and indeed she begged Octavian, unless for other reasons he had decided to declare war on Antony, to ignore her situation, declaring that it was an ugly thing to hear that the two greatest generals, one out of love for a woman, the other because of jealous rivalry, immersed the Romans in civil war. The things she said were confirmed by her deeds. For she lived in her husband's house as if he were present, and splendidly and magnificently raised his children, not only those born from her but also those [previously] born from Fulvia. Receiving friends of Antony's who were sent [to Rome] to seek political offices or on business, she helped them in their requests to Caesar. Through this she unintentionally hurt Antony, for he was hated because of his mistreatment of such a woman.

C
Julia

Suetonius, *Life of Augustus* chapter 64.2

In bringing up his daughter and granddaughters he even had them trained in weaving, and he forbade them to say or do anything except openly and what might be recorded in the household diary. Indeed, he forbade contact with outsiders to such an extent that he once wrote Lucius Vinicius, a distinguished and proper youth, that he had not behaved with propriety because he had come to Baiae to pay his respects to his daughter [without permission].

Macrobius, *Saturnalia* Book 2 chapter 5.2–9

Julia was thirty-eight years old, a period in life, if she had kept any good sense, [she would have regarded as] verging on old age. But she often abused her good fortune and the indulgence of her father. On the other hand, she had a sincere love for literature and great learning, which were easy to obtain in that household. In addition to these qualities, a gentle regard for humanity and a disposition not in the least cruel gained great respect for the woman from those who were aware of her vices and yet marveled as well at the great diversity in her.

Again and again, in language balanced between gentle indulgence and severity, her father admonished her to restrain her extravagant life-style and her notorious companions. At the same time, whenever he looked at his numerous grandchildren and noticed their resemblance to Agrippa, he was ashamed to have doubted his daughter's virtue.

So Augustus flattered himself that, despite her cheerful exuberant spirits, seemingly wanton, his daughter was completely free of any guilt.... Therefore, among friends he said that he had of necessity two spoiled daughters to put up with — the government and Julia.

She once came to him dressed somewhat indecently. Her father kept quiet although he was offended by the sight. On the following day, changing the style of her dress, she pleased her father, whom she embraced with affected primness. But whereas the day before he had restraind his distress, he could now no longer restrain his joy, saying: "How much more suitable is this dress for the daughter of Augustus." Julia was not without a defense, as follows: "Today I have dressed for the eyes of my father, yesterday for my husband's."

The following is a well-known anecdote. At a gladiatorial show Livia's and Julia's dissimilar styles in their respective retinues caught the attention of the people. Distinguished men attended Livia, but Julia was seated surrounded by a group of young men of the self-indulgent type. Her father admonished her in writing to take notice of the vast difference between the two most prominent women of the state. Her reply was a neat one: "These young men will grow old along with me."...

Moreover, when Julia heard a conservative friend trying to convince her that she would be better off if she accommodated herself to the example of the simple life-style of her father, she said: "He forgets that he is Caesar, but I remember that I am Caesar's daughter."

Velleius, *Roman History* Book 2 chapter 100.2 – 5

But in the city in the very same year in which Augustus was consul with Gallus Caninius [2 BC] ... in Augustus's own household a storm broke loose, indecent even to mention and horrible to recall. For his daughter Julia, completely unmindful of her distinguished father and husband [Tiberius], left unperformed not a single act tainted by excess and sexual passion which a woman could do or experience in disgrace. She was in the habit of measuring the magnitude of her fortune by the grossness of her sin, championing as licit anything that was her desire. Iullus Antonius, the outstanding example of Caesar's clemency, violated his house, but then himself avenged the crime he had committed. When his father [Marcus Antonius] had been defeated, Augustus had not only granted Iullus life, but also honored him with a priesthood, praetorship, consulship, and administration of provinces; and by marriage with the daughter of his sister,[62] he had brought him into a very close relationship. Quintus Crispinus also, who covered up his extraordinary depravity with a stern brow, Appius Claudius, Sempronius Gracchus, a Scipio, and other men of both ranks but of lesser prestige, debauched the daughter of Caesar and wife of Nero [Tiberius], and they paid the penalty which they would have suffered if they had violated the wife of any man. Julia was relegated to an island and removed form the sight of her fatherland and parents, although her natural mother Scribonia voluntarily accompanied her and remained a constant companion in her exile.

Dio Cassius, *History of Rome* Book 55 chapters 10–12

Detecting at length that his daughter Julia was so licentious in her behavior that she reveled and engaged in late night drinking bouts in the Forum and even on the Rostra, Augustus became enraged. For he had suspected even before this that she was not living an upright life, but he refused to believe it.... Having learned what was going on, he flew into such a rage that he did not keep the matters within the household but communicated them to the Senate. Thereupon Julia was exiled to the island of Pandateria near Campania, and her mother Scribonia voluntarily accompanied her. Of those who had been intimate with her, Iullus Antonius, on the grounds that he had acted out of aspirations for monarchy, was put to death along with other distinguished men, while the others were banished to islands. And since among them was a tribune, he was not put on trial before he had completed his term of office.

Seneca, *On Benefits* Book 6 chapter 32.1–2

The deified Augustus exiled his daughter, lewd beyond reproach of shamelessness, and he made public the acts that disgraced the house of the *princeps*: that she had admitted adulterers in droves and had roamed through the city at night in revels, and that the Forum itself and the Rostra, from which her father had sponsored the law on adultery, had been chosen by the daughter for debauchery; she had daily resorted to the Statue of Marsyas,[63] where she turned from adultery to selling her favors and sought the right of all license with unknown adulterers. Not being able to restrain his anger, he made the matter public…. After some time had elapsed, and shame slowly replaced his anger, he lamented that he had not suppressed in silence things he had not known for such a long time until it was disgraceful to mention them. As a result, he often exclaimed: "None of these things would have happened to me if either Agrippa or Maecenas had lived…."

18

'RES GESTAE' THE ACHIEVEMENTS OF AUGUSTUS

Of the many writings of Augustus during his long life the only one that has survived intact is what has come to be called the *Res Gestae Divi Augusti* ("Achievements of the Deified Augustus"). This personally prepared "obituary notice" was found among his papers (see no. 19 below) when he died, just before reaching his seventy-sixth birthday. It was originally inscribed on bronze tablets, now lost, set up before his mausoleum in Rome. The text is known from three copies (in Latin and a Greek version) found in Asia Minor, in what was then the Province of Galatia: at Ancyra (modern Ankara), Antioch, and Apollonia. This autobiographical "Achievements of Augustus" is our most important inscription dealing with Roman affairs — "the queen of Latin inscriptions" it was called by the great historian of Rome, Theodor Mommsen.

In purpose and contents the *Res Gestae* of Augustus is a unique and unprecedented document, the closest to it being the eulogies prepared to commemorate the deeds of eminent Romans and the vainglorious inscriptions of Oriental monarchs. Augustus intended this summary of his career mostly for the eyes of the Roman plebs. Had he prepared it for Roman senators or the leading men in the provinces, he would have stressed other achievements and contributions. Here Augustus does not deal with constitutional theory, nor is he reflective or philosophical, but pragmatic, matter-of-fact. It is, however, a tendentious document, for Augustus is deliberately selective in his account, omitting much. But, as Samuel Johnson once said, "In lapidary inscriptions a man is not upon oath." Augustus' purpose was to set forth the record of himself as an extraordinary person, a man of unique qualities, virtues, and achievements, a leader unparalleled in Roman history, indeed in the history of the world.

CIL, Vol. III, pp. 769–799 = Ehrenberg-Jones, pp. 1–31 = *ADA,* pp. 20–63

Below is a copy of the achievements of the deified Augustus, whereby he subjected the world to the empire of the Roman people, and of the expenditures he made on behalf of the country and the Roman people, as inscribed on two pillars set up in Rome.

1 At the age of nineteen, on my own initiative and at private expense, I raised an army through which I championed the liberty of the country, which was oppressed by the tyranny of a faction.[64] For this reason the Senate decreed honors to me and coopted me into its body, in the consulship of Gaius Pansa and Aulus Hirtius [43 BC], according me consular status in debates, and it granted me *imperium*. It ordered me with the rank of propraetor to take measures, together with the consuls, to protect the state from harm.[65] Moreover, in the same year, when both consuls had died in war, the people chose me consul and triumvir for regulating the state.

2 Those who assassinated my father[66] I drove into exile, a- venging their crime through trials with due process; and after- wards I defeated them twice in battle,[67] when they waged war against the country.

3 I often waged wars on land and sea, both civil and foreign, in the whole world, and as victor I spared all citizens who asked pardon. Those foreign peoples who could safely be pardoned I preferred to preserve rather than exterminate. Roman citizens who were under military oath to me numbered about 500,000. From this number I settled in colonies or sent back to their municipalities, after completion of their terms of service, some- what more than 300,000, and I assigned them lands or granted them money as rewards for their military service. I captured 600 ships, not including vessels smaller than triremes.[68]

4 I celebrated an ovation twice and three curule triumphs[69] and was hailed *imperator* twenty-one times. When the Senate decreed still more triumphs to me, I declined them all. I depo- sited in the Capitol the laurels decorating my *fasces*,[70] after fulfil- ling the vows I had pronounced in each war. For exploits success- fully accomplished on land and sea by me or through my legates acting under my auspices, the Senate fifty-five times decreed thanksgivings to the immortal gods. Moreover, the number of days on which thanskgivings were made by decree of the Senate was 890. In my triumphs there were led before my chariot nine kings or children of kings. At this writing [14 AD] I had been

consul thirteen times, and I was in the thirty-seventh year of my tribunician power.

5 The dictatorship offered to me, both in my absence and in my presence, by both the people and the Senate in the consulship of Marcus Marcellus and Lucius Arruntius [22 BC] I did not accept. I did not decline in a time of extreme scarcity of grain the care of the grain supply, which I administered in such a manner that within the space of a few days I freed the entire citizen body from fear and immediate danger by my personal expenditures and my supervision. The consulship also proffered to me at that time, to be held annually and in perpetuity, I refused.

6 In the consulship of Marcus Vinicius and Quintus Lucretius [19 BC], and afterwards of Publius Lentulus and Gnaeus Lentulus [18 BC], and a third time in that of Paullus Fabius Maximus and Quintus Tubero [11 BC], when the Senate and the Roman people agreed that I be made sole guardian of the laws and morals with supreme power, I did not accept any magistracy proffered to me that was contrary to the traditions of our ancestors. The measures the Senate at that time desired to be taken through me, I carried out through the tribunician power. In this power I voluntarily requested and received from the Senate a colleague five times.[71]

7 I was triumvir for the regulation of the state for ten consecutive years [43–33 BC]. I was ranking senator for forty years, up to the date of the present writing. I was *pontifex maximus,* augur, member of the College of Fifteen for Making Sacrifices, member of the College of Seven for Conducting Sacred Feasts, Arval Brother, Sodalis Titius, and Fetial.[72]

8 I increased the number of patricians in my fifth consulship by order of the people and Senate. I revised the list of senators three times. And in my sixth consulship [28 BC], together with my colleague Marcus Agrippa, I conducted a census of the people and I performed the *lustrum*[73] after a lapse of forty-two years. At that *lustrum* there were counted 4,063,000 Roman citizens. Then a second time I performed the *lustrum* alone, with consular power, in the consulship of Gaius Censorinus and Gaius Asinius [8 BC]. At that *lustrum* there were counted 4,233,000 Roman citizens. And a third time, with consular power and with Tiberius Caesar my son as colleague, in the consulship of Sextus Pompeius and Sextus Appulcius [14 AD]. At this *lustrum* there were counted

4,937,000 Roman citizens. By new laws sponsored by me I restored many traditions of our ancestors which were becoming obsolete in our generation, and I myself handed down traditions in many spheres for imitation by posterity.

9 Vows for my health were decreed by the Senate to be undertaken every fifth year through the consuls and priests. In accordance with these vows games were given in my lifetime, sometimes by the four most distinguished colleges of priests, sometimes by the consuls. Moreover, the whole body of the citizens, individually and by towns, with one accord prayed continuously at all the shrines for my health.

10 My name, by decree of the Senate, was included in the Salian Hymn, and it was enacted by law that I be sacrosanct in perpetuity, and that I possess the tribunician power as long as I live. As for the office of *pontifex maximus,* I refused to accept this in place of a colleague while he was still alive,[74] although the people proffered this priestly office to me, which my father had held. This priesthood some years later, when the man died who had seized it in a time of civil disturbance, I accepted in the consulship of Publius Sulpicius and Gaius Valgius [12 BC]. For my election a multitude flocked from all of Italy such as never before previously had been recorded at Rome.

11 The altar of Fortuna the Home-bringer before the temples of Honor and Virtue at the Porta Capena was consecrated by the Senate in honor of my return, and it ordered the pontiffs and Vestal Virgins to make annual sacrifice on the anniversary of the day on which, in the consulship of Quintus Lucretius and Marcus Vinicius [19 BC], I returned to the city from Syria, and it named the day Augustalia from my name.

12 By authority of the Senate, a part of the praetors and the tribunes of the plebs, together with the consul Quintus Lucretius, and the leading men were sent to meet me in Campania, an honor which hitherto had been decreed to no one besides myself. When I returned to Rome from Spain and the Gauls, after successfully settling affairs in those provinces in the consulship of Tiberius Nero and Publius Quintilius [13 BC], the Senate voted in honor of my return to consecrate the Altar of Peace in the Campus Martius, on which it ordered the magistrates, priests, and Vestals to make an annual anniversary sacrifice.

13 The temple of Janus Quirinus, which our ancestors desired to be closed when peace through victories had been won on land and sea throughout the whole empire of the Roman people, although before my birth from the founding of the city it is recorded that it was closed twice in all, the Senate in my Principate decreed three times that it be closed.

14 My sons, whom fortune took from me when they were but youths, Gaius and Lucius Caesar, the Senate and the Roman people in my honor named consuls-designate when they were in their fifteenth year, with the understanding that they were to enter that magistracy five years later. And from the day on which they were conducted into the Forum,[75] the Senate decreed that they were to participate in the councils of state. Moreover, the whole body of Roman equestrians hailed them *principes iuventutis* ("Leaders of the Youth") and presented them with silver shields and spears.

15 To each man of the Roman plebs I paid 300 sesterces under my father's will, and in my own name when I was consul for the fifth time I gave them 400 sesterces each from spoils of war. And again in my tenth consulship I paid out to each man 400 sesterces as largess from my own patrimony; and in my eleventh consulship I bought up grain out of my private funds and made twelve distributions of grain; and in the twelfth year of my tribunician power I gave each man 400 sesterces for a third time. These largesses of mine never reached less than 250,000 persons. In the eighteenth year of my tribunician power, when I was consul for the twelfth time, I gave each man of the urban plebs, to the number of 320,000, 60 denarii. When I was consul for the fifth time I gave to each of the colonists from my soldiers 1,000 sesterces out of booty. About 120,000 men in the colonies received this triumphal largess. In my thirteenth consulship I gave 60 denarii apiece to the plebs who were then receiving public grain. These numbered a little over 200,000 persons.

16 In my fourth consulship, and afterwards in the consulship of Marcus Crassus and Gnaeus Lentulus Augur [14 BC], I paid cash to the municipalities for the lands which I assigned to the soldiers. This sum was about 600,000,000 sesterces which I paid out for Italian lands, and about 260,000,000 sesterces for provincial lands. Of all those who established colonies of soldiers in Italy

and the provinces I was the first and only one to have done this in the memory of my generation. And afterwards, in the consulship of Tiberius Nero and Gnaeus Piso [7 BC], likewise in that of Gaius Antistius and Decimus Laelius [6 BC], of Gaius Calvisius and Lucius Pasienus [4 BC], of Lucius Lentulus and Marcus Messalla [3 BC], and of Lucius Caninius and Quintus Fabricius [2 BC], to the soldiers whom, on completion of their service, I settled in their municipalities, I paid monetary bonuses, and for this I spent about 400,000,000 sesterces.

17 Four times I assisted the public treasury with my own funds, transferring to those in charge of the treasury for this purpose 150,000,000 sesterces. And in the consulship of Marcus Lepidus and Lucius Arruntius [6 AD] I transferred from my own patrimony 170,000,000 sesterces to the Military Treasury, which was founded at my advice for the purpose of giving bonuses to soldiers who had completed twenty or more years of service.

18 From the year when Gnaeus and Publius Lentulus were consuls [18 BC], whenever public revenues were insufficient, I made distributions from my own granary and patrimony in the form of grain and money, sometimes to 100,000 persons, sometimes to many more.

19 I built the Senate House, and the Chalcidicum next to it, and the temple of Apollo on the Palatine with its porticoes, the temple of the Deified Julius, the Lupercal, the portico at the Circus Flaminius, which I permitted to be named Octavia after the name of the person who had previously built it on the same site, the *pulvinar* at the Circus Maximus, the temples of Jupiter Smiter and Jupiter the Thunderer on the Capitoline, the temple of Quirinus, the temple of Minerva and Juno the Queen and Jupiter Freedom on the Aventine, the temple of the Lares at the top of the Sacred Way, the temple of the Penates Gods on the Velia, the temple of Youth, the temple of the Great Mother on the Palatine.

20 I restored the Capitol and the Theater of Pompey, both works at great expense, without inscribing my own name. I restored the channels of the aqueducts, which were falling into disrepair through age in several places, and I doubled the water of the aqueduct called Marcia by bringing in a new source into its channel. The Forum Julium and the basilica which was between the temple of Castor and the temple of Saturn, works which had

been begun and carried well along by my father, I completed; and when the same basilica was destroyed by fire, I began to rebuild it on an enlarged site in the name of my sons, and in case I do not complete it in my lifetime, I ordered it to be completed by my heirs. I restored eighty-two temples of the gods in the city when I was consul for the sixth time, overlooking none which required repair at that time. When I was consul for the seventh time, I rebuilt the Via Flaminia from the city to Ariminum, as well as all the bridges except the Mulvian and Minucian.

21 On a private site I built from booty the temple of Mars the Avenger and the Forum Augustum. The theater at the temple of Apollo I built on ground in large part purchased from private persons, in the name of Marcus Marcellus, my son-in-law. From booty I dedicated gifts in the Capitol and in the temple of the Deified Julius and in the temple of Apollo and in the temple of Vesta and in the temple of Mars the Avenger, which cost me about 100,000,000 sesterces. In my fifth consulship, I remitted to municipalities and colonies in Italy 35,000 pounds of crown gold[76] which they were contributing to my triumphs; and afterwards, whenever I was hailed *imperator,* I refused the crown gold which the municipalities and colonies decreed as graciously as previously.

22 I gave gladiatorial games three times in my own name, and five times in the name of my sons or grandsons. At these games about 10,000 men fought. Twice in my own name and a third time in the name of a grandson I gave a display of athletes summoned from all parts. Four times I produced shows in my own name, and twenty-three times in place of other magistrates. On behalf of the College of Fifteen, at its head, with Marcus Agrippa as colleague, I gave the Secular Games in the consulship of Gaius Furnius and Gaius Silanus [17 BC] When I was consul for the thirteenth time, I was first to give the Games of Mars, which after that time in each subsequent year were given by the consuls in accordance with a decree of the Senate and a law. I gave for the people hunts of African beasts in the Circus or in the Forum or in the amphitheaters, in my own name or that of my sons and grandsons, on twenty-six occasions, during which about 3,500 beasts were destroyed.

23 I gave the people a display of a naval battle across the Tiber in the place where there is now the grove of the Caesars, having excavated a site 1,800 feet in length and 1,200 in width. Here thirty beaked ships, triremes, or biremes, and still more smaller vessels, engaged in combat. In these fleets about 3,000 men, aside from the rowers, fought.

24 After my victory, in the temples of all the cities of the Province of Asia I replaced the ornaments which the person with whom I had waged war[77] had, after despoiling the temples, taken into his private possession. About eighty silver statues of mine, on foot, horse, and in chariots, once stood in the city. These I myself removed, and from the money I set up gifts of gold in the temple of Apollo in my name and the names of those who had honored me with the statues.

25 I pacified the sea by suppressing the pirates.[78] In that war, of the slaves who had fled from their masters and had taken up arms against the state, about 30,000 I handed over to their masters for punishment. All of Italy took an oath of allegiance to me voluntarily and requested me as leader of the war in which I was victorious at Actium. The same oath was taken by the provinces of the Gauls, Spains, Africa, Sicily, and Sardinia. Among those who campaigned then under my standards there were more than 700 senators, from whom those who either had been consuls before or afterwards became consuls there were, up to the day of this writing, eighty-three, and of priests about 170.

26 I enlarged the territory of all the provinces of the Roman people that neighbored upon peoples who were not subject to our empire. The Gallic and Spanish provinces, likewise Germany — that is, the territory bounded by the Ocean from Gades to the mouth of the Elbe River — I pacified. The Alps from the region bordering on the Adriatic up to the Tuscan Sea I pacified, without bringing an unjustified war against any people. My fleet sailed through the Ocean from the mouth of the Rhine to the East as far as the territory of the Cimbri, into which no Roman, either on land or sea, had previously penetrated. The Cimbri, Charydes, and Semnones, and other peoples of the Germans in the same territory sought my friendship and that of the Roman people through envoys. At my order and under my auspices two

armies were led at almost the same time into Ethiopia and Arabia called Fortunate, and very great numbers of the forces of the enemy in each people were killed in battle, and a number of towns captured. In Ethiopia an advance was made as far as Napata, which is very close to Meroe; in Arabia an army advanced into the territory of the Sabaeans as far as the town of Mariba.

27 I annexed Egypt to the empire of the Roman people. As for Greater Armenia, after the assassination of her king Artaxes, though I might have made it a province, I preferred, following the precedent of our ancestors, to hand this kingdom over to Tigranes (son of Artavasdes, grandson of King Tigranes) through Tiberius Nero, who was then my stepson. And the same people, when it revolted and rebelled and was subdued through my son Gaius, I handed over to the rule of King Ariobarzanes (son of Artabazenes), King of the Medes, and after his death to his son Artavasdes. When he was killed, I sent to that kingdom Tigranes, who was a scion of the royal family of the Armenians. All the provinces which extend across the Adriatic Sea eastward and Cyrene, which for the most part were already in the hands of kings, as well as Sicily and Sardinia, which had been seized in the slave war, I recovered.

28 I established colonies of soldiers in Africa, Sicily, Macedonia, in each of the Spains, Achaea, Asia, Syria, Narbonese Gaul, and Pisidia. Italy, moreover, contains, established by my authority, twenty-eight colonies which in my lifetime became famous and populous.

29 A number of military standards lost by other generals I recovered after defeating the enemy, from Spain, and Gaul, and the Dalmatians. The Parthians I compelled to restore to me the spoils and standards of three Roman armies, and to seek the friendship of the Roman people as suppliants.[79] Moreover, those standards I deposited in the inner shrine of the Temple of Mars the Avenger.

30 The Pannonian peoples, whom before my Principate the army of the Roman people never approached, were conquered through Tiberius Nero, who was then my stepson and legate. I brought them into the empire of the Roman people and extended the frontier of Illyricum to the banks of the Danube River. When an army of Dacians crossed the Danube, it was defeated and

overwhelmed under my auspices, and afterwards my army was led across the Danube and compelled the Dacian peoples to submit to the commands of the Roman people.

31 From India were often send to me royal embassies, previously not seen in the presence of any Roman general. Our friendship was sought through envoys by the Bastarnians, the Scythians, and by the kings of the Sarmatians on both sides of the Don River, and also by the kings of the Albanians, the Hiberians, and the Medes.

32 There fled to me for protection [two] kings of the Parthians — Tiridates, and afterwards Phraates (son of King Phraates) — Artavasdes of the Medes, Artaxares of the Adiabenians, Dumnobellaunus and Tincommius of the Britons, Maelo of the Sugambrians, and ... of the Marcomanian Suebians. Phraates, King of the Parthians, son of Orodes, sent me all of his sons and grandsons to Italy, though not conquered in war, seeking my friendship through the use of his children as pledges. A number of other peoples with whom previously there had existed no exchange of embassies and friendship, experienced the good faith of the Roman people in my Principate.

33 The Parthian and Median peoples, through ambassadors who were the leading men of those people, sought and received kings from me: the Parthians received Vonones, son of King Phraates, grandson of King Orodes; the Medes Ariobarzanes, son of King Artavasdes, grandson of King Ariobarzanes.

34 In my sixth and seventh consulships, after I had ended the civil wars and by universal consent had obtained complete power, I handed over the state from my power to the will of the Senate and the Roman people. For this service, by decree of the Senate I was named Augustus, and the doorposts of my house were publicly decorated with laurels, and the civic crown was attached to my doorway, and a golden shield was placed in the Julian Senate House, which on its inscription testified that it was given to me by the Senate and the Roman people for my virtue, clemency, justice, and devotion. After this time I had priority over all in authority, but had no more power than any others who were also my colleagues in magistracies.

35 When I was holding the consulship for the thirteenth time, the Senate, the Equestrian Order, and the Roman people unani-

mously named me "Father of Our Country" and decreed that this title be inscribed in the vestibule of my house, in the Julian Senate House, in the Forum Augustum, and on the pedestal of the four-horse chariot which had been set up in my honor in accordance with a decree of the Senate.

At this writing I was in my seventy-sixth year.

There are also four appendices to the *Res Gestae,* which are here omitted. They were not part of the original document, but summarize the sums expended by Augustus and recapitulate his public works.

From the *Res Gestae* of Augustus at Ancyra:
beginning of the Latin text.
Courtesy of Walter de Gruyter, from M. Schede and H. St. Schulz,
Ankara und Augustus (Berlin 1937) Plate 36

19
AUGUSTUS' WILL AND LAST DOCUMENTS

Suetonius, *Life of Augustus* chapter 101

He made a will in the consulship of Lucius Plancus and Gaius Silius [13 AD] on the third of April, one year and four months before his death.... As his chief heirs he named Tiberius to two-thirds and Livia to one-third, and he ordered both of them to assume his name. As heirs in the second degree he named Drusus, son of Tiberius, to one-third, and for the rest Germanicus and his three sons; in the third degree he named many of his relatives and friends. He left to the Roman people 40,000,000 sesterces, to the tribes 3,500,000, to each soldier of the Praetorian Guard 1,000, to the soldiers of the urban cohorts 500 each, and to the soldiers of the legions 300. He ordered this sum to be paid at once, for he had this in a separate account and always set aside. He ordered the remaining legacies to be paid at various times (some amounted to 20,000 sesterces), setting one year as the final date for paying these and giving as explanation the smallness of his private estate, declaring that not more than 150,000,000 sesterces would come to his heirs. For though he had received from the wills of friends 1,400,000,000 sesterces in the preceding twenty years, all this, together with the two paternal patrimonies and other inheritances, he had spent on behalf of the state. His daughter Julia and his granddaughter Julia, if anything happened to them, he forbade to be buried in his mausoleum.

Dio Cassius, *History of Rome* Book 56 chapters 32–33

Drusus took his will from the Vestal Virgins, with whom it had been deposited, and brought it into the Senate. Those who had witnessed the will examined its seals, and it was then read in the hearing of the Senate... Polybius, an imperial freedman, read the will, since it was not proper for a senator to read any such document. In it two-thirds was left to Tiberius, the rest to Livia (so some say).... These two then were designated his heirs. He also instructed that many items and sums of money be given to many persons, both relatives and others who were not related, not only to senators and those of the Equestrian Order but also to kings. To the people he left 40,000,000 sesterces, to the Praetorian soliders 1,000 sesterces each, and half that amount to every member of the urban cohorts, and to each of the rest of the citizen soldiers 300 sesterces. In addition, he ordered that in the case of children whose fathers' estates he had inherited while they were minors, the whole sum with accrued interest be restored to them when they reached majority. This was his policy even in his lifetime. For, whenever he inherited the estate of anyone having children, he restored all of it to his children, immediately if they were already grownup, otherwise later. Although such was his position toward the children of others, he did not restore his daughter from exile (yet he considered her worthy of gifts), and he instructed that she not be buried in his mausoleum....

Four rolls were then brought in, from which Drusus read the contents. In the first Augustus had detailed all the arrangements of his funeral; in the second were recorded all his accomplishments, which he ordered to be inscribed upon bronze tablets set up in front of his mausoleum. The third contained details of military matters, revenues, and public expenditures, the sum of money in the treasuries, and whatever else of the sort that related to administration. The fourth contained directives and commands for Tiberius and the state, such as not to free many slaves, lest the city be filled with a motley rabble, and not to admit too many into citizenship, so that the distance between them and subjects might be considerable. He urged them to entrust public business to those who were capable both in intelligence and action, and not to let these matters depend upon a single man. In this way no one would aspire to monarchy, nor in turn would the public sector collapse if one man fell. He added the view that they be content with their present possessions and under no circumstances wish to expand the Empire farther; for, he said, it would be difficult to guard it and they would run the risk as a result of losing even their present territory.

20

DEIFICATION OF AUGUSTUS

Dio Cassius, *History of Rome* Book 56 chapter 46

At that time [Sept. 17, 14 AD] they proclaimed Augustus immortal, allocated to him a body of priests and sacred rites, and made Livia, already called Julia and Augusta, his priestess. They also granted her the use of a lictor in the exercise of her sacred duties. And she bestowed 1,000,000 sesterces upon a certain Numerius Atticus, a senator who was an ex-praetor, because, as in the accounts concerning Proculus and Romulus, he swore that he had seen Augustus ascending to heaven.[80] A shrine voted by the Senate and built by Livia and Tiberius was erected to him in Rome; other shrines were constructed in many different places, some communities building them voluntarily and others unwillingly. Also, the house at Nola where he died was consecrated to him. Now, during the time in which the shrine was being constructed in Rome, they placed a golden death mask of him on a couch in the temple of Mars, and to this they paid all the honors that they were later to accord to his statue. The following were additional honors voted him: that his image should not be displayed in somebody else's funeral procession, that the consuls should celebrate his birthday with games like the *Ludi Martiales,* and that the tribunes of the plebs, since they were sacrosanct too, should be in charge of the Augustan Games. These persons conducted everything else in the customary manner.... Besides this, Livia observed a private festival in his honor for three days in the palace, a ceremony which is still continued up to the present by whoever happens to be emperor.

The Pantheon, Rome, built by Agrippa, reconstructed by Hadrian.
Courtesy of Anton Schroll & Co., Vienna

II
LIFE IN ROME
AND ITALY

21
'A CITY OF MARBLE'

A
The Imperial Capital

Suetonius, *Life of Augustus* chapters 28–30

The city, which was not adorned in a manner suitable to the grandeur of the Empire and was liable to flooding and fires, he so beautified that he could rightly boast that he found the city built of brick and left it marble....

He built many public works, among them in particular the following: his forum, with the temple of Mars the Avenger; the temple of Apollo on the Palatine; and the temple of Jupiter the Thunderer on the Capitoline.... He had vowed to build the temple of Mars in the war of Philippi, which was undertaken to avenge his father; therefore he decreed that here the Senate should deliberate on wars and triumphs, and that from it those who were on their way to the provinces with *imperium* should be escorted, and those who had returned victorious should bring here the trophies of their triumphs. He built the temple of Apollo in that part of his home on the Palatine which had been struck by lightning and therefore, according to the pronouncements of soothsayers, was requested by the god. He added porticoes with a Latin and a Greek library, where, as an old man, he often also convened the Senate and reorganized the panels of jurors. He dedicated the shrine to Jupiter the Thunderer because of an escape from danger: for during the Cantabrian expedition on a night march lightning struck near his litter, killing instantaneously a slave lighting his way. He also had some works done under the name of others, namely his grandchildren, wife, and sister, such as the portico and basilica of Gaius and Lucius Caesar, likewise the porticoes of Livia and Octavia, and the theater of Marcellus....[1]

He divided the city into regions and wards, and arranged that officials chosen annually by lot should watch over the regions, and that these officials should be elected by the people of the respective neighborhoods. Against fires he devised a system of stations and night watchmen; to curb flooding he widened and cleared the Tiber's bed, which for some time had been filled with rubbish and narrowed by the protruding sides of buildings. To make the approach to the city easier from every direction he assumed personally the rebuilding of the Flaminian Way all the way to Ariminum, and he assigned to men who had held triumphs the task of paving the rest of the highways out of the money from spoils. He restored sacred shrines that had collapsed from age or had been gutted by fire, and adorned these and others with most expensive gifts....

Strabo, *Geography* Book 5 chapter 3.8

The early Romans neglected the beauty of Rome, being concerned with other greater and more necessary matters; the later Romans, especially those now and in my time..., have filled the city with many beautiful monuments. In fact, Pompey and the deified Caesar, Augustus, his children, his friends, wife, and sister have surpassed all in zeal and expense for these structures. The Campus Martius contains most of these; in addition to its natural beauty, it has acquired planned adornment. As a matter of fact, the size of the Campus is remarkable, providing open space as it does for both chariot racing and other equestrian exercises, and for the large mass of people exercising with balls, hoops, and wrestling. And the works of art scattered around, and the ground grass covered all year round, and the crowning hills above the river and extending up to the bed present a view like a scene-painting and afford an alluring spectacle.

Near this Campus is another all filled with stoas around it, and groves, and three theaters, and an amphitheater, and very costly temples contiguous to one another, as if appearing to proclaim the rest of the city something incidental. Accordingly, considering this place as their holiest, they have also erected there the tombs of their most famous men and women. The most noteworthy is the so-called Mausoleum, a great mound on a high foundation of white marble near the river, thickly covered up to the summit with evergreen trees. On the summit is a bronze statue of Augustus Caesar, and under the mound the tombs of himself, his kinsmen, and family....

B
The Quinctian Law on Aqueducts, 9 BC

Frontinus, *On Aqueducts* Book 2 chapter 129

Tiberius Quinctius Crispinus, consul, duly proposed to the people, and the people duly voted in the Forum, before the Rostra at the temple of the deified Julius, June 30. The Sergian tribe voted first, on behalf of the tribe Sextus ... Virro, son of Lucius, cast the first ballot.

Whoever after the passage of this law, with regard to the channels, mains, arches, pipes, tubes, reservoirs, cisterns of the public water supply that leads into the city, with malice aforethought pierces or breaks them, or causes them to be pierced or broken, or causes them to deteriorate, so as to prevent those aqueducts or any parts thereof from going, falling, flowing, arriving, or being led into the city of Rome, or so as to prevent in the city of Rome and in those places and in those buildings which are now or in the future will border on the city, or in those gardens, estates, and places to whose owners or possessors the water is now or in the future will be granted or assigned, from flowing, being distributed, piped, or let into reservoirs and cisterns, that persons shall be condemned to pay a fine to the Roman people of 100,000 sesterces. And he who with malice aforethought does any such thing shall be condemned to repair, rebuild, restore, construct, replace all [he has damaged], and speedily demolish [what he has built] without malice aforethought.

And whoever is or shall be curator of the water supply, or if there is no curator of the water supply then the praetor who has jurisdiction over cases between citizens and aliens, shall impose and execute fines, with pledges therefor. And the said curator, or if there is no curator then the said praetor, shall have the authority and power by virtue of this [law] to collect and execute the stated fine or the pledge to be taken. If a slave does any of these things, his master shall pay a fine of 100,000 sesterces to the Roman people. If any place abutting the channels, mains, arches, pipes, tubes, reservoirs, cisterns of the public water supply which is or will be brought into the city of Rome, has been or will be indicated by markers, no one in that place, after the passage of this law, shall obstruct, construct, fence in, fix, place, set up, locate, plow, sow [there]; and let no one bring anything into that place except what will be permitted or necessary, in accordance with this law, for the sake of doing and making repairs. Whoever does anything to the contrary, the same law, jurisdiction, and prosecution in all respects shall be available to everybody against that person, as would be or ought to be if contrary to this law he had broken or pierced a channel or main. Nothing has been passed in accordance with this law to deny permission to pasture in this place, to cut grass or hay, or to remove thorn bushes.

The present or future curators of the water supply in this place which has been marked off abutting the springs, arches, walls, channels, and mains, shall provide that trees, vines, briar bushes, thorn bushes, banks, enclosures, willow thickets, reeds be removed, cut out, dug out, uprooted, as they deem proper. And by virtue of this they possess the power of taking a pledge, the declaration and execution of a fine, and they shall be permitted to do this, and they shall have the jurisdiction and power without personal liability. No action has been taken in accordance with this law to prevent vines and trees which are in the confines of villas, buildings, or enclosures, from remaining if the curators of the water supply, after an investigation, have granted to the owners that such enclosures are not to be demolished on which there have been inscribed or engraved the names of those curators who granted the permission. No action has been taken in accordance with this law to prevent those to whom the curators of the water supply have granted or will grant permission to take or draw water from those springs, channels, mains, or arches, except that it is permitted with a wheel, water screw, mechanical device, provided no new well and no new opening is made.

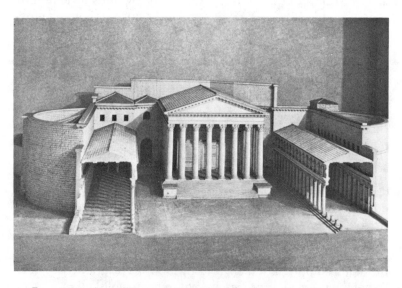

Reconstruction of Forum of Augustus, with Temple of Mars the Avenger.
Courtesy of Fototeca Unione, Rome

22
GREAT FORTUNES OF THE AUGUSTAN AGE

Despite the summons to self-sacrifice and a return to ancestral virtues, the Augustan Age was the scene of the greatest concentration of wealth in private hands in all antiquity. Besides the incalculable wealth of the *princeps,* the fortunes of Livia, Octavia, Agrippa, and many senators and equestrians close to the *princeps* were fabulously large.

After the instability of the civil wars, Augustus, in his bid for the minds and loyalty of the Roman upper classes, reaffirmed the sanctity of private property, rejected the overt statism of the Hellenistic monarchies, and sought — not completely successfully — to discourage self-indulgence and display of luxury. In his efforts to prevent the uses of wealth for personal political ambitions and to reestablish a substantial nucleus of propertied families to staff the imperial service, Augustus assumed the role of grand patron. He garnered numerous clients among the senatorial nobility by providing families with subsides, through a kind of "imperial charity," to assure them the property qualifications and style of life expected of the aristocracy.

Thus, most of the great fortunes of the early principate came to rest in the hands of Augustus' family and the adherents of the new regime. It was expected, however, that the wealth of the upper classes be used extensively for public purposes. Much of the surviving wealth tended to flow back into the hands of the *princeps* through legacies left to him by the holders of the great fortunes. Despite the desires of the *princeps,* the more stable conditions after the end of the civil wars led to an explosion of new building for private pleasure, and to luxury spending on a scale that elicited expressions of concern from commentators of the age.

A
Some Rich Men of the Time

Pliny, *Natural History*

(Book 18 chapter 37.) Lucius Tarius Rufus, though a man of

lowest birth, obtained the consulship [17 BC] through his military efficiency. In other respects a man of old-fashioned frugality, he used up a fortune of about 100,000,000 sesterces which he accumulated through the generosity of the deified Augustus and exhausted by buying up and cultivating land in Picenum to win fame, so that his heir refused to accept the inheritance.

(Book 33 chapter 135.) Gaius Caecilius Isidorus, freedman of Gaius, in the consulship of Gaius Asinius Gallus and Gaius Marcius Censorinus [8 BC], January 27, left a will in which he declared that, although he had suffered heavy losses in the civil war, he nevertheless left 4,116 slaves, 3,600 yokes of oxen, other cattle to the number of 257,000, and 60,000,000 sesterces in cash; and he left instructions that 1,100,000 sesterces be spent on his funeral.

Seneca, *On Benefits* Book 2 chapter 27.1–2

Gnaeus Lentulus, the augur, [consul 14 BC], was the greatest example of wealth before his freedmen made him a poor man. He was a man who saw 400,000,000 sesterces (I have given this figure accurately, for he did no more than just see them), but was as devoid of and insignificant in intellect as he was in spirit.... He owed all his advancement to the deified Augustus, to whom he contributed his poverty laboring under the burden of his nobility. Yet, when he was already a leader of the state, both in wealth and influence, he used constantly to complain to Augustus, saying that Augustus had diverted him from his studies, and that he had not heaped upon him as much [wealth] as he had lost by abandoning rhetoric.

B
Public Uses of Wealth

The ideal use of wealth in the Augustan Age was that attributed to Augustus himself: "a man poor in private life, rich in public life." (Dio Cassius *History of Rome* Book 56 chapter 41.5.)

Suetonius, *Life of Augustus* chapter 29.4–5

Augustus often urged other leading men, in proportion to their resources, each one to adorn the city with monuments either new or rebuilt or improved. Many structures were built then by men such as Marcius Philippus (temple of Hercules of the Muses), Lucius Cornificius (temple of Diana), Asinius Pollio (Atrium of Liberty), Munatius Plancus (temple of Saturn), Cornelius Balbus (a theater), Statilius Taurus (an amphitheater), and by Marcus Agrippa, of course, many sumptuous structures.[2]

Dio Cassius, *History of Rome*

(Book 53 chapter 23.4.) Agrippa not only did not incur any envy for this but was even greatly honored by Augustus himself and by all the rest. The reason for this is that he consulted and cooperated with him on the most generous, distinguished, and beneficial projects and did not in the least claim glory for them. He used the offices bestowed by Augustus not for personal aggrandizement or personal pleasures but for the advantage of Augustus and the public.

(Book 54 chapter 29.3–5.) Agrippa won over the people by his benefactions, as if he were indeed a fervent advocate of popular government. At any rate, at that time [12 BC] he willed to them gardens and the baths named after him, so that they might bathe without charge, and for this he gave some estates to Augustus. And Augustus not only made these public property, but also distributed to the people 400 sesterces apiece, as Agrippa had instructed. And indeed he inherited most of Agrippa's estate, including, among other bequests, the Chersonesus on the Hellespont, which in some way came into Agrippa's possession.

C
The Dangers of Luxury
Horace, *Odes*

(Book 2 no. 15.) Soon the regal structures will leave few acres for the plow; everywhere will be seen ponds more extensive than the Lucrine Lake, and the unwedded plane tree will crowd out the elms. Then violet beds and myrtle and the whole array of perfumes will scatter their fragrance over the olive groves, fruitful to their previous owner. Then the laurel trees with their thick branches will shut out the burning rays of the sun. Not so was it ordained under the auspices of Romulus and unbarbered Cato, and by the standard of our ancestors. For them the property rating was a small thing, but common good something great. No private persons had porticoes, measured by tens of feet, which faced the shady north. And the laws did not allow them to spurn the chance turf, but instructed them to adorn their towns at public expense and the temples of the gods with marble stone.

(Book 3 no. 24.) Though you may be richer than the unplundered treasures of the Arabs and the riches of India, and with your buildings occupy the whole of the Tuscan and Apulian Seas, if dread Necessity drives her adamantine nails into your topmost roofs, you will not free your mind from fear nor your head from the noose of death.

The Scythians of the steppes live better, with their wagons, as is their custom, dragging their homes from place to place, and so do the stern Getae, whose unassigned fields bear fruits and wheat free to all. Nor do they care for tilling longer than a year; when one has completed his labors, a substitute works the land anew on equal terms. There a matron treats with compassion her stepchildren, who have lost their mother, nor does the wife with a dowry rule her husband and rely on a glamorous adulterer. The great dowry there is the virtue of parents, and chastity that, in steadfast loyalty, spurns a second husband, and to sin is a crime, or the penalty is death....

Let us send to the Capitol, where the shouting crowd summons us with applause, or into the nearest sea, our jewels and precious stones and useless gold, the source of our greatest evil, if we truly regret our crimes. The roots of our base greed must be eradicated and over-indulgent spirits must be moulded in sterner pursuits....[3]

Livy, *History of Rome* Preface

Titus Livius (59 BC – 17 AD) was the author of a grandiose *History of Rome*, in 142 books, from the founding of the city to 9 BC (death of Drusus). Unfortunately, his treatment of the Augustan principate is lost. Livy's history reflects a joyful acceptance of the new order and is virtually a prose epic of Rome's past, rivalling Vergil's *Aeneid* in the fervor of its moral message and its idealization of ancient Roman virtues and Rome's grandeur.

...If it is granted to any people to consecrate their origins and to allude to the gods as their founders, so great is the glory of the Roman people in war that when they relate that their father and the father of their founder was none other than Mars, the peoples of the world may accept this with as much grace as they accept our empire. [Our empire grew mighty through the virtues of our people, but eventually] morality more and more declined, and then began the precipitous plunge to the present times, when we can endure neither our vices nor the remedies.... But either love of the task I have undertaken deceives me, or there never has been a country either greater or more righteous or richer in good examples, nor one into which avarice and luxury penetrated so late, one in which there was so much humble means and thrift for so long a time.... Lately riches have brought in avarice, and overflowing pleasures have produced the desire, through luxury and lust, to ruin and destroy everything.

23
A PROGRAM
FOR REGENERATION

The "Roman Odes" of Horace were issued in the first few years after Augustus' victory over Antony, as a sort of manifesto for the moral regeneration of the Roman aristocracy. Assuming the role of *vates* — poet prophet — as spokesman for the country, Horace addressed in particular the younger generation on the question of values. While he urged a return to the values of the past, the older Roman moral standards, he was painfully aware of the prevalent greed, ambition, and immorality. Horace thus lets us see in a sequence of poems — the first six odes of Book 3 — the dual aspects of the Augustan Age: the idealized past of official policy, and the realities of the present.

Horace, *Odes*

(Book 3 no. 1.) I have nothing to do with the uninitiated common people, and keep them at a distance. Keep a holy silence! I as priest of the Muses sing to the girls and boys songs never before heard.

The power of dread kings is over their own people, but that of Jupiter is over the kings themselves. Jupiter, famous for his triumph over the Giants, moves all by his mere nod.

It is true that one person sets out his vineyards on furrowed land that is more extensive than that of another. One man comes down to the Campus Martius a candidate for office of nobler descent; still another contends for office with a better character and reputation; and another has a larger throng of clients. But Fate with impartial law dooms the eminent and the lowest; its spacious urn shakes every name.

The one over whose arrogant neck a drawn sword hangs will not have a pleasant appetite aroused by Sicilian feasts, nor have his sleep restored by the music of birds and the lyre. Gentle sleep does not disdain the humble abodes of farming folk, the shady bank, or the valley fanned by the zephyrs.

The man who desires just what is enough is not disturbed by the tumultuous sea, nor the fierce weather when Arcturus is setting or Haedus is rising, nor when vineyards are lashed by hail, nor by a deceitful farm while the trees complain now of too much water, now of the constellations that scorch the fields, now of the destructive winters.

The fish feel that the waters have been contracted by foundation piers set into the sea; here many a contractor with his gang of workmen and many a master disdainful of the land pours building material. But the threats that come from fear climb to the same place the master does, and fear does not abandon the bronze-beaked warship, and dread worry sits behind the horseman.

But if neither Phrygian marble, nor the use of purple robes that glisten more than stars, nor Falernian wine, nor Persian perfume soothe a distressed person, why should I build a lofty atrium in the new fashion, with columns that cause envy? Why should I exchange my Sabine valley for more troublesome riches?

(Book 3 no. 2.) Let the boy grown sturdy in tough military training learn to endure cheerfully austere circumstances, and let him harass the fierce Parthian as a cavalryman feared because of his spear, and let him spend his time under the open sky and in dangerous circumstances. Let the wife of the warring prince and the nubile maiden looking down on him from the walls of the enemy sigh with fear that the royal fiance, inexperienced in the ranks, may annoy the lion rough to the touch, whom bloody anger rushes through the midst of the enemy. It is sweet and glorious to die for one's country. Death pursues also the man who flees and does not spare the hamstrings and the timid back of faint-hearted youth.

Virtue has no knowledge of humiliating defeat in office, and shines with undefiled offices, and does not assume or place down the *fasces* by decision of popular favor. Virtue opening up the heavens to those not deserving to die seeks a journey on a path denied to most and spurns common company and the earth below with flying wings.

There is also a sure reward for those who keep a loyal silence. I shall forbid a person who has disclosed the sacred rites of the mysteries of Demeter to be with me in the same room, or to sail the same fragile boat with me. Often Jupiter, if neglected, has involved the pure man with the impure. Rarely has punishment, though lame of foot, failed to catch up with the criminal who runs ahead.

(Book 3 no. 6.) O Roman, though you do not deserve it, you will pay for the sins of your ancestors until you restore the temples and decaying shrines of the gods, and the statues ugly with black smoke. You have an empire because you conduct yourself as subject to the gods. From this comes every beginning, to this every end. The neglected gods have given many woes to sorrowing Italy. Already twice have Monaeses and the troops of Pacorus[4] crushed our inauspicious attacks, and they gloat to have added our booty to their slender bracelets. The Dacian and the Ethiopian have come near to destroying our city invested with insurrections, the latter feared because of his fleet, the former superior in arrows as missiles.

Our age rich in sin has taken the lead in defiling marriages, the family line, and domestic life. This is the source of the slaughter that has flowed upon our country and people. The nubile maiden is happy to be taught Ionic dances, and is made up by artificial means, and now plans even incestuous amours, naughty to her finger tips. Soon she seeks out younger adulterers, while her husband is in his wine cups, and does not even choose stealthily to whom she should give impermissible pleasures when the lamps are removed, but at the order of her husband and with his complicity she stands up boldly, whether a peddler calls her, or the captain of a Spanish ship, the generous purchaser of debauchery.

It was not a younger generation born of such parents that dyed the sea with Punic blood and cut down Pyrrhus and Antiochus the Great and dread Hannibal, but the virile offspring of rustic soldiers, taught to till the soil with Sabine mattocks, to carry cut logs at the command of a stern mother, when the sun lengthened its shadows on the mountains, to remove the yokes from the weary cattle, bringing a welcome time as the wagon was taken away.

What has not destructive time deteriorated? The age of our parents, worse than our grandparents, has made us worse, and presently will produce a generation even more corrupt.

24
REBIRTH OF ITALY UNDER AUGUSTUS

In the critical years from 36 to 29 BC Vergil immersed himself in writing his exquisitely wrought poem the *Georgics*, ostensibly a didactic poem on agricultural life, but intended by him as a sort of summons to rededication to national mission, moral reformation, and shared values. Vergil actually read the entire poem to Augustus over a period of four days in 29 BC. The work emphasizes redemption of man through useful honest toil as a substitute for war, and the need for order if civilization is to survive. The normal grim conditions of human life require man's integration with nature. And to evoke a rebirth out of the ashes of the civil wars Vergil suggests the following desiderata: love of country; the ideal of the Italian yeoman farmer; the cardinal Roman virtues; atonement for past mistakes; and the regenerative potential of communal life though harmonious cooperation and public service.

Vergil, *Georgics*

It is noteworthy that in his invocation Vergil does not call on the Muses, as was customary, but on twelve traditional deities, all beneficent forces of nature, and finally on Augustus as the thirteenth god, savior of the world.

(Book 1 verses 1–42) What makes wheat fields productive, under what constellation, Maecenas, it is advantageous to till the earth, to wed the vines to the elm trees, what is the proper care of cattle, what procedure for keeping a flock, how much expertise for keeping frugal bees, these are the themes of the poem I shall begin.

You, O brightest lights of the world, who guide the year gliding through the heaven; and you, O Bacchus and gracious Ceres, if by your bounty the earth exchanged the fruitful wheat stalk for the primitive acorn and mixed water with newly discovered grapes; and you, O Fauns, present deities of country folk; come together, O Fauns and Dryad maidens: it is your gifts I sing. And you, too, for whom the earth, struck with your mighty trident, produced a neighing horse, O Neptune; and you, O Aristaeus, guardian of the groves, whose three hundred snow-white bullocks will crop the luxuriant thickets of Cea; and you yourself, Pan, protector of sheep, leaving your native grove and the pastures of Mt. Lycaeus, if you love your own Arcadian hills, may you be here propitiously, O dweller in Tegea; and you, Minerva, inventor of the olive; and you, O boy [Triptolemus], who display the curved plow; and you, Silvanus, carrying a young cypress with its roots; and you gods and goddesses all, whose concern it is to look after the fields, and who nourish the new fruits though no seed has been sown, and who send down upon the crops abundant rain from the sky. And you, above all, O Caesar, about whom we know not yet what assemblies of the gods will eventually possess you, whether you wish to visit cities and watch over the lands, and the mighty earth will receive you as increaser of fruits and master of seasons, garlanding your head with your mother's myrtle;[5] and whether as god of the immense sea you come, and sailors venerate your divinity only; and Thule at the end of the world is subject to you; and Tethys is giving all the waves as dowry to you as son-in-law; or whether you join the lingering months as a new constellation, where place is made between Virgo and the Claws of Scorpio pursuing her; already fiery Scorpio of its own accord is drawing in its arms to make a place for you and has left you more than just a share of heaven.[6] Whatever you will be (of course, the Underworld does not expect you as king, nor does so dread a desire of ruling overcome you, however much Greece marvels at the Elysian Fields, and Proserpina does not desire to follow her mother, who has been seeking for her, back to earth), grant me a smooth course and nod assent to my bold endeavors, pitying with me the farming folk ignorant of the way, advance and even now become accustomed to being invoked with vows.

This is Vergil's message to a generation that has lost its way in idleness, absence of purpose, immorality. The need for challenges is emphasized. The guideline is, "By the sweat of your brow."

(Book 1 verses 118–146.) Still, though these are the labors of both men and cattle working hard to turn the soil, the troublesome goose, and the Thracian cranes, and the endives with their bitter fibres do much harm, or the shade is injurious. Jupiter himself did not wish the path of tilling to be easy, and was the first to cause fields to be worked by skill, sharpening men's wits with worries, and did not allow his dominion to be idle with troublesome sloth. Before the time of Jupiter no farmer subdued the fields; nor was it lawful even to mark out or parcel out a field with a boundary stone. They gathered for the common store, and the earth of her own accord bore all more freely with no one asking. Jupiter added dangerous venom to deadly snakes and ordered wolves to be predatory and the sea to be restless, and he shook away the honey from the leaves, and removed fire, and inhibited wine from running in streams everywhere, so that man might hammer out little by little the various skills by study and experience, and seek the blade of corn in furrows, and strike out fire hidden away in the veins of flint. The streams then first experienced boats from hollowed-out tree trunks. Then the sailor made calculations and gave names to the constellations — the Pleiades, the Hyades, and the bright Bear of Lycaon. Then it was discovered how to hunt wild beasts with nooses, and to trap them with birdlime, and to surround great pastures with dogs. And now one man lashes the broad stream with a net, seeking the deep parts, and another drags his dripping net from the sea. Then came hard iron and the blades of the noisy saw — for at first they split logs with wedges. Then came the various arts. Relentless work conquered all, and pressing need in harsh conditions.

(Book 2 verses 136–176.) But neither the forests of the Parthians, a very rich land, nor the beautiful Ganges and the Hermus River muddy with gold can rival the praises of Italy, nor Bactria, nor India, nor all of fabled Panchaea, rich with incense-bearing sands. Not these places have been plowed by bulls breathing fire from their nostrils, nor planted with the teeth of the monstrous hydra; nor do the wheat fields bristle with helmets and masses of spears. But abundant crops and the juice of Massic wine fill them; olive orchards and prolific flocks possess them. From here comes the war horse that proudly prances in the Campus Martius. Here white flocks and the bull, the supreme sacrificial victim, O Clitumnus, into whose sacred waters their blood has often been poured, have led Roman triumphs to the temples of the gods. Here there is perpetual spring, and summer in months that do not belong to it. Twice a year the cattle are with young, twice the tree produces fruits. But there are not wild tigers or the breeding places of cruel lions; nor does poison deceive, to their woe, those picking in the fields; nor does the scaly snake drag its immense coils along the ground, nor does it gather itself into a coil of great length.

Add so many famous cities and the construction of works, so many towns heaped up by hand on towering rocks, and rivers running beneath ancient walls. And need I mention the Adriatic Sea and the Tyrrhenian Sea? Or such great lakes? You, great Lake Como, and you, Lake Garda, rising up with waves and the roar of the sea? Or need I mention the harbors?... Italy too exhibits lodes of silver and veins of bronze metal, and abundant gold has flowed there.

She has raised a spirited species of man, the Marsians, and the Sabine folk, and the Ligurians accustomed to hardship, and the Volscians armed with javelins. And she has produced the Decii, the Marii, and the great Camilli, and the Scipios, tough in war, and you, O mighty Caesar, who now, as victor in the farthest lands of Asia, turn aside the unwarlike Indians with Roman weapons.

Hail, O great mother of crops, land of Saturn, great mother of men! For you I have entered upon themes and art of ancient fame, daring to unlock the holy sources; and I sing the song of Hesiod[7] throughout the towns of Italy.

(Book 2 verses 458–540.) O how fortunate beyond measure are farmers, if they only knew their blessings. Upon them, far away from discordant arms, the very just earth by herself pours out on the ground an easy livelihood. If a lofty town-house, huge with proud doors, does not belch forth in the morning in the entire house a mob to give the morning greeting, and people do not gape at the pillars inlaid with beautiful tortoise shell and at curtains tricked out with gold and at Corinthian bronzes, and the woolen garment is white and not dyed with Phoenician purple, and the enjoyment of olive oil is not spoiled with cinnamon, but one's rest is secure, and life is incapable of deceiving, then there are riches of various kinds: peace in the spacious fields, caves, natural lakes, cool valleys, and the lowing of cattle, and soothing sleep under a tree. There one finds woodlands and the lairs of wild animals, and the younger generation assumes its tasks, accustomed to the simple life. There are shrines of the gods, and the fathers are revered. The goddess Justice when she left the earth walked her last steps among them....

Happy the man who could know the causes of things and trampled on all fears, and inexorable death, and the din of greedy Hades. Happy he too who knows the country gods, Pan, and aged Silvanus, and the sister Nymphs. Such a one is not swayed by the *fasces* offered by the people, nor by the purple of kings, nor by the discord which embroils unfaithful brothers, nor by the Dacians descending from the Danube in conspiracy, nor by the affairs of Rome, nor by kingdoms on the verge of collapse. Nor does he either pity and grieve for the poor man or envy the rich man. The fruits which the branches and the field readily have born spontaneously he plucks, and he does not experience harsh laws, the insane Forum, or the public record offices. Others stir up the hidden waters with oars and rush into arms, penetrate the palaces and rooms of kings. One person attacks a city and its pitiable homes with destructive means, so that he may drink from a jeweled cup and sleep on Phoenician purple; another hoards his wealth and watches over his buried gold. Another person is amazed and astonished at the speakers' platform; still another has been thrilled and left gaping by the redoubled applause in the theater of the people and the Senate. Others rejoice when they have been drenched in the blood of their brothers, and exchange their homes and sweet abodes for exile, and seek a country lying in another clime.

The farmer tills the earth with his curved plow — this is his toil of the year; with this he supports his country and small grandchildren, with this the herds of cattle and the hard-working bullocks. And there is no end to the year's abundance of fruits, or of the offspring of the flocks, or of the sheaves of wheat heaped up; and he loads the furrows and stuffs to overflowing his storerooms. When winter comes, the olive is crushed in olive mills, and the pigs return fattened with acorns, and the woods provide wild strawberries. And autumn yields her varied crops, and high up on the sunny rocks the tender grape harvest is ripened.

Meanwhile sweet children hang upon his kisses, the chaste home preserves its modesty, the cows have udders distended with milk, and the fat kids on lush grass fight one another with butting horns. The master observes the holidays, and, lying on the grass, where there is a fire in the midst and his companions wreathe the mixing bowls, he invokes you, O Bacchus, and sets up competitions for the shepherds of the flock with swift missiles into an elm tree target, and the farming folk bare their bodies for the rough wrestling match. This was the life that once the ancient Sabines lived, and Remus and his brother [Romulus]; thus Etruria grew brave, and, of course, Rome became the loveliest thing in the world and made one city by surrounding its seven hills with a wall. Before the reign of Jupiter, and before sacrilegious people feasted on slain bullocks, this was the life that Saturn in the Golden Age provided. Not yet had they even heard the trumpet blast of war nor yet swords on hard anvils clanking.

25

ROMAN WOMEN

Dramatic examples of sexual freedom among upper-class Roman women and the ease and frequency of divorce have created an exaggerated popular impression about the lives of most Roman women. The norm is to be found in such women as Augustus' sister Octavia (see no. 17 B above) and in the happy marriages of three eminent women commemorated in sources of the Augustan Age given below; contrasting with them are Augustus's daughter Julia (no. 17 C above) and Sulpicia, below.

A
Cornelia

Cornelia, the wife of Lucius Aemilius Paullus, was a half-sister of Julia. She was the daughter of a Cornelius Scipio and of Augustus's first wife Scribonia. Cornelia is depicted here as speaking from the tomb.

Propertius, *Elegies* Book 4 no. 11

Cease, Paullus, importuning my tomb with tears; the gate of darkness is not opened to any prayers....

What help was there in my marriage to Paullus, in the triumphs of my ancestors, in such illustrious offspring that are witnesses to my fame? The Fates were no less cruel to Cornelia, and I am but a handful of dust....

If ancestral trophies have ever brought fame and glory to anyone, our statues bespeak ancestors at Numantia,[8] a second line gives equal share to the Libones on my mother's side, and my house is upheld on both sides by their own achievements. Later, when my girl's attire gave way to marriage, another kind of ribbon caught up and bound my hair. I was joined to your bed, Paullus, destined to leave it thus. On this stone the inscription will read that I was married to one man only. I call to witness the ashes of my ancestors, revered by you, O Rome....

Cornelia never tarnished such spoils of war. Nay, even in that great house hers was a role to be emulated. My life was never altered, it is wholly without censure. I have lived with distinction between the torch of marriage and the torch of death. Nature gave me laws derived from blood, not to be virtuous through pressure of fear or criticism... Nor have I shamed you, my sweet mother Scribonia. What would you have wished changed in me except my fate? I am praised by my mother's tears and the laments of the city, and my ashes are covered also by the grief of Caesar. He is saddened because I lived as a worthy half-sister to his daughter, and we saw tears come from a god.

And yet I deserved the dress of honor that is the mark of a fertile woman, nor was I snatched away from a sterile house. You, Lepidus, and you, Paullus, are my solace after death. My eyes were closed in your bosom.

We have also seen my brother in the curule chair twice, and I, his sister, was snatched away in the happy time when he was consul [16 BC]. And, you, my daughter, born to be the token of your father's censorship [22 BC], be sure you imitate me and have but one husband. And, my children, support the house with a line. I am ready for the boat of death to sail, now that I have so many who will prolong my deeds. This is the highest reward of a woman, her triumph, that common talk praises her in death after a life well lived.

And now to you, Paullus, I commend our children, our mutual pledges; this concern of mine still breathes, burned even into my ashes. Father, play the part of a mother's role; the host of all my children must be the burden of your shoulders. When you kiss them as they weep, add the kisses of their mother. The whole house has begun to be your burden now. And if you are going to weep, do it far away from their eyes. When they come, cheat their kisses with dry cheeks....

B
Turia

This long inscription is thought to record the funeral eulogy delivered by

Quintus Lucretius Vespillo (consul 19 BC) for his wife Turia, who died between 8 and 2 BC. Only about one-half of the inscription has survived. Technical matters connected with the complications attending the will of Turia's parents are here omitted.

CIL, Vol. VI no. 1527 & 31670 = Dessau, *ILS* 8393 = *FIRA,* Vol. III no. 69 = Ehrenberg-Jones no. 357

Before our marriage day you were suddenly orphaned by the murder of both of your parents at the same time.... It was chiefly through you that the death of your parents did not remain unavenged, at a time when I had gone away to Macedonia, and Gaius Cluvius, your sister's husband, into the Province of Africa.

So zealously did you perform this pious duty, hounding, investigating, punishing the guilty that we could not have done any more, even if we had been present. And that saintly woman, your sister, shared this with you.

While you were engaged in this matter, for protection, after the guilty were punished, you went at once from your father's house to my mother's house, where you awaited my arrival....

Marriages that are so lasting, ended by death and not terminated by divorce, are rare.[9] For it was our good fortune that ours was prolonged unclouded for forty-one years. Would that our long union had come to its final change by my death, for it would have been more just for me, the older one, to yield to fate.

Why should I mention your domestic qualities of modesty, deference, and charm, your amiable disposition, your diligence in making clothing, your liberal religion, your inconspicuous adornments, your modest dress? Why should I speak of the attachment of your kinfolk, the devotion of your family, since you cherished my mother as you did your parents, and looked after her comfort as you would for your own parents, and shared countless other virtues with all matrons who cherish a fair reputation? Those are your very own which I claim for you, and few have come to have similar ones to hold on to and exhibit, for human fortune admonishes how rare they are.

All the estate you received from your parents we have preserved with joint diligence. And you entrusted it to me entire, with no concern for increasing it. We shared our duties so that I looked after the protection of your fortune and you maintained guard over mine....

You showed your generosity both to very many of your relatives and especially in your devotion at home.... Worthy girls of your relatives...you brought up at our home. You provided them with dowries, so they might be able to acquire a match worthy of your family. I and Gaius Cluvius, in accord, provided the dowries arranged by you, and approving your generosity, we offered our own family property and gave our own estates so that you might not be embarrassed in your own estate. I have related this not to glorify myself but to show that we considered it a matter of honor to carry out from our own wealth the plans conceived by you with pious generosity....

You helped my escape by selling your jewels, and you turned over to me all the gold and pearls removed from your own person, and, continuously getting money from your household, you deceived the guards of my opponents and made me comfortable in my absence. You stopped exposing yourself to the violence of the soldiery, as your sense of honor kept urging you to try. For fortune protected you by the clemency of those against whom you were planning this. In all this your spirit was so steadfast that no unworthy word escaped your lips....

Then when evil men were stirred up by Milo, whose house I bought and equipped for myself, and when he, though an exile, hoped that he would break into it during the turmoil of the civil war, you vigorouly defended our home....

Rightly did Caesar say that you were responsible for my restoration to my country by him. For unless you had made preparations for what he saved, even Caesar's promised help would have been in vain. And so I owe my preservation as much to your dutifulness as to his clemency....

I shall confess, however, that I had the most bitter experience in my life because of what happened to you. When the favorable decision of Caesar Augustus, then absent from Rome, restored me to my country as a still useful citizen, his colleague Marcus Lepidus,[10] who was present, interposed objection to my restoration. When you prostrated yourself at his feet, he not only did not lift you up, but dragged you and abused you, as if you were a slave, so that your body was covered with bruises; with great firmness of spirit you called to his attention Caesar's edict with its words of congratulation on my restoration. You endured his insulting words also, and the shameless wounds, and made these things public, so that he became known as the author of the dangers to me. He was soon punished for what he did....[11]

When the whole world was pacified, and the republic restored, then peaceful and happy times were our good fortune. There were the longed-for children, whom fate had denied to us for some time. If fortune, smiling on us, had permitted them to grow up in the customary fashion, what would either of us have lacked? Advancing age put an end to our hopes.... Despairing of your fertility and grieving because of my childlessness, so that I should not abandon the hope of having children by continuing our marriage and so that I should not be unhappy on this account, you spoke of divorce. And you declared that you would yield our home to another, fertile woman, with no other intention but to seek for and provide another match for me worthy of our well-known affection for each other, and that you would consider future children as our common children and as your own..., and that you would from then on render to me the duties and devotion of a sister or mother-in-law.

I shall admit that I was so furious that I lost my mind and was so horrified at your proposals that I scarcely recovered my senses....

Would that our marriage could have lasted, the age of each of us permitting, until I, as the older — something that is more just — had passed away, and that you might have performed the last rites for me, and that I had departed leaving you behind with a daughter to substitute for me in your widowhood.

By fate's will you have preceded me, and you have bequeathed to me grief out of longing for you, and left your husband alone without children....

The end of this oration will be that you have deserved all, and that it was not given to me to repay all to you. Your instructions are law to me. Whatever in addition I have the opportunity to do, I shall offer it.

I pray that your *Manes*[12] may assure and protect your repose.

C
Ovid's Devoted Wife

Ovid, *Tristia* Book 1 no. 6

Not so beloved was Lyde by the poet of Claros [Antimachus], or Bittis by the poet of Cos [Philetas], as you, my wife, are fixed in my heart, worthy you of a less wretched husband, not a better one. My ruin is propped up by you as a supporting pillar; if I am still anything, it is all your gift. It is all your doing that I have not been plundered or stripped bare by those who have attacked the timbers of my shipwreck.... Someone, unfaithful in my bitter circumstances, would have come into my property if you had allowed it. Your virtue, with the aid of courageous friends, drove him off, friends to whom it is not possible to render proper thanks.

Thus you are approved by a witness who is as reliable as he is wretched, if only this witness carries any weight. Neither Hector's wife excels you in uprightness, nor Laodamia, who joined her dead husband in death. If you had been fated to have Homer as your poet, the fame of Penelope would be second to yours. I don't know whether you owe this to yourself, made into a devoted woman without a teacher, or whether such character was bestowed on you at birth, or whether the first lady [i.e., Livia], revered by you through all the years, teaches you to be the exemplar of a good wife and by long training has made you like herself, if it is proper to compare great things with small.

Woe is me that my poems do not have great powers, and my lips are no match for your merits! If ever I had in the past stirring vigor (it has all been extinguished by my long troubles), you would hold first place among the saintly heroines, you would be the first in reputation for the goodness of your heart. Yet, however much my praise will have power, you will live on in my songs forever.

D
Sulpicia in Love

A minor but remarkable figure in the literature of the Augustan Age is

Sulpicia, a young poetess of the literary circle of Messalla, whose niece she was. Her few extant poems — "The Garland of Sulpicia" — are preserved among the elegies attributed to Tibullus.

"Tibullus," *Elegies* Book 3

(No. 13.) At last love has come — and such a love that I would be more ashamed of a rumor that I concealed it than that I bared it to someone. Venus in answer to my songs brought him to me and put him into my arms; Venus fulfilled her promises. Let anyone tell of my joys who does not have his own. It irks me to have to entrust anything to sealed letters, so that no one may read it before my darling. On the contrary, I glory in my sin, and loathe having to put on appearances for the sake of reputation. Let people say of me that I was worthy of him as he was of me.

(No. 14.) The dreaded birthday is here which in sadness I must observe, bored by the country and without my Cerinthus. What is sweeter than the city? Is a country villa the right place for a girl? or some chilly brook in a field near Arezzo? Messalla, you are too fond of me; now relax, journeys, my kinsman, are often untimely. Secluded, I leave here my heart and my feelings; compulsion does not allow me my own judgment.

(No. 18.) My sweeetheart, I hope I may not be again such a burning concern to you as I seemed to have been a few days ago, if in my entire life I did anything foolishly for which I would confess more regret than the fact that I left you alone last night, wishing to conceal my passion.

26

EDUCATION: TRAINING IN ORATORY

During the last century of the Roman Republic, rhetorical training was the highest goal of Roman education. Under the Principate of Augustus eloquence was still valued as a noble art; men still made their mark in the law courts, and political oratory continued to have a place in the Senate despite the inhibiting power of the *princeps*. School exercises continued to stress declamation, and rhetoric played an important role in the life of educated Romans. The custom of recitation, or oral presentation of new works in public, was invented and became popular. The best source for the rhetorical practices of the Augustan Principate is Lucius Annaeus Seneca (Seneca the Elder), who has preserved numerous examples of declamations in his book *The Orators' and Rhetors' Aphorisms, Divisions and Colors*. The two types of school exercises in declamation were the *controversia*, based on imaginary, often bizarre, legal problems, and the *suasoria*, in which an historical or mythological person gives advice on a problem at a public meeting.

Seneca the Elder, *Suasoria* no. 6

Cicero Deliberates Whether to Beg Antony's Pardon

QUINTUS HATERIUS:[13] Let posterity know that the country could be slave to Antony, but Cicero could not. You have to praise Antony; in this sort of cause words will fail even Cicero. Believe me, though you watch yourself carefully, Antony will still do something about which Cicero cannot be silent. If you understand him, O Cicero, he is not saying, "Beg that you may live," but "Beg that you may be a slave." How, moreover, will you be able to enter this kind of Senate, cruelly drained, as it was shamefully filled? Will you really want to enter a Senate in which you will see neither Gnaeus Pompey, nor Marcus Cato, nor the Luculli, nor Hortensius, nor Lentulus and Marcellus, nor your, I repeat *your,* consuls

Hirtius and Pansa?[14] Cicero, what belongs to you in an alien generation? Now our work is done. Marcus Cato,[15] uniquely the greatest exemplar of living and dying, preferred to die rather than to beg; and there was no Antony for him to beg. And he armed those hands, to the last day undefiled with the blood of citizens, for his own most venerable breast....

PORCIUS LATRO.[16] And so does Cicero ever speak without Antony being afraid; does Antony say anything to cause Cicero to be afraid? Sulla's thirst for the blood of citizens has returned to the state, and the deaths of Roman citizens are contracted for at the auctions of the triumvirs like state revenues. On one public list the carnage at Pharsalus, of Munda, of Mutina is surpassed; the heads of consuls are weighed with gold. Your own words, Cicero, can be used: *O tempora, O mores!* [Oh the times, oh the morality!]. You will see eyes blazing with cruelty as well as arrogance. You will see the face not of a man but of civil war....

ARELLIUS FUSCUS THE ELDER.[17] We rush from arms to arms; victorious abroad, we are butchered at home; at home an internal enemy sucks our blood. Who does not think that, with this state of affairs of the Roman people, Cicero is being constrained to remain alive? Cicero, it will be a disgrace for us to beg Antony, and it will be in vain. It will not be an ignoble tomb that will cover you over, nor will there be the same end of your virtue as of your life. Remembrance, the immortal guardian of men's deeds, through which everlasting life is granted to great men, will hand you down undefiled to all future generations....

Seneca the Elder, *Controversiae* Book 1, Preface, chapters 6–9

Though Seneca the Elder composed his work in the 30s and 40s of the first century AD, his observations on the decline of oratory and of vigor among the Roman youth are also applicable to the second half of the reign of Augustus.

How greatly ability is declining daily! Through some adversity of nature eloquence has retrogressed. Whatever Roman eloquence possessed to challenge or surpass the arrogant Greeks came to flower in Cicero's time. All the talented men who brought brilliance to our field were born then. From that time things have become worse daily — either from the luxury of the age (nothing is so deadly to talent as luxury), or, since the value of this elegant field has fallen, from competition having been entirely transferred to base activities that flourish with great prestige and profit....

Look how the talents of our lazy youths are asleep; they do not stay awake to make an effort in a single honorable pursuit; sleep, dullness, and industriousness in evil that is more shameful than these have taken hold of their minds. Indecent pursuit of singing and dancing grips these effeminate young men; they soften their hair, make the voice high pitched so that it has the allure of a woman; they compete in softness of body with women and adorn themselves with the foulest finery. That is the model of our youth. Which of your generation is sufficiently a man (not to speak of talent and dedication)? They are born effeminate and spineless, and remain that way throughout life....

27

ROMAN HOLIDAYS

A
Calendar of Holidays

These items have been selected from upwards of twenty calendars of Augustan holidays found in Italy.

Ehrenberg-Jones, pp. 44–55

January 7 On this day [in 43 BC] Caesar first assumed the *fasces*. Thanksgiving to Jupiter the Eternal.

January 13 [27 BC] The Senate decreed that an oak wreath be placed on the doorway of the house of Imperator Caesar Augustus because he restored the Republic of the Roman people.

January 16 On this day [in 27 BC] Caesar was named Augustus. Thanksgiving to Augustus.

January 17 Holiday because on that day [in 38 BC] Augusta [i.e., Livia] married the deified Augustus.

January 30 On that day [in 9 BC] the Altar of Peace was dedicated. Thanksgiving to the *imperium* of Caesar Augustus, guardian of the Roman citizens and the world.

February 5 Holiday because on that day [in 2 BC] Imperator Caesar Augustus, *pontifex maximus,* holding the tribunician power for the twenty-first year, consul thirteen times, was named by the Senate and the Roman people "Father of Our Country."

March 6 On this day [in 12 BC] Caesar was made *pontifex maximus.* Thanksgiving to Vesta, to the public household gods of the Roman people, the Quirites.

June 26 (or 27) Holiday because on that day Imperator Augustus adopted as his son Tiberius Caesar in the consulship of Aelius and Sentius [4 AD].

August 1 Egypt was subjected to the power of the Roman people.... Holiday because on that day [in 30 BC] Imperator Caesar liberated the state from the gravest danger.

September 2 Holiday by decree of the Senate in honor of Imperator Caesar, because on that day [in 31 BC] he was victorious at Actium.

September 17 Holiday by decree of the Senate because on that day divine honors were decreed by the Senate to the deified Augustus in the consulship of Pompeius and Appuleius [14 AD].

September 23and 24 Birthday of Caesar [Augustus]. Sacrifice of animals to Caesar. Thanksgiving.

December 15 On that day [in 19 BC] was dedicated the Altar of Fortuna the Home-bringer, who brought back Augustus Caesar from the transmarine provinces. Thanksgiving to Fortuna the Home-bringer.

B
Holiday Tradition

Ovid, *Fasti*

(Book 1 verses 185–287.) [January 1.] What is the meaning of gifts of dates and wrinkled figs? ... and of the honey glistening in the snow-white jar? "For the sake of a good omen," said Janus, "so the savor may linger on what happens after, and that the year may run its course sweet as it began." "I see," I said, "why sweets are given. Tell me also the reason for the cash...." Janus laughed and said, "O how ignorant you are of your times if you think that honey is sweeter than cash that is acquired. Even in the reign of Saturn I hardly saw anyone in whose heart money was not sweet. The love of possessions grew with time, and now it is at its height, and now there is scarcely any room for it to advance farther. Wealth is now more valued than in ancient times, when the people were poor, when Rome was new.... But after the fortune of the place raised its head, and Rome with her head has touched the highest gods, wealth has increased and also the frantic desire for wealth, and when they possess the most, they seek even more. They strive to acquire so that they may use it up, and when they have done so, to acquire again; and the vices themselves nourish their vices.... Now money is all: one's property rating gives one offices and friendships; the poor man is everywhere prostrate.... We gods too delight in our golden temples, though we approve the ancient ones. Such majesty befits a god. We praise the olden times, but we reap the advantage of the present. Yet both customs are equally worthy of respect...."

[Janus continues:] "My doorway is completely open without any bars, that the people, when they have gone forth to war, may have a place to return to. In peace I bar the doors, so that it cannot depart, and under Caesar's divine power I shall long remain closed." He spoke, and lifting up his eyes that looked in opposite directions,[18] he surveyed everything in the world. There was peace.... O Janus, make peace and the ministers of peace eternal!...

(Book 1 verses 587–616.) [January 13.] On the Ides the chaste priest in the temple of great Jupiter offers in the flames the entrails of a gelded ram, for on that day the whole empire was restored to our people, and your grandfather was given the name Augustus.[19] Read the inscriptions on the wax images set up in the halls of the nobility — such great titles were never any man's glory before.... But all these were glorified with human honors. Augustus has a title ranking with supreme Jupiter. The fathers call holy things august, and august are called temples duly dedicated by the hands of the priests.... May Jupiter augment the *imperium* of our *princeps,* may he augment his years, and may an oaken crown[20] protect his doors; and under the auspices of the gods may the heir[21] of so great a name take up his burden under the same omens as did his father.

(Book 1 verses 709–722.) [January 30.] My poem has led me to the Altar of Peace. This day will be the day before the end of the month. O Peace, your hair wreathed in laurel of Actium, be present and remain in gentleness in the whole world. So long as there are no enemies, and no reason for triumphs, you will be for our leaders a glory greater than war. May the soldier bear arms only to restrain arms, and may the fierce trumpet blow only for processions. May the world, nearest and farthest, fear the Romans, and if any land did not fear Rome, let it love her. Add incense, O priests, to the flames of the Altar of Peace, and let a white victim be struck on the head and sacrificed, and pray to the gods, indulgent to pious prayers, that the house which provides peace may last forever along with the peace.

(Book 2 verses 122–142.) [February 5.] This is the greatest honor heaped on the calendar; my genius fails, my strength is not equal to such great things. This day in particular is to be sung by my lips. Madman, that I wished to impose so great a weight on elegiac verse; this theme belongs to heroic meter. O holy Father of Our Country, this name the people have given you, and the Senate, and us, the Equestrians. But history had already given it. Late did you receive your true titles; long before had you been the father of the world. Throughout the earth you bear the name which Jupiter bears in the high heaven; you are the father of men, he of the gods. O Romulus, yield.... You possessed but some little bit of conquered land; whatever there is under Jupiter above Caesar holds. You raped women;[22] under his leadership he bids them be chaste wives.... Force was pleasing to you; under Caesar the laws flourish. You had the name of master; he has that of *princeps*.

(Book 2 verses 617–638.) [February 22.] The next day is called Caristia, from *cari* ["dear"] relatives. A crowd of kinsfolk comes to the family gods.[23].... Give incense, good people, to the gods of the family (on that day, especially gentle Concord is said to be present), and offer food that — as a pledge of the pleasing honor — the *Lares,* with robes girt up, may take nourishment from the platter offered them. And now, when damp night invites to gentle sleep, take up generous measures of wine in your hand as you pray, and say, as you pour out the wine, these sacred words: "Blessing on you, blessing on you, Father of Our Country, excellent Caesar." And with these sacred words pour out the wine.

(Book 3 verses 697–710.) [March 15.] I was about to pass over the swords plunged into the leader [i.e., Julius Caesar], when Vesta

141

from her chaste hearth spoke thus: "Do not hesitate to recall it. He was my priest,[24] and sacrilegious hands struck me with the weapons. I myself snatched the man away; and I left behind an empty image. What fell by the sword was Caesar's shade." He indeed was placed in the sky and saw the halls of Jupiter; and he has a temple dedicated to him in the great Forum. But whoever dared the crime, defying the will of the gods, polluted the pontiff's head, and they lie dead deservedly. Philippi shall be the witness, and those whose scattered bones whiten the ground there. This was Augustus's work, this his duty, this his first task, to avenge his father with righteous arms.

(Book 5 verses 551–590.) [May 12.] Mars the Avenger himself descends from heaven to behold his honors and the temple in the Forum of Augustus. The god is huge and so is the structure; not otherwise should Mars dwell in the city of his son [Romulus].... the god examines the weapons of varied shape on the doors, and the arms of lands conquered by his soldiers. Here he sees Aeneas shouldering the dear burden, and the many ancestors of the noble Julian line. On the other side he sees Romulus carrying on his shoulders the arms of a [conquered] leader, and their famous deeds below the statues of the men arranged in order. He views also the name of Augustus on the facade, and the structure seems greater when the name Caesar is read....

And Augustus is not satisfied to have earned once for all the name Avenger for Mars; he pursues the standards held in the hands of the Parthians.... The Parthians kept the Roman standards, the glory of war, and an enemy was standard bearer of the Roman eagle. That shame would still have remained, were the resources of Italy not protected by Caesar's mighty arms. He removed the old stains and the disgrace of a long time. The recovered standards recognized their rightful owners.

28

LIFE OF THE ROMAN SMART SET

Ovid, *Amores*

(Book 1 no. 4.) Your husband is going to be at the same party as we are. (I hope that it may be your husband's last meal.) And so am I as a guest merely to gaze at the girl I love? Will some other man enjoy your touch? Will you cuddle up close to another's chest and fondle him? Will he put his arm around your neck whenever he wishes? Do not be surprised that the pretty daughter of Atrax aroused those men-creatures of double form to arms when wine had been served.[25] My home is not the forest, nor are my limbs joined to a horse — yet I scarcely seem able to keep my hands off you.

But learn what you must do, and don't give my words to the East Wind or the balmy South Wind to carry away. Come before your husband does; I do not see what can be achieved if you come first, but come before him anyway. When he reclines on the couch and when you, accompanying him with innocent expression, go to lie beside him, secretly touch my foot. Look at me, my nods, my expressive face; notice my secret signs and return them. With my eyebrows I shall say words that speak without a sound; you will read, marked out by my fingers, words traced in wine. When that lustful notion for our love-making comes over you, touch your rosy cheeks with your tender thumb; if you find something to complain about me in the silence of your mind, let your soft fingers touch your earlobe; but when I say or do something that pleases you, my darling, turn your ring again and again with your fingers; touch the table with your hand the way those do who pray, when you wish many ills upon your husband (it will serve him right!). Be smart and order him to drink himself whatever he mixes for you. Quietly ask a slave boy for what you yourself want.

I shall be the first to take the cup that you hand back to him, and I shall drink from the spot where you set your lips. If he happens to give you some food that he has tasted first, refuse it because it has been touched by his mouth; do not allow him to put his onerous arms around your neck, and do not rest your soft head on his hard chest; don't let him put his hand in your dress or on your breasts (ah, so caressable!), and refuse, above all else, to give kisses; for if you do give him kisses, I shall openly reveal myself as lover and exclaim, "Those are mine," and lay my claim. Yet these things I shall see, but those favors which the robe conceals will cause blind fear. Do not press thigh to thigh, nor hold together leg to leg, nor link your tender foot with his hard one.

Poor me, I fear many things because I have engaged in numerous wanton affairs, and I am tormented by fear of my example. Often for me and my mistress a hurried passion has found its pleasure under a tunic thrown over us. You will not do this; but lest you be thought to have done such a thing, take off the guilty robe from your shoulders. Keep asking your husband to drink up (only don't mix kisses with your requests), and while he drinks, secretly, if you can, add more wine — unmixed. If he lies lulled to sleep by wine, the circumstance and place will offer us a plan. When you rise to go home, and we all rise, remember to make your way in the middle of the milling crowd; in the crowd you will find me (or I'll find you there!); whatever part of me you can touch, touch it.

O poor me, I have given advice that helps for only a few hours. The night commands that I be separated from my mistress. At night your husband will shut you in; sadly with rising tears I shall follow, where it is possible, right up to the cruel doors. Now he will take kisses, then he will take not just kisses; what you give to me in secret, forced by law you will give to him. But give unwillingly (you can do this) like a woman who has been compelled to do it: speak no sweet nothings, and let love be grudging. If my prayers have any power, I pray that he does not enjoy it either; if not, at least may you not enjoy him at all. But in any case, whatever fate the night brings, tomorrow tell me with unwavering voice that you did not give in.

(Book 3 no. 2.) I do not sit here because I am interested in thorough-bred horses, yet I pray the one you favor wins. I have come to speak with you, to sit beside you, lest the love which you arouse in me go unnoticed. While you watch the race, I watch you; let each of us look and feed our eyes upon what pleases each the most. Oh, lucky the driver you favor, whoever he is! Do you then happen to have some affection for him, lucky fellow? If only I had such luck as to be on the chariot with fearless heart, urging on the horses released from the starting booths, sometimes slackening the reins, other times lashing their backs, now grazing the turnpost with the inside wheel. If I catch sight of you during my ride, I'll hesitate, the reins will flap falling from my hands. Ah, how close Pelops was to dying from the Pisean spear while he was gazing upon your features, Hippodamia! Yet, of course, with the favor of his girl he won. Let each of us win the favor of his mistress. Why do you retreat? It's useless — the line[26] forces us to sit touching. The stadium has this convenience by the rule of space; but you there, on the right, whoever you are, watch out for the girl; you are hurting her by pressing against her side. And you who are sitting behind us, pull in your legs; if you have any sense of decency, don't press her back with your bony knee. Your cloak has slipped and is dragging along the ground; raise it up, or better, look, I'll lift it with my fingers. Hateful clothing, to cover such pretty legs (you can see more, too, hateful cloak!) ... Do you wish meanwhile to fan gentle breezes, which I shall produce by waving the fan in my hand? Or is this the heat of my passion, not of the air, and the love for a woman that burns my heart possessed? While I am talking, dust lightly sprinkles on your white dress; get off this snow-white body, dirty dust!

But the procession is coming now — observe religious silence and be attentive! The time for applause is at hand: the golden procession is coming. At the head is carried Victory with wings outspread. Be present here, and bring my love in a winner, O goddess. Applaud Neptune, you who put too much trust in the sea; I have nothing to do with the sea; land that is mine keeps me. Applaud your Mars, O soldier. I hate arms; peace and love found in the midst of peace are my pleasures. May Apollo aid the augurs; Diana aid hunters; O Minerva, direct toward you the applause of craftsmen; country dwellers, rise to Ceres and tender Bacchus; boxers delight in Pollux; the horsemen in Castor. We applaud you, O bewitching Venus, and your children who are potent with the bow. Goddess, nod assent to my undertakings, make my new mistress inclined to allow herself to be loved. She nodded, and by this movement granted favorable signs. What the goddess promised, I beg that you too promise. With the permission of Venus I shall speak: you will be a greater goddess than she is. By all these witnesses and by the procession of gods, I swear to you, please, be my mistress for the rest of time. But your feet are dangling; you can, if you want, stick your toes into the railing.

With the track now empty for the prime event, the praetor has dispatched from an equal start the four-horse chariots. The one you're interested in I see; he will win, whomever you favor. Even the horses seem to know what you want. Poor me, he has turned the post in a wide curve; you, what are you doing? The nearest charioteer closes in with gaining wheels. What are you doing, you wretch? You are wrecking the fine prayers of my girl. I beg you, pull the reins with your left hand. We have been backing a lazy driver. I ask you, call them back, Romans;[27] wave your togas as signal everywhere. Look! They are calling them back! But lest you get your hair messed up by a waving toga, here, you may hide yourself in my cloak. And now, once again, the bolt of the starting block is removed and the gates fly open. In a blur of colors an array of horses let loose rushes out. Now, you, pass them at least, and rush into the open track. Fulfill my vows, and my mistress'. My girl's vows are fulfilled, but mine remains unsettled. The charioteer has his prize; my prize still is to be won. She smiled and made some promise or other with her sparkling eyes. Enough here now; in some other place relate the rest.

Propertius, *Elegies* Book 1 no. 11

As you loiter in the thick of Baiae,[28]... does love for me, Cynthia, steal upon you so that you pass nights remembering me? Is there any place left for me on the edges of your love? Or has some rival or other with feigned passion taken you, Cynthia, away from my songs? And I pray you are lingering on Lake Lucrine entrusting yourself to a small boat with tiny oars, or that you are swimming in calm waters.... But I fear you are listening at ease to another's enticing whispers, displaying yourself on the quiet beach. How often a faithless girl sneaks out and eludes her chaperon, forgetting shared gods. Not that I do not know your well-known reputation, but in this place every love has cause to fear. Therefore, pardon me if my books have brought you some grief; the fault is my fear. Indeed, my care for my dear mother is no greater; without you would my life mean anything? You, Cynthia, are my only home, you alone my parents. You are my joy at every moment. If I come upon friends, whether I'm sad or in a happy mood, whatever shape I'm in, I'll say, "Cynthia was the cause." Only I ask you as soon as possible to leave corrupt Baiae; those shores will cause separations to many, shores that have been the undoing of virtuous girls. Damn those waters of Baiae, that offence against love!

III
LIFE IN THE EMPIRE

29

ORGANIZATION OF THE EMPIRE

A
Administration of the Provinces

The tendencies of the Roman Empire, centrifugal because of flagrant abuses by Roman officials and businessmen during the last decades of the Republic, were reversed with the dominance of Augustus and the efficiency and credibility of his policies for administering the multi-cultural, far-flung empire. The historic division of the empire, in 27 BC, into imperial and senatorial provinces effectively transferred to the *princeps* the bulk of the imperial armed forces and the foreign policy of the empire. As titular proconsul, his *imperium* extended over many strategically important areas as well as Rome's numerous client-states on the borders, while the Senate administered the more peaceful provinces. Moreover, his *imperium* took precedence over the authority of all other proconsuls, and throughout the empire provincials looked to the *princeps* (as a father figure in Rome) to help them with their problems.

Strabo, *Geography* Book 17 chapter 3.25

The provinces had been divided differently at different times; but at the present time they are as Caesar Augustus arranged them. For when his country entrusted to him the Principate, and he was established for life as lord of war and peace, he divided all the territory into two parts. One part he assigned to himself, the other to the Roman people — to himself whatever required a military guard (this area is the barbarian country and that neigh-boring on tribes not yet subdued, or land sterile and difficult to cultivate, so that, lacking everything else but possessing an abun-dance of strongholds, they might rebel and refuse obedience); to the people the rest, whatever was peaceful and easy to rule without arms.

Each part he divided into several provinces, of which some are called provinces of Caesar, others provinces of the people. Into the provinces of Caesar he sends *legati* and procurators, administering the regions differently at different times, as conditions require. On the other hand, into the provinces of the people, the people sends propraetors or proconsuls, and these are arranged in different divisions, as expediency demands. But among the provinces of the people Caesar organized two as consular: Libya (whatever part of it was under the Romans, except that part previously subject to Juba and now to Ptolemy, his son), and Asia on this side of the Halys River and the Taurus Mts. (except the Galatians and the tribes under Amyntas, and also Bithynia and the Propontis). And then ten praetorian provinces: in Europe and the islands near it, Farther Spain as it is called (whatever is in the neighborhood of the Baetis River and the Anas); Narbonese Gaul; third, Sardinia (together with Corsica); fourth, Sicily; fifth and sixth, in Illyria the part next to Epirus, and Macedonia; seventh, Achaea, as far as Thessaly and Aetolia and Acarnania, and some Epirote tribes, which are bounded by Macedonia; eighth, Crete together with Cyrene; ninth, Cyprus; tenth, Bithynia, together with the Propontis and some parts of Pontus. The other provinces are held by Caesar, into some of which he sends as caretakers men of consular rank, to some men of praetorian rank, and to others men of the Equestrian Order. Kings, dynasts, and decarchs are now and have always belonged to Caesar's portion.

Dio Cassius, *History of Rome* Book 53 chapters 12–15

Augustus accepted the care and complete administration of public affairs on the grounds that they were in need of attention. However, he declared that he would not personally govern all the provinces, and in the case of the ones he should control, he would not do so permanently. And in fact he gave back to senatorial control the weaker provinces on the ground that they were peaceful and unwarlike, while he kept control over the stronger ones because (as he said) they were unstable and precarious and either had enemies along their borders or had the power of their own accord to start a rebellion. Ostensibly the Senate could enjoy without fear the best fruits of the empire, and he would have the trouble spots and risks; in reality, however, by this pretext the senators would be without arms and without experience in war, and he alone would retain arms and maintain soldiers.

Accordingly, Africa, Numidia, Asia, Greece with Epirus, Dalmatian and Macedonian territory, Sicily, Crete and the district of Cyrene in Libya, Bithynia and Pontus contiguous to it, Sardinia and Baetica were counted to belong to the people and the Senate; Caesar's portion, on the other hand, was the remainder of Spain (the territory of Tarraco and Lusitania), all the Gauls — Narbonensis, Lugdunensis, Aquitania, and Belgica — with their inhabitants and aliens. For some of the Celts, whom we call Germans, took control of all Belgian country along the Rhine and called it Germany, the upper territory extending to the source of the river, and the lower section extending as far as the British ocean. These provinces, and the country they call Syria Coele, and Phoenicia, Cilicia, Cyprus, and Egypt became Caesar's share of the provinces at that time; for, later, he gave Cyprus and Narbonese Gaul back to the people and took Dalmatia in return....

Augustus ordered that some governors of provinces were to be annual and chosen by lot, except when someone had special privilege because of many children or marriage,[1] and such governors were to be sent out at a public meeting of the Senate. They were to wear no swords or military dress; and the title proconsul was to belong not only to the two ex-consuls but also to the others who had completed the praetorship or were only deemed to have done so. Each of these men was to employ as many lictors as is customary in the city; and they were to have the insignia of their offices from the moment they left the *pomerium* and were to use them continuously until they returned. He arranged that the other governors be chosen by himself and be called *legati propraetores* even if they were ex-consuls.... These he caused to hold office for more than a year, at his pleasure, and they were to wear the military uniform and sword, inasmuch as they have the authority

to pass judgment upon soldiers. For no one else, neither proconsul, nor propraetor, nor procurator has been given the right to
wear a sword without being granted the right to put even a soldier
to death. This has been granted not only to senators but also the
equestrians who wear the sword....

Concerning the provinces of the people, this is the method
used. To the others, called imperial provinces and having more
than one citizen-legion, are sent his legates, who are chosen by the
emperor himself, for the most part from ex-praetors, but also
from ex-quaestors or those who have held some intermediate
office.

These are the offices of the senators. From among the equestrians the emperor despatches the military tribunes..., some to
strictly legionary garrisons, some to those manned also by auxiliary troops.... Procurators (this is the title we give to those who
collect the public revenues and disburse payments according to
their instruction) he sends to all the provinces alike, both his own
and the people's; some come from the equestrians, some also
from the freedman class. But proconsuls exact the tribute from
those they govern. The *princeps* gives instructions to the procurators, the proconsuls, and the propraetors, so that they may go
out to their provinces under specific orders. For this system and
the payment of salary, both to these and to other officials, were
established then.... Under Augustus these offices for the first
time began to receive a definite salary.... The following regulations were established for all of them alike: not to levy soldiers or
exact money in excess of what has been assigned to them, unless
the Senate so votes or the emperor so orders; when their successor arrives, to depart from their provinces at once, and not to
delay on the return but to come back within three months.

B
The Province of Egypt

Suetonius, *Life of Augustus* chapters 17.3−18.2

[After Actium] he proceeded to Egypt, and laid siege to Alexandria, whither Antony and Cleopatra had fled, and he took the city

in a short time. Though Antony tried to obtain last-minute terms of peace, Augustus drove him to suicide and viewed his body. Cleopatra he greatly desired to save for his triumph, and even brought in Psylli[2] to suck out the poisonous venom, because she was thought to have died from the bite of an asp. He granted them both the honor of joint burial and ordered the mausoleum begun by them to be completed. The young Antony, the elder of the two sons born from Fulvia, he dragged away from the statue of the deified Julius at which he had sought asylum, after many vain entreaties, and killed him. Likewise, Caesarion, whom Cleopatra had fathered upon Caesar, he brought back after he had fled and executed him. The rest of the children of Antony and the queen he spared, as if they were related to him, and then reared and cherished them according to the status of each.

At this same time he had the sarcophagus and body of Alexander the Great brought forth from its inner shrine, and he viewed it; he placed a gold crown on it and strewed it with flowers. When he was asked whether he wished also to view the tomb of the Ptolemies, he said he wished to see a king, not corpses. He organized Egypt into the form of a province, and, to render it more fertile and suitable for the grain supply of Rome, he had all the canals into which the Nile overflowed cleaned out by the army, for they had been filled with mud over a long period of time....

Dio Cassius, *History of Rome* Book 51 chapter 17

Augustus made Egypt tributary[3] and put Cornelius Gallus[4] in charge. For in view of the large population of both the cities and the country, and in view of the easy-going and fickle character of the people, and in view of the grain supply and wealth, he not only did not entrust it to any senator, but did not even grant anyone of them permission to visit it, unless he himself granted permission by name.... In the palace [of Cleopatra] much treasure was found. She had removed practically all the dedications from the most sacred shrines and thus helped the Romans increase their booty without any defilement to themsleves. Large sums were collected from everyone against whom charges were brought. And, in addition, all the rest, even though no personal charge could be proven, were fined two-thirds of their property. From these sums all the soldiers received what was owed to them, and those with Caesar at the time received, in addition, 1,000 sesterces not to plunder the city. Full payment was made to all those who had previously made loans, and to those senators and equestrians who had taken part in the war with him very large sums were given. In sum, the Roman empire was enriched and its temples adorned.

C
Oath of Allegiance to the Princeps

The oath of allegiance by the military had long been established Roman practice. Augustus extended the ritual to the civilian population throughout the empire, taking as precedent the oath sworn to himself in 32 BC by all of Italy and the western provinces (see no. 18, sec. 25, above). In 6 BC Paphlagonia in Asia Minor was transferred from a client-kingdom to provincial status, and the population soon after swore allegiance to the *princeps* as their new ruler. This oath by civilians remained standard ritual for all subsequent emperors (cf. Dessau, *ILS* no. 190 [37 AD]).

Dessau, *ILS* no. 8781

In the third year after the twelfth consulship of Caesar Augustus, son of a god, on the sixth of March at Gangra, in the civic center, the following oath was taken by the inhabitants of Paphlagonia and the Roman businessmen among them:

I swear by Zeus, Ge, Helios, by all the gods and goddesses, and by Augustus himself that I shall be faithful to Caesar Augustus and his children and descendants all my life, in word, deed, and thought, considering as friends those whom they so consider, and counting as enemies those whom they so deem. And on behalf of their interests, I shall spare neither body nor soul nor life nor children, but in every way undergo every danger. And whatever I observe or hear being said or plotted or done against these, I shall give information about this and will be an enemy to whoever says or plots or does any such thing. Whomsoever they deem to be enemies, these I shall pursue and punish with weapons and sword by land and sea. And if I do anything contrary to this oath, or not in conformity with what I swore, I call down upon myself, my body, soul, life, children, all my family, and property utter ruin and destruction, unto all my issue and those issuing from them, and may neither earth nor sea receive the bodies of my family or those issuing from me or yield fruits to them.

D
Treaty with Mytilene

The city of Mytilene, a famous resort center on the island of Lesbos in the Aegean Sea, had been caught up in the conflicting allegiances spawned by the civil wars. Since it was technically a "free" city, its privileges, which may have been put in jeopardy, needed to be reaffirmed and regularized by the following decree of the Senate in 25 BC.

IGRR, Vol. IV no. 33, Col. B, line 37 — Col. D, line 17
Decree of the Senate Concerning the Treaty

In the consulship of Imperator Caesar Augustus for the ninth time, and of Marcus Silanus.... Present in the Julian Senate House at the writing of the decree were Paulus Aemilius Lepidus, son of Lucius, Palatine tribe, Gaius Asinius Pollio, son of Gnaeus.... Lucius Sempronius Atratinus, son of Lucius, Falerian tribe, Marcus Terentius Varro, son of Marcus, Papirian tribe, Gaius Junius ... Silanus, Quintus Acutius..., son of Quintus....

Concerning these matters Marcus Silanus stated that a letter must be sent to his colleague Imperator Caesar Augustus, if it pleases the Senate..., what it deems best concerning this matter.... Concerning this matter it was decreed as follows: That Marcus Silanus..., consul, if he deems ... treaty..., and any other matter as he deems best, in accordance with the public interest and his own good faith. So decreed....

The people of Mytilene shall not officially permit the enemies of the Roman people to go through their own territory, so as to make war on the Roman people, or their subjects or the allies of the Roman people, and shall not aid them with weapons, money, ships.

The Roman people shall not officially permit the enemies of the people of Mytilene to go through their own land and their own territory, so as to make war on the people of Mytilene, or their subjects or the allies of the people of Mytilene, and shall not aid them with weapons, money, ships.

If anyone makes aggressive war against the people of Mytilene or the Roman people and the allies of the Roman people, the Roman people shall bring aid to the people of Mytilene, and the people of Mytilene shall bring aid to the Roman people and the allies of the Roman people.... And this shall be valid.... Let there be peace [between them] for all time. [The rest is fragmentary.]

E
Client-Kings

Tacitus (*Agricola* chapter 14) speaks of the "age-old long-established policy of the Roman people of using kings also as instruments of enslavement." The polciy of establishing "soft" frontiers for the empire was continued by Augustus through a system of Roman protectorates ruled by native princes, who were called "friends and allies of the Roman people." These rulers were invested with their royal insignia by the *princeps* and the Roman Senate, but they were effectively "clients" of Augustus himself. Among the Roman client-rulers were such eminent figures as Cleopatra of Egypt and Herod of Judaea. Such vassal states were especially expedient in North Africa, on the Romano-Parthian frontier, and along the Thracian border, regions that were economically backward and culturally unsuited for the introduction of the Roman administrative machinery. When sufficiently Romanized, they tended to be annexed and transformed into provinces.

Suetonius, *Life of Augustus* chapter 48

With a few exceptions, Augustus either restored the kingdoms he had obtained by right of conquest to the same men from whom he had removed them, or added them to other client states. He also united with mutual ties the kings to whom he granted alliance and was very eager to suggest and foster marriages or friendships among them. He always treated them with all consideration as integral parts of the empire; it was his regular practice to appoint a guardian for those who were too young to rule or were mentally incompetent, until they grew up or recovered. And he brought up the children of many of them, educating them together with his own children.

Strabo, *Geography* Book 14 chapter 5.6

[Cilicia Trachaea] was a region naturally well suited for piracy by land and sea. By land this was so because of the high mountains and the populous tribes living on the other side on easily overrun plains and farms; by sea because of the abundance of timber for ship building, or harbors, fortresses, and secret coves. Considering all this, the Romans deemed it better for this region to be ruled by kings than to be under Roman prefects sent to administer justice, for these were not likely to be present at all times or to have troops with them.

CIL, Vol. v no. 7231 = Dessau, *ILS* no. 94 = Ehrenberg-Jones no. 166

Inscription on an arch at Segusio [Susa] in Cottian Alps, erected 9/8 BC.

To Imperator Caesar Augustus, son of a god, *pontifex maximus,* holding the tribunician power for the fifteenth year, hailed imperator thirteen times, [dedicated by] Marcus Julius Cottius, son of King Donnus, prefect[5] of the following tribes: Segovii, Segusini, Belacori, Caturiges, Medulli, Tebavii, Adanates, Savincates, Ecdinii, Veaminii, Venisami, Iemerii, Vesubianii, and Quadiates, and by the tribes under his command.

IGRR, Vol. 1 no. 901 = Ehrenberg-Jones no. 171; Phanagoria, Cimmerian Bosporus

In honor of Imperator Caesar Augustus, son of a god, ruler of all the land and all the sea, her savior and benefactor, from Queen Dynamis,[6] loyal to the Romans.

IGRR, Vol. 1 no. 879 = Ehrenberg-Jones no. 172; Panticapaeum, Cimmerian Bosporus

In honor of the great king Aspurgus,[7] loyal to the Romans and to Caesar [Augustus], descended from King Asandrochus, king of the whole Bosporus, of Theodosia, and of the Sindians, Maetians, Tarpeitians, Toretians, Psesians, and Tanaitians, holding under his power the Scythians and Taurians, by Menestratus II, administrator of the island, to his savior and benefactor.

Ehrenberg-Jones no. 168; Philippi, Macedonia

To King Gaius Julius Rhoemetalces,[8] son of King Rhascuporis, Marcus Acculeius, son of Marcus, of the Voltinian tribe, made this in honor of his well-deserving friend.

30
EXPANSIONIST PLANS

In the first decade of the "Augustan Peace" enthusiastic plans were in the air for massive expansion of the empire on all frontiers.

By orders of Augustus ca. 26–25 BC aggressive campaigns to extend the empire into Ethiopia and Arabia Felix (in the southwest of the Arabian peninsula) were undertaken by successive prefects of Egypt, Aelius Gallus and Gaius Petronius. The aim was not only territorial expansion for strategic reasons, but booty, tribute, and military prestige for Augustus. Both expeditions failed. (Plans for invading Britain also were in the air about this time.) After these abortive attempts, the policy of Augustus in the East was to refrain from new conquests.

Anonymous, *Panegyric on Messalla* verses 135–150

The *Panegyric on Messalla* was composed in the years 31–27 BC.

Encouraged by a god, begin to devote yourself to mighty exploits. Your triumphs will be greater than those of others. Neither Gaul will stand in your way and delay you with war nearby, nor aggressive Spain with its broad lands, nor the savage country [i.e., Cyrene] settled by colonists from Thera, nor where the Nile or the royal stream Choaspes [in Persia] flows, nor the swift Gyndes, object of Cyrus' madness, nor the kingdom which Queen Tamyris adjoins at the meandering Araxes River, nor the country occupied by the Padaeans, at the end of the world near Apollo, who celebrate impious feasts on savage tables, nor where the Hebrus River and the Don water the lands of the Getans and Maynians. Why do I hesitate to say it? Where the Ocean surrounds the world with its waters no region opposes you with hostile arms. The Briton unconquered by Roman might and the other part of the world separated from us by the sun await you.

Suetonius, *Life of Augustus* chapter 21

Partly under his own leadership, partly by others under his auspices, he subdued Cantabria, Aquitania, Pannonia, Dalmatia and all of Illyria, Raetia and the Alpine tribes of the Vendelici and Salassi.[9] He also curbed Dacian incursions, killing a great number of them along with three leaders, and he drove back the Germans beyond the River Elbe. Among the Germans, the Suebi and Sugambri who surrendered he transported to Gaul and settled on lands near the Rhine. He also reduced to submission other peoples that were not peaceful and brought war upon no people without just and proper reasons, and so far was he from any desire to increase the empire at any cost or of military glory that he compelled the chiefs of some barbarians to swear in the temple of Mars the Avenger that they would keep their word and maintain the peace which they were seeking. From some peoples he tried to exact a new kind of hostages, that is, women, because he realized they disregarded pledges secured by male hostages; however, he always granted them the right of taking back their hostages as often as they wanted. And upon those who rebelled frequently and who were particularly treacherous he never exacted any severer punishment than selling the prisoners, with the restriction that they not serve as slaves in a region near their own, nor be freed within thirty years. His reputation for military prowess and moderation induced the Indians and Scythians (peoples known only by hearsay) on their own accord to send envoys to sue for his friendship and that of the Roman people. The Parthians also readily yielded to him as he was laying claim to Armenia, and at his demand they restored the military standards which they had taken from Marcus Crassus and Marcus Antonius; in addition, they offered him hostages, and finally, when there were several contestants for their throne, they approved the one chosen by him.

Strabo, *Geography*

(Book 16 chapter 4.22–24.) Many of the peculiarities of Arabia were revealed by the recent expedition of the Romans against the

Arabians in our time. The leader of the expedition was Aelius Gallus, who was sent by Caesar Augustus to explore the tribes and the places both in Arabia and in Ethiopia, since he saw that the Troglodytic region adjoining Egypt neighbors on the Arabians, and that the Arabian Gulf [i.e. the Red Sea], which separates the Arabians from the Troglodytes, is quite narrow. His plan was to make allies of them or to subjugate them. There was also the age-old report that they were very wealthy, and that they offered aromatics and very precious stones for silver and gold, but exchanged nothing of what they received with those outside. Augustus indeed expected to deal with wealthy friends or conquer wealthy enemies....

Gallus built 130 transport vessels, on which he sailed with about 10,000 infantry from the Romans in Egypt, and also with allies among whom were 500 Jews and 1,000 Nabataeans.... Gallus put into Leuce Kome,[10] his army distressed by scurvy of the gums, lameness in the leg, and local ailments, the symptoms of which were a kind of paralysis around the mouth and legs, resulting from the water and plants. At any rate, he was compelled to spend the summer and winter there, looking after the sick.... He [later] advanced to the city of Marsiaba of the tribe of the Rhammantians.... For six days he attacked and besieged this city, but abandoned the siege for lack of water. He was now a two-days' journey from the aromatic-producing country, as was learned from captives. But he had expended a time of six months on his marches, being poorly guided. He realized this when he turned back ... for on the return journey he completed the whole trek in sixty days, having expended six months on the original journey. From here he crossed his army in eleven days over to Myus Harbor, and then marched overland to Coptus with those able to survive, and arrived at Alexandria. The rest he lost not in battle but from illnesses, fatigue, hunger, and deception concerning the roads. Indeed, it happened that only seven men were lost in war....

(Book 17 chapter 1.54.) The Ethiopians, emboldened by the withdrawal of part of the force in Egypt to fight with Aelius Gallus against the Arabians, attacked the Thebaïd and the garrison of the three cohorts at Syene and, by a surprise attack, suddenly captured Syene, and Elephantine, and Philae; they took slaves and dismantled the statues of Caesar. Petronius, attacking with less than 10,000 infantry and 800 cavalry against 30,000 men, first forced them to retreat to Pselchis, an Ethiopian city, and sent envoys to demand what they had seized and to ask for what reasons they began the war. When they said that they were wronged by the nomarchs, he stated that these were not the rulers of the country but Caesar. When they requested three days for consultation and did nothing expected of them, Petronius attacked.... [Invading Ethiopia] he set out for Napata. This was the royal residence of Candace, and her son was there; but she herself was stationed in some place nearby. Though she sent envoys concerning friendship and gave back the captives and the statues taken from Syene, Petronius attacked and captured Napata also, after her son fled, and he razed the city. Taking slaves, he turned back again with the booty, judging the regions farther on to be difficult to cross.

But he fortified Premnis better and, introducing a garrison and food for two years for 400 men, he set out for Alexandria. Of the captives, he sold some as booty and sent 1,000 to Caesar, who was just coming back from Cantabria [25 BC], and some were destroyed by diseases. Meanwhile, Candace marched against the garrison with many thousands. But Petronius went out to their assistance and arrived at the fortress first. After he had completely secured the place with many means, envoys came, and Petronius ordered them to go as envoys to Caesar. When they stated that they did not know who Caesar was, or where they had to go to him, he gave them escorts. And they went to Samos[11] when Caesar was on the point of going ahead from there to Syria, after sending Tiberius to Armenia. When they obtained all they asked, he remitted to them also the tribute which he had imposed.[12]

31

THE MAJOR
TROUBLE SPOTS

A
The Parthian Problem

Augustus inherited from the ambitions, mistakes, and failures of the military leaders of the last decades of the Republic the knotty problem of viable relations with the only other neighboring world power, the Parthian Empire, which ruled from the Euphrates River to the Indus. The efforts of even Sulla, Pompey, Crassus, and Antony had not effectively blunted the threat of the Parthians at Rome's eastern frontier, particularly to the Province of Syria. Roman world prestige had been damaged; anti-Parthian sentiment was intense in Rome; and the "drums of Carrhae," Crassus's stunning military debacle in 53 BC, still rang in the ears of the Romans. However, working to Rome's advantage was the weakness of the Parthian monarchy of the Arsacids: the feudal looseness of organization and the recurrent bloody dynastic intrigues. The flash point of dispute at the Romano-Parthian frontier was the Roman sphere of influence over the strategically important client-kingdom of Armenia — which was, however, culturally Iranian.

Augustus' solution to the Eastern question was diplomatic, not military: in 20 BC captured Roman military standards and prisoners were returned; Roman suzerainty over Armenia was reaffirmed; and the Euphrates was fixed as the natural limit of the two empires. This was hailed by Augustus as a diplomatic victory of the first order. Nevertheless, conditions at the frontier remained unstable, and in 1 BC Augustus sent Gaius Caesar on a special mission to the East in this connection. While he was there military intervention was necessary when Armenia revolted in 2 AD. Peaceful coexistence, cold war, and limited military engagements between the two world powers continued for centuries.

Strabo, *Geography* Book 6 chapter 4.2

The Parthians, having common borders with the Romans and

being very powerful, have nevertheless yielded to the superiority of the Romans and the leaders of my time to such a degree that they have not only sent to Rome the trophies which they once set up over the Romans, but also Phraates entrusted his children and grandchildren to Augustus Caesar, obsequiously giving hostages to win his friendship. The present Parthians have often sent from their country a candidate for their king and are quite close to placing all their power in the hands of the Romans.

Dio Cassius, *History of Rome* Book 54 chapter 8

Meanwhile Phraates [King of Parthia], fearing that Augustus would lead an army against him because he had not yet carried out any of the terms of agreement, sent back to him both the military standards and the prisoners, except for a few who had killed themselves out of shame or remained in the country in hiding. Augustus accepted them as if he had conquered the Parthians in war and, as a matter of fact, took pride in this, stating that what had previously been lost in battles he recovered without a struggle. And indeed, he ordered that sacrifices be voted for this, and that a temple of Mars the Avenger be built on the Capitoline, to rival the temple of Jupiter Feretrius, for the depositing of the standards, and he carried this out. In addition, he celebrated an ovation, and was honored with a triumphal arch.[13]

Velleius, *Roman History* Book 2 chapters 101−102

Gaius Caesar ... was sent to Syria..., where he conducted himself in such a mixed manner that he furnished a great deal of material for praise and not a little for fault-finding. He met with the king of the Parthians, a very distinguished youth, on an island in the Euphrates River, with an equal number on each side. This spectacle of the armies standing on different sides, the Roman army on one, the Parthian on the other, while the two most eminent leaders of empires and of mankind met — a spectacle truly famous and memorable — it was my good fortune to witness at the begining of my military career, as tribune of soldiers....

At first the Parthian dined with Gaius on our bank, later Gaius with the king on the enemy's side.... Subsequently Gaius entered Armenia and, in the first part of his campaign, conducted matters successfully. Later, in a parley to which he had rashly entrusted himself near Artagira, he was seriously wounded by a certain Adduus. As a result of this, not only was his body less fit, but he also began to be mentally less useful to the state. Besides, he had as companions men who nourished his weaknesses by flattery (for flattery is always the attendant of high status), and he was so influenced by them that he preferred to live out his life in a remote and far-distant corner of the world rather than return to Rome. Then, after resisting it for a long time, he began unwillingly to return to Italy but died of illness in a city of Lycia called Limyra, his brother Lucius having died about a year before at Massilia on his way to Spain.

B
The German Problem

Augustus strove to extend the boundaries of the empire in Germany from the Rhine to the Elbe River. After some initial successes under Drusus, from 12 to 9 BC, the Romans were eventually forced to pull back to the Rhine. With the loss of three legions under Quintilius Varus in 9 AD Augustus abandoned all hope of extending Rome's German frontier beyond the Rhine. By 14 AD the Rhine legions were all on the left bank. Augustus' advice in 14 AD to "confine the empire within its [existing] borders" acknowledged the failure of his earlier adventurous policy in the East (see no. 30 above) and the abandonment of his grand strategy beyond the Rhine as not worth the price. The dream of a "limitless empire" (Vergil, *Aeneid* Book 1 verse 279) was at an end.

Dio Cassius, *History of Rome* Book 54 chapters 54–55

The Sugambri and their allies undertook war [12 BC] because of Augustus' absence and the fact that the Gauls resented their subjection. Drusus seized the subject territory first, sending for their chiefs on the pretext of the festival which even now they observe around the altar of Augustus at Lugdunum. He also watched and waited for the Germans to cross the Rhine and then drove them back. After this he crossed over to the territory of the Usipetes right along the island of the Batavians, and from there he proceeded along the river to the Sugambrian region and devastated much of the area.... At the beginning of spring [11 BC] he set out again for the war, crossed the Rhine, and subjugated the Usipetes. He bridged the Lippe River, invaded the territory of the Sugambri, and proceeded through it to the country of the Cherusci as far as the Weser River.... He would also have crossed the Weser if he had not run short of supplies, and if winter had not been upon him.... Therefore, he proceeded no farther, but marching back to friendlier parts he encountered grave risks en route. For these exploits Drusus received triumphal honors, the right to celebrate an ovation, and the *imperium* of a proconsul when he completed the praetorship....

Drusus [9 BC] invaded the territory of the Chatti and proceeded as far as the land of the Suebi, conquering after some difficulty all the territory on his march, and defeating after some bloodshed all those that attacked him. From there he advanced to the land of the Cherusci, crossed the Weser, and marched as far as the Elbe, plundering everything. This river flows from the mountains of the Vandals and empties in great size into the northern ocean. He attempted to cross over but was unable to do so. Therefore, he set up trophies and withdrew.

Velleius, *Roman History* Book 2 chapters 106, 109

All of Germany was traversed by our armies [5 AD], tribes were conquered whose names were almost completely unknown, and the Cauchi people were subjugated: all their young men, infinite in number, huge in physique, and well protected by their terrain, handed over their arms, and, surrounded by a line of our soldiers gleaming in their armor, along with their leaders fell on their knees before the tribunal of the general. The Langobardi were broken, one of the fiercer tribes in savage Germany; finally — something never conceived even as a hope, much less undertaken — the Roman army with its standards was led 400 miles beyond the Rhine as far as the Elbe River, which flows past the boundaries of the Semnones and Hermunduri. And because of the surprising good fortune and planning of the general, and by a careful observance of the seasons, a fleet, which had sailed around along the bays of the Ocean, sailed from a sea previously unheard of and unknown up the Elbe River. Gaining victory over many tribes, it joined up with Caesar and his army, bringing a great abundance of all kinds of supplies....

I, too, shall try, as others have, to explain in adequate volumes the sequence of events of the most terrible defeat the Romans ever suffered among foreign people since the disaster of Crassus in Parthia. Here the entire episode must be lamented. An army, the very bravest of all, the very best in discipline, the most energetic, the most experiencnienccced in war among all Roman soldiers, because of the negligence of its general, the treachery of the enemy, and the quirks of fortune, was surrounded. Little opportunity, indeed, and not as much as they wanted was given for fighting or withdrawal, except at a disadvantage; some soldiers were punished severely when they used Roman arms and showed a Roman spirit. Hemmed in by forests, bogs, and attacks from ambush, the army was slaughtered to a man by an enemy which it had always slaughtered like cattle, and for whom life or death was determined by the anger or pity of the Romans. The general (Varus) showed more courage in dying than in fighting: following the precedent of his father and grandfather, he stabbed himself.

Suetonius, *Life of Augustus* chapter 23

Augustus suffered only two serious and ignominious defeats, both in Germany — those of Lollius and of Varus. The Lollian disaster caused greater humiliation than loss, the Varian defeat was almost fatal because three legions with their general, his lieutenants, and all the auxiliaries were wiped out. When this was reported, Augustus posted night watches throughout the city to prevent the outbreak of any disturbance, and he prolonged the *imperium* of provincial governors so that the allies could be controlled by known experienced men. He vowed great games to

Jupiter Best and Greatest if the condition of the state should improve; this had also been done in the Cimbric and Marsic wars. Indeed, they say that he was so dismayed that month after month he let his beard and hair grow and would sometimes pound his head against the door and shout, "Quintilius Varus, give back my legions." Every year he observed the day of the disaster as one of sorrow and mourning.

32
AUGUSTUS' POLICY ON CITIZENSHIP

After Actium, the stabilization of the eastern provinces and the reconciliation of the Greek East to Roman rule made it possible for Augustus to continue Julius Caesar's policy of large-scale planting of Roman citizen colonies, consisting mostly of veterans, in these provinces, as well as in Italy and the western provinces. But in other respects Augustus reversed Caesar's cosmopolitan vision by a more conservative policy regarding Greeks and freedmen (see no. 10D above), demanding careful scrutiny of the credentials of each individual to whom citizenship and its privileges were given.

Grants of citizenship to Greeks raised the problem of dual citizenship (see no. 35A below). Under traditional Roman law, Roman citizenship was not compatible with another citizenship, but beginning in the first century BC, following Hellenistic practice, the Romans accepted the concept of multiple citizenship in their empire. The provisions, given below, of Octavian's grant to Seleucus of Rhosus, a city in the province of Asia, illustrate Augustan policy and practice.

Suetonius, *Life of Augustus* chapter 40.3−4

Deeming it of great importance to preserve the people pure and untainted by any mixture of the blood of foreigners and slaves, he bestowed Roman citizenship very sparingly and set a limit on manumissions. When Tiberius asked for citizenship for a Greek client of his, he wrote back that he would not grant it unless the individual convinced him in person that he had just causes for the request. And when Livia asked it for a certain Gaul who was subject to payment of tribute, he denied the request for citizenship but offered immunity from tribute, asserting that he would be more willing to endure a loss to the treasury than to cheapen the honor of Roman citizenship. Not content to have put many difficulties in the way of slaves' acquiring freedom — and, still more, freedom with full rights — by making careful provisions regarding the number, condition, and status differences of those who were manumitted, he added this restriction also: that no one who had ever been put in chains or tortured should acquire citizenship with any type of freedom.

FIRA, Vol. 1 no. 55

Letter of Octavian concerning Seleucus of Rhosus, 30 BC.

Imperator Caesar, son of a god, imperator for the sixth time, consul for the fourth time, to the magistrates, council, and people of the sacred, inviolate, and autonomous city of the Rhosians, greeting. If you are well, it is well. I too and my army are in good health. Seleucus, your fellow citizen and my ship captain, accompanied me in all my campaigns, and gave many proofs both of his good will and of loyalty and courage. As is befitting for those who campaigned with us and exhibited deeds of valor in the war, he has been decorated with privileges: exemption from taxation and Roman citizenship. I therefore commend him to you. For such men make us more ready to show good will toward their native lands. Rest assured that I shall more readily do everything possible for you on account of Seleucus, and you may send to me with confidence regarding whatever matters you wish. Farewell.

There follows an edict of Octavian on Seleucus, 41—36 BC.

Imperator Caesar, triumvir for regulating the state, in accordance with the Munatian-Aemilian Law[14] granted citizenship and exemption from taxation in regard to all property in the following terms:

Whereas Seleucus of Rhosus, son of Theodotus, campaigned with us in the wars in..., under our command, and underwent many great hardships and dangers on our behalf, sparing himself not at all in enduring perils and exhibited complete devotion and loyalty to the affairs of the republic, and joined his own fortunes to our safety, and underwent all kinds of sacrifice on behalf of the Republic of the Roman people, and both in our presence and elsewhere was useful to us;

To him and his parents, to his children and descendants, and to the wife he shall have with him..., we grant citizenship and exemption from taxation, with the same privileges as those who are tax-exempt citizens with fullest rights, and exemption from military service and all compulsory public services.

The aforementioned and his parents, children, and descendants shall belong to the Cornelian tribe....

Insofar as the aforementioned and his wife and parents, children, and descendants, before he became a tax-exempt Roman citizen, enjoyed tax-exemption [elsewhere], if, even after he has become a tax-exempt Roman citizen, he wishes to enjoy those privileges, it shall be permitted to him to hold priesthoods..., offices, privileges....

If anyone wishes to bring an accusation against them, or to lodge a complaint, or to seek a judgment against them and institute proceedings..., in all such matters, if they wish to be tried at home according to their own laws, or in autonomous cities, or before our magistrates or promagistrates..., the choice shall be theirs; and no one shall act contrary to what has been prescribed in this document, or give judgment concerning them..., or pronounce sentence. And if any proceeding is held concerning them contrary to his document, it shall not be valid.

If anyone, however, is minded to accept an accusation against the aforesaid, his parents, wife, children, and descendants, or to make a prior judgment involving their status..., it is ordered that it be their right to come personally as appellants to our Senate and our magistrates and promagistrates, or to send envoys concerning their personal affairs....

Whatever city or magistrate does not carry out whatever is required according to this document, or acts contrary to it..., or with malice aforethought prevents the aforesaid from enjoying the privileges granted to them..., shall be liable to pay to the Roman people a fine of 100,000 sesterces; and there shall be the right to anyone, to prosecute and sue for this sum in the province before our magistrates and promagistrates, or at Rome.... It is ordered that concerning these sums, whoever is minded to sue shall provide adequate sureties. Our magistrates and promagistrates, whichever have jurisdiction, shall make decisions and see to it that the aforementioned are carried out as prescribed.

33

PROTECTION OF
ESTABLISHED RELIGIONS

After the decades of turmoil in which respect for traditional religious places and institutions had decayed, Augustus presented himself all over the empire as the champion of religious freedom and established cults, thereby winning the loyalty of millions. He pursued a restorative policy in Rome and Italy with regard to traditional cults and shrines there (see nos. 9 and 18 above). The following documents illustrate Augustus' religious policy in the empire.

A
Restoration of Sacred Property

SEG, Vol. xviii no. 555 =*Greek, Roman and Byzantine Studies* Vol. iv (1963), pp. 115−122

This inscription, the first part in Greek, the second in Latin, was first published in 1958. It reveals Augustus and Agrippa, in 27 BC, intervening as consuls in the affairs of Cyme, a city of the senatorial Province of Asia.

Imperator Caesar Augustus, son of a god..., Marcus Agrippa, son of Lucius, consuls.... With regard to any public or sacred places that are under the jurisdiction of the prefecture of each city, if there are or will be any dedications belonging to these places, let no one remove these or buy them or accept them as security or gift. With regard to whatever has been removed from those places or bought or received as gift, whoever may be in charge of the prefecture shall see to it that these are restored to the public or sacred account of the city; and with regard to any security that has been given, let him not recognize this as legitimate.

 ... Vinicius, proconsul, sends greetings to the magistrates of

Cyme. Apollonides, son of Lucius, a Noracean, your citizen, approached me and deposed that a shrine of Dionysus was in the possession of Lysias, son of Diogenes, a Tycallean, your citizen, by title of sale. And when the devotees, in accordance with the order of Caesar Augustus, desired to restore the sacred places to the god by paying the price inscribed on the shrine of Dionysus, it was witheld by Lysias. It is my wish, if such are the facts, that you see to it that Lysias accept the price which has been set for the shrine, and that he restore the shrine to the god, and that there be inscribed on it: "Imperator Caesar Augustus, son of a god, restored it." If however, Lysias objects to what Apollonides demands, let him give him security wherever I shall be. I regard it as more proper for Lysias to release the shrine....

B
Protection of Freedom of Worship by Jews

Though monotheists, the Jews had enjoyed protection of their religion and customs by the Romans ever since their alliance with the Romans in the Maccabean revolt against the Seleucid kings. They had enjoyed Caesar's favor, and under Augustus they continued to receive equality of civic status with the Greeks in the Asiatic provinces. Marcus Agrippa visited Jerusalem in 15 BC at the invitation of Rome's client-king Herod, was hailed there with enthusiastic acclaim by the populace, and offered a sacrifice of 100 oxen to Yahweh. In 14 BC he reaffirmed Jewish privileges in the provinces. The privileges of the Jews in the diaspora were frequently challenged in the provinces by Greeks, whose need for money for civic purpose was never-ending, and Roman officials were called upon frequently to reaffirm these privileges. The one exception was the Jewish population of Roman Egypt, even those in Alexandria, who were ranked by Augustus as politically and juridically inferior to Greeks, and reduced to a social status closer to native Egyptians.

Josephus, *Jewish Antiquities*

Flavius Josephus (37/8–ca. 100 AD) was a prominent Jewish leader who settled in Rome after the fall of Jerusalem in 70 AD, receiving Roman citizenship. Here he wrote, in the Greek language, his greatest work, *Jewish Antiquities,* in twenty books.

(Book 16 chapters 167–168.) Agrippa to the magistrates, council, and people of the Ephesians, greeting. It is my will that the Jews in the [Province of] Asia, in accordance with their ancestral custom, should provide for the care and protection of the sacred monies transmitted to the temple in Jerusalem. And as for those who steal sacred monies of the Jews and flee to places of asylum, it is my will that they be removed and handed over to the Jews, in accordance with the law by which sacrilegious persons are removed. I have also written to the proconsul Silanus that no one shall compel a Jew to give sureties for appearance in court on the Sabbath.

(Book 16 chapters 169–170.) Marcus Agrippa, to the magistrates, council and people of the Cyrenaeans, greeting. The Jews in Cyrene — on behalf of whom Augustus had already sent orders to Flavius [or Fabius], then proconsul in Libya, and to the others in charge of the province that the sacred monies be transmitted without hindrance to Jerusalem, as is their ancestral practice — appealed to me now that they are being harassed by some informers and are being prevented from sending the monies on the pretext of taxes due that are not actually owed. I order that restitution be made to them, and that they not be molested in any way. And if sacred monies have been removed from any cities, I order those persons responsible for these matters to correct these matters for the Jews there.

(Book 16 chapters 162–165.) Caesar Augustus, *pontifex maximus*, holding the tribunician power..., decrees: Whereas the Jewish people have been found well-disposed to the Roman people, not only at the present time but also in the past and especially in the time of my father Imperator Caesar, as was their high priest Hyrcanus, it has been decided by me and my council, in accord with the treaty rights passed by the Roman people, that the Jews are to enjoy their own customs in accordance with their ancestral law, just as they enjoyed them under Hyrcanus the high priest of the most high god, and that their sacred monies are to be inviolate, and transmitted to Jerusalem, and be delivered to the financial officials of Jerusalem, and that they not have to give surety for appearance in court on the Sabbath or on the day of preparation for it from the ninth hour. And if anyone is caught stealing their sacred books or their sacred monies from a synagogue or from an ark of the Law, he shall be deemed sacrilegious, and his property is to be confiscated to the treasury of the Roman people.

And with regard to the decree granted to me by them on account of the piety I have toward all men, and also concerning Gaius Marcius Censorinus,[15] I order it and this edict to be set up in a most conspicuous place, that prepared for me by the provincial council of Asia in Ancyra. And if anyone violates any of the aforesaid, he shall suffer a severe penalty.

C
Protection of Burial Places

This Greek inscription, first published in 1930, was reported to have come from Nazareth, but its provenience is far from certain. It has been assigned to the reign of Augustus by most scholars on the basis of the forms of the letters, but it may be as much as a century later. In late Greek law violation of sepulture was a crime punishable by a fine; in early Roman law it was only a civil offense subject to monetary fine. Augustus (if the "Caesar" here is indeed he), as in so many other cases, continued traditional legal institutions in the eastern provinces, but in this case he sharply increased the rigor of existing local law. In the Roman imperial period thereafter violation of sepulture was treated as a serious crime, with severe penalties, including capital penalties, such as condemnation to the mines, deportation, even death. Efforts to connect this edict with Jesus are without substance.

SEG Vol. viii no. 13 =*FIRA,* Vol. i no. 69

Ordinance of Caesar. It is my pleasure that graves and tombs which any persons have constructed for the cult of ancestors or children or relatives shall remain undisturbed in perpetuity. But if anyone deposes that someone has either destroyed them or in any other way caused the buried persons to be thrown out or transferred to other places with malice aforethought to the dishonor of the buried dead, or has removed the inscriptions or other stones, I order that a trial of such a person be held with regard to the cult of human beings as if it were a matter concerning divine beings. For much more respect in the future must be accorded the buried dead. No one whatsoever shall be permitted to disturb them. If any one does, I desire him to be condemned to a capital offense for violation of sepulture.

D
Egyptian Cults

Though Augustus succeeded Cleopatra as pharaoh of Egypt in 30 BC, the traditional Egyptian cults continued undisturbed. In addition to the cults of Sarapis and Isis, this papyrus emphasizes the cult of Thoëris, the hippopotamus goddess at Oxyrhynchus. This is the earliest extant papyrus of the Roman period; the date is 30–29 BC.

Oxyrhynchus Papyri, Vol. XII no. 1453

Copy of oath. Thonis (also called Patoiphis), son of Thonis, and Heraclides, son of Totoës, both lamplighters of the temple of Sarapis, the most great god, and of the shrine of Isis in the same place, and Paapis, son of Thonis, and Petosiris, son of the aforementioned Patoiphis, both lamplighters of the temple at Oxyrhynchus of Thoëris, the most great goddess, all four swear by Caesar, god, son of a god, to Heliodorus, son of Heliodorus, and to Heliodorus, son of Ptolemaeus, caretakers of the temples of the Oxyrhynchite and Cynopolite nomes, that we will carefully look after the lamplighting of the aforementioned temples as prescribed and will provide the proper oil for the daily lamps burning in the indicated temples from Thoth 1 to Mesore [intercalary] 5[16] of the present first year of Caesar.... If I observe the oath, may it be well with me; if I swear falsely, the opposite. First year of Caesar....

34
EMPEROR WORSHIP

A complex of factors resulted in the growth of ceremonial veneration of Augustus and the members of his family: his use of the appellation *divi filius*, "son of a god"; his status in Egypt of god-king, as successor of the pharaohs; the centuries-old practice in the Greek East of according cult honors to the ruling house. There was, however, no formal, empire-wide, official cult of the ruler in the Roman Empire. Freedom of worship in a highly polytheistic world was the norm: provinces, cities, groups, individuals expressed their homage to Augustus at their own discretion. Often the ruler cult was merely an expression of loyalty and gratitude to the *princeps* and his family, or an act of political and diplomatic expediency, not genuine religious worship. In the eastern provinces there were outpourings of good will to Augustus as successor of the traditional divine monarchs, especially as "savior" and "benefactor"; but Augustus instructed that such worship be maintained as a joint cult of the Goddess Roma and himself. In the western provinces there was no such spontaneous cult; it was created deliberately by imperial direction, from 12 BC on, through the establishment of altars in provincial centers to serve as focal points of the cult. In Rome and Italy, where religious tradition did not know the cult of living men, worship was directed to the *genius* or *numen* (guardian spirit) of Augustus, a practice that did not clash with Roman tradition. There was an anticipation in Rome of the apotheosis of Augustus throughout his reign (Vergil had written as early as 41 BC: "For he will always be a god to me"), but deification came to him posthumously.

Dio Cassius, *History of Rome* Book 51 chapter 20.6–8

Caesar, meanwhile, in addition to attending to other matters, gave permission for the establishment of sacred precincts in Ephesus and Nicaea to Roma and to his father Caesar, naming him the hero Julius [i.e., *divus Julius*]. These cities at that time were the foremost in Asia and Bithynia. And he instructed the Romans resident in those cities to honor these divinities. But he permitted the aliens, whom he called Hellenes, to establish precincts to himself, those in Asia at Pergamum, the Bithynians at Nicomedia. And this practice, beginning with him, prevailed under other emperors, not only among the Hellenic peoples but also among the others subject to the Romans. For in the city of Rome itself and the rest of Italy no one has dared to do this, not even those worthy of any renown. However, even there various divine honors are bestowed upon those who have passed away and have been good emperors, and indeed shrines are built to them.

SEG Vol. IV no. 490 = *Orientis Graeci Inscriptiones Selectae* no. 458 = Ehrenberg-Jones no. 98

In 10/9 BC the governor of the Province of Asia, Paullus Fabius Maximus, intimate friend and kinsman of Augustus, helped to reorganize the province's calendar (long based on a Macedonian lunar calendar) making it a Roman-style, Julian solar calendar. In so doing, he proposed that the first day of the year in this provincial calendar coincide with the birthday of Augustus. Of this long document, in both Greek and Latin, copies of which have been found in five cities of the province, only the letter of the governor and the decree of the provincial assembly are given here. Such provincial assemblies, attended by leading men representing the various communities, were established in the East in 29 BC and in the western province beginning in 12 BC. Beside maintaining the local imperial cult, the assemblies were the channel for appeals to the emperor on general provincial matters.

[*Letter of the Proconsul*]

... whether the birthday of the most divine Caesar is more delightful or more beneficial. We should justly assume his birthday to be equivalent to the beginning of all things; and he has restored to usefulness, if not to their natural state, whatever institutions have become imperfect or fallen into misfortune; and he has given a different appearance to the whole world, which would merrily have accepted destruction if Caesar had not been born for the common blessing of all. Therefore could a man rightly deem this to have been the beginning of life itself for him, that is, the final end of regret that he had been born. And since from no other day can each person obtain more auspicious beginnings for the public and private advantage than from that one which has been fortunate for all; and since it happens that in almost all the cities in Asia there exists the same day for assuming magistracies — a system obviously prearranged according to some divine plan, so that it might be the starting point of honor to Augustus; and since it is difficult to render thanks properly for his great benefactions, unless in each case we should devise some novel manner of repaying him; therefore, men should celebrate his birthday with greater pleasure as a holiday common to all. Since personal benefit has come to them through his rule, it seems to me that the birthday of the most divine Caesar should be for all citizens one and the same New Year's day, and that they should all assume their magistracies on that day, which is September 23, so that it might be honored the more elaborately by drawing to itself some religious observance, and that it may become better known to all, which I think will afford the greatest benefit to the province.

It will be necessary for a decree to be prepared by the assembly of the Province of Asia embracing all his virtues, so that what has been devised by us for the honor of Augustus may abide forever. I shall order that the decree be inscribed on a stele and posted in the temple, with instructions that the decree be written in both languages [i.e., Greek and Latin].

[Decree of the Provincial Assembly]

It was decreed by the Greeks in the Province of Asia, on motion of the high priest Apollonius, son of Menophilus, of Azanium: Whereas providence which divinely has arranged our lives has with special zeal and munificence devised the most perfect good for our lives by creating Augustus, filling him with virtue for the benefit of mankind, blessing us and those to come after us with a savior who put an end to war and established peace; and whereas Caesar, when he appeared, surpassed the hopes of all who had anticipated good tidings, not only surpassing the benefactors before him, but not even leaving any hope of surpassing him to those to come; and whereas the birthday of the god was the beginning for the world of good tidings through him; and whereas the Province of Asia decreed in Smyrna in the governorship of Lucius Vulcacius Tullus, when Papias, son of Diosieritos, was secretary, that a crown be awarded to the one devising the greatest honors for the god; and whereas Paullus Fabius Maximus, proconsul of the province, sent as our benefactor by his right hand and purpose, not only benefited the province in other ways — benefits the greatness of which no one could succeed in recounting adequately — but also devised for the honor of Augustus a thing unknown to the Greeks up to this time, namely, to begin their calendar with his nativity;

Now, therefore, with good fortune and for our own safety, it has been decreed by the Greeks of Asia to begin the New Year in all the cities on September 23, which is the birthday of Augustus; and that day be coordinated in every city; that they use jointly the Roman date and the Greek date; and that the first month, called Caesar, as previously decreed, begin with September 23, the birthday of Caesar; and that the crown voted for the one devising the greatest honors for Caesar be granted to the proconsul Maximus; and that he always be proclaimed in the athletic games at Pergamum in honor of Roma and Augustus, as follows: "Asia crowns Paullus Fabius Maximus for having most piously devised the honors for Augustus." And likewise that it be announced also in the games conducted in the city in honor of Caesar; and that the communication of the proconsul and the decree of Asia be inscribed on a stele of white marble, which is to be set up in the sacred precinct of Roma and Augustus [in Pergamum]; and that the current public advocates are to provide that in the leading cities of the administrative districts the communication of Maximus and the decree of Asia be inscribed on steles of white marble, and that these steles be set up in the temples of Caesar.

[The rest of the decree deals with specific months and days of the new calendar.]

Berlin papyrus 1137 = U. Wilcken, *Grundzüge und Chrestomathie der Papyrusurkunde,* Vol I, Part 2: *Chrestomathie* (Leipzig, 1912) no. 112; Alexandria, 6 BC

Year 25 of Caesar, month Hathyr 22, at the meeting that took place in the Paratomus of the association honoring the god Imperator Augustus Caesar, of which Primus, slave of Caesar, is communer and chairman, Iucundus, slave of Caesar, is priest, and Alexander is gymnasiarch, with most members present.... [The rest deals with payment of funds.]

Wilcken, *ibid.* no. 111

Oath in the name of Augustus, from Fayum, Egypt, 6 AD. The form continues the Ptolemaic practice of giving oaths by the king, not by his *genius* as in Rome and Italy.

Copy of declaration. The 35th year of Caesar, month Pachon 2, I swear by Imperator Caesar Zeus Eleutherios Augustus, son of a god, I, Heraclides, son of Paniscus, a Macedonian of the military settlement, to Areius, son of Herodes, Macedonian of the military settlement, that I shall adhere to all the stipulations in accordance with the contract of the agreement which I contracted for.... [The rest concerns property matters.]

Ovid, *Metamorphoses* Book 15 verses 750–870 (selections)

There is no greater work among [Julius] Caesar's achievements than that he became the father of this one [Caesar Augustus]....

With him as governor of all the world, O gods above, you generously showered your favors upon the human race! And so that this one might not be born of mortal seed, the former had to be made a god....

As heir to his name he will bear alone the burden placed upon him, and, most brave avenger of his slain father, he shall have us gods on his side....

When peace has been granted to the earth, he shall turn his mind to civil justice, and as most just innovator shall pass laws and by his own example shall guide public morals, and, looking forward to future time and future generations, he shall bid his son [Tiberius], born of his chaste wife, to bear both his name and cares, but not until as an old man he has equalled Nestor's years shall he reach the heavenly abodes and the stars of his kinsfolk....

Far off be that day and later than our own age when Augustus, leaving the world which he rules, shall go to heaven, and there, though away froyers.

CIL, Vol. XII no. 4333 = Dessau, *ILS* no. 112 = Ehrenberg-Jones no. 100

Altars instead of temples were erected in Italy and the western provinces in Augustus' lifetime; they were dedicated to his divine spirit. Such an altar at Narbonne, in southern France, was erected in 11 AD and dedicated in 12/13.

i.

In the consulship of Titus Statilius Taurus and Lucius Cassius Longinus [11 AD], September 22, the following vow in perpetuity was undertaken by the populace of the Narbonensians to the divine spirit of Augustus:

May it be good, favorable, and auspicious to Imperator Caesar Augustus, son of a god, father of our country, *pontifex maximus,* holding the tribunician power for the thirty-fourth year, to his wife, children, and house, and to the Senate and Roman people and the colonists and residents of the colony Julia Paterna of Narbo Martius, who have bound themselves to worship his divine spirit in perpetuity. The populace of the Narbonensians has erected an altar at Narbo in the Forum, at which annually on September 23, the day on which the good fortune of the age produced him to be ruler of the world, three equestrians from the populace and three freedmen shall sacrifice one animal apiece and shall on that day, at their own expense, provide incense and wine to the colonists and residents for the supplication to his divine spirit. And on September 24,[17] they shall likewise provide incense and wine to the colonists and residents. Also on January 1 they shall provide incense and wine to the colonists and residents.[18] Also on January 7, the day on which he first entered upon the command of the world,[19] they shall make supplications with incense and wine and sacrifice an animal apiece, and provide incense and wine to the colonists and residents on that day. And on May 31, because on that day in the consulship of Titus Statilius Taurus and Manius Aemilius Lepidus[20] he made judicial actions involving the populace uniform with those of the members of the municipal council, they shall sacrifice an animal apiece and provide incense and wine to the colonists and residents for supplicating his divine spirit. And from among these, three Roman equestrians or three freedmen, one.... [The rest is lost.]

ii.

The populace of the Narbonensians had dedicated the altar of the divine spirit of Augustus... in accordance with the regulations written below:

O divine spirit of Caesar Augustus, father of our country! When I shall give and dedicate today this altar to you, I shall give and dedicate it in accordance with those regulations and rules which I shall declare publicly here today as the groundwork of this altar and its inscriptions. If anyone wishes to clean, decorate, or repair it as a benefaction, it shall be lawful and permissible. If anyone makes a sacrifice of an animal, without providing in advance the additional offering, it shall nevertheless be properly done. If anyone wishes to give a gift to this altar and to embellish it, it shall be permitted, and the same regulation applies to the gift as to the altar itself. The rest of the regulations for this altar and its inscriptions shall be the same as for the altar of Diana on the Aventine [in Rome]. In accordance with these regulations and rules, as I have said, on behalf of Imperator Caesar Augustus, father of our country, *pontifex maximus,* holding the tribunician power for the 35th year, his wife, children and house, and the Senate and Roman people, and colonists and residents of the

Colony Julia Paterna of Narbo Martius, who have bound themselves to worship his divine spirit in perpetuity, I give and dedicate this altar to you, that you may be favorably and kindly disposed.

Révue de Philologie, Vol. IX (1935) pp. 182−185
= Ehrenberg-Jones no. 98a

This inscription, found at Halicarnassus in the Province of Asia, is a copy of a decree of the provincial council of the province passed, probably in 15 AD, shortly after the death of Augustus.

[It was decreed by the Greeks in Asia on motion of Gaius Julius M..., loyal to the emperor, high priest of the Goddess Roma and Imperator Caesar Augustus, son of a god, *pontifex maximus*, father of his country and of the whole world.]

Whereas the eternal and immortal nature of the universe, in addition to other immense benefactions, has bestowed the greatest good upon mankind by producing Caesar Augustus for a happy life for us, the father of his own country, namely, the Goddess Roma, Zeus Patroos, and the savior of the whole human race. Whereas his providence has not only fulfilled the vows of all, but exceeded them ... for peace has been brought to land and sea; cities flourish, well governed, harmonious, and prosperous, and there is the height and prosperity of all that is good. Whereas there are high hopes for the future, good cheer in the present, with men showing their loyalty in full measure with games, poems, sacrifices, and hymns.... [The rest is lost.]

35
ADMINISTRATION
OF JUSTICE

A
The Cyrene Edicts, 6–4 BC

The five edicts of Augustus concerning the senatorial Province of Crete-Cyrene, which are preserved in a long Greek inscription, constitute the most important evidence we have for the administration of justice in the heterogeneous empire under the first *princeps.* We may note the *princeps'* concern for protecting provincials from officials and Roman citizens, his provision for judicial equity for Greeks, and the growing coalescence of Roman and Hellenistic legal principles and procedures. Augustus' intervention in a senatorial province was accomplished by virtue of his *maius imperium* ("power superior to that of all governors") and of his personal *auctoritas.*

SEG Vol. IX no. 8 =*FIRA* Vol. I no. 68
= Ehrenberg-Jones no. 311

[Edict 1]

To insure fair trials in capital cases in a province with a large Greek population, in 6 BC Augustus ordered the establishment of mixed juries to try such cases.

Imperator Caesar Augustus, *pontifex maximus,* holding the tribunician power for the seventeenth year hailed imperator fourteen times, declares:

Since I find the total number of Romans in the provincial district of Cyrene to be 215 of all ages who have a census rating of 2,500 denarii or more, the rating of those from whom jurors are chosen,[21] and since envoys from the cities of the provincial district have complained bitterly that among these Romans there are some conspiracies to oppress the Greeks in cases involving the death penalty, the same persons taking turns in accusing and acting as witnesses for each other; and since I myself have ascertained that some innocent persons have been oppressed in this fashion and subjected to the supreme penalty; until the Senate takes action concerning this or I myself find some better procedure, it seems to me to be proper and suitable procedure for those in charge of the Province of Crete and Cyrene to impanel in the provincial district of Cyrene an equal number of Greek jurors from the highest property rating as Roman, no one, Roman or Greek, to be younger than twenty-five years, and no one to have a census rating in property of less than 7,500 denarii, and if there be a deficiency of such men, or if on this basis the number of jurors that are required to be impaneled cannot be filled, then they shall impanel as jurors men having half this census rating, but not less, in trials of Greeks in cases involving the death penalty.

If a Greek is indicted, a day before the prosecutor begins his case the defendant shall be given the right to decide whether he wishes all his jurors to be Romans or half of them Greeks. And if he opts for half Greeks, then the lottery balls shall be weighed[22] and the names written on them, and from one lottery box the names of the Romans, from the other those of the Greeks shall be drawn at random, until a total of twenty-five is completed from each group. Of these the prosecutor may challenge peremptorily one from each group if he desires, the defendant three out of the total, with the proviso that he not peremptorily dismiss either all Romans or all Greeks. Then [after the case is heard], all the remaining jurors shall be separated for casting their ballots, and the Romans shall cast their ballots separately in one box, the Greeks in a second one. Then a separate count of the ballots on either side shall be made, and the governor shall declare in open court whatever the verdict of the majority of all the jurors was.

Moreover, since the relatives of those who have been killed do not generally leave unjust deaths unavenged, and it is likely that those involved will not fail to have Greeks to prosecute them and demand justice on behalf of their slain relatives or fellow-citizens, it seems to me proper and suitable procedure for those who will govern Crete and Cyrene that in the provincial district of Cyrene they do not permit a Roman to act as prosecutor of a Greek in the case of the death of a Greek man or woman, unless the person who goes to law concerning the death of one of his relatives or fellow-citizens is someone honored with Roman citizenship.

[Edict 2]

A landmark decision concerning "treason" to the emperor (see no. 13 above) in connection with statues of the emperor.

Imperator Caesar Augustus, *pontifex maximus,* having the tribunician power for the seventeenth year, declares:

Publius Sextius Scaeva ought not to be criticized or censured for seeing to it that there be sent to me under custody from the provincial district of Cyrene, Aulus Stlaccius Maximus, son of Lucius, and Lucius Stlaccius Macedo, son of Lucius, and Publius Lacutanius Phileros, freedman of Publius, since they stated that they had knowledge of and wished to declare something that affected my security and that of the state. Sextius acted properly and conscientiously. However, since they have no information pertaining to me or to the state, but declared that they had misrepresented this in the provincial district, and made it clear to me that they had lied, I set them free and released them from custody.[23] But, as for Aulus Stlaccius Maximus, whom the envoys of the Cyrenaeans accuse of removing statues from public places, among them also the one on the base of which the citizens had inscribed my name, until I investigate this matter, I forbid him to leave without my order.

[Edict 3]

This measure defines the rights and privileges of persons in Cyrene who have been granted Roman citizenship.

Imperator Caesar Augustus, *pontifex maximus,* having the tribunician power for the seventeenth year, declares:

If any persons of the provincial district of Cyrene have been honored with [Roman] citizenship, I order these nonetheless to perform the public services in their turn to the Greek community, except those to whom, in accordance with a law or decree of the Senate or by decree of my father or myself, exemption was granted together with citizenship.[24] And even for those to whom exemption has been granted, it is my pleasure that they be exempt only for the property they possessed at that time; but for all additional property they shall be subject to the existing obligations.

[Edict 4]

An amendment to the first edict concerning jury trials.

Imperator Caesar Augustus, *pontifex maximus,* having the tribunician power for the seventeenth year, declares:

As regards any future disputes between Greeks in the provincial district of Cyrene — excluding indictments involving capital punishment, concerning which whoever administers the provincial district must himself conduct the inquiry and give decision or provide a panel of jurors — in all other matters it is my pleasure that Greeks be assigned as jurors, unless some defendant or the one accused desires to have Roman citizens as jurors; and for those among them to whom, in accordance with this decree of mine, Greek jurors will be assigned, it is my pleasure that not a single juror be assigned from the city from which the plaintiff or accuser, or the defendant or accused, comes.

[Edict 5]

This edict and decree of the Senate established a new, more efficient and speedy procedure for trying public officials accused of extortion. The procedures during the last decades of the Republic allowed sixty days for constituting the jury; gave the parties the right to summon many witnesses from all over the empire; and allowed months of time to gather evidence and witnesses.

Imperator Caesar Augustus, *pontifex maximus,* having the tribunician power for the nineteenth year, declares:

A decree of the Senate was passed in the consulship of Gaius Calvisius and Lucius Passienus [4 BC], with me present and participating in the preparation of it. Since it pertains to the welfare of the allies of the Roman people, and so that it may be known to all for whom I have a care, I had decided to send it into all the provinces and to attach to it my preface. From this it will be evident to all the inhabitants of the provinces how much I and the Senate are concerned that none of our subjects should suffer any impropriety or any extortion.

[Decree of the Senate]

Whereas the consuls, Gaius Calvisius Sabinus and Lucius Passienus Rufus, spoke concerning matters which Imperator Caesar Augustus, our *princeps,* in accordance with the recommendation of his council drawn by lot from the Senate,[25] wished to be referred through us to the Senate, matters affecting the welfare of the allies of the Roman people, it was decreed by the Senate as follows:

Whereas our ancestors established legal process for recovery of money extorted, so that it would be easier for our allies to be able to proceed concerning wrongs done to them and to recover money extorted from them; and whereas this type of legal action is sometimes very costly and inconvenient for those on whose behalf the law was enacted, because poor persons and some weak through illness or age are dragged as witnesses from distant provinces; therefore the Senate decrees:

If, after this decree of the Senate has been passed, any of the allies desirous of recovering extorted money, either public or private (except where the defendant is subject to a capital penalty), shall make deposition and revelation concerning such matters to one of the magistrates who is authorized to convene the Senate, the magistrate shall bring these persons as quickly as possible before the Senate and shall assign an advocate who will speak on their behalf before the Senate, whoever they themselves request. But no one who has been excused from this duty shall be advocate against his will.

In order that those bringing charges may be heard in the Senate, the magistrate who grants them access to the Senate shall on the same day, if the Senate is in session, provided no less than 200 are present, choose by lot four from all those of consular rank, either those who are in Rome itself or within twenty miles from the city; and likewise three from all those of praetorian rank, from those in Rome itself or within twenty miles of the city; likewise two from all the other senators or those permitted to participate in the debates of the Senate,[26] whoever are then either in Rome or within twenty miles of the city. But he shall choose no one who is seventy years or older; or who is a magistrate or assigned to some authority; or who is presiding officer of a court or curator of the grain supply; or who is prevented by illness from performing this duty, after excusing himself on oath before the Senate and presenting three members of the Senate to attest to this on oath; or anyone who is related by kinship or marriage to the accused, that he may not against his will be compelled to be a witness in a public trial, in accordance with the Julian Judiciary Law;[27] or anyone who the accused swears before the Senate is hostile to him, though he may not give such oath against more than three. From the nine chosen by lot in this fashion, the magistrate who does the drawing shall see to it that within two days those who claim the money and those from whom the money is claimed shall make peremptory rejections in turn until five remain. If any one of these judges dies before the matter is adjudicated, or some other cause prevents him from giving a decision, and his excuse is approved by five men from the Senate under oath, then the magistrate, in the presence of the judges and those claiming the money and the one from whom the money is claimed, shall choose a substitute by lot from those men who are of the same rank and have held the same magistracies as the person who is being replaced happened to have held, provided that he does not select a man who may not, in accordance with this decree of the Senate, be selected to try the accused.

The judges selected concerning these matters shall hear and investigate only those matters in which someone is accused of having appropriated money, public or private; and such sums of money, public or private, as the accusers prove was taken from them, they shall order him to return, and the judges shall render their decision within thirty days. Those whose duty it is to investigate and pronounce judgment on these matters shall, until they complete their investigation and render judgment, be excused from all public services except public worship.

The Senate also decrees that the magistrate who does the drawing by lot of the judges, or, if he is unable to, the consul who has priority, shall preside over this proceeding and shall give permission to summon witnesses who are in Italy, with the proviso that he shall permit those making a private claim to summon not more than five, and those making a public claim not more than ten.

Likewise, the Senate decrees that the judges who are chosen by lot, in accordance with this decree, shall pronounce in open court what each one of them has decided; and whatever the majority pronounces shall stand as the verdict.

B
Augustus Adjudicates a Criminal Case

IGRR Vol. IV no. 1031 = H. Dittenberger, *Sylloge Inscriptionum Graecarum* (4th Ed.) no. 780

Cnidus was a *civitas libera* ("free state"), like Mytilene (see no. 29 D above), hence not subject to the jurisdiction of the proconsul of the Province of Asia. Two defendants in a homicide case in 6 BC, having no confidence in obtaining a fair trial at home, requested a "change of venue," asking that the matter be adjudicated by the *princeps* personally. The Cnidians sent representatives to Rome to present the city's case to the emperor.

Imperator Caesar Augustus, son of a god, *pontifex maximus,* consul designate for the twelfth time, possessing the tribunician power for the eighteenth year, to the magistrates, council, and people of the Cnidians, greeting. Your envoys Dionysius and a second Dionysius, son of Dionysius, appeared before me in Rome and, after giving me your decree, accused Eubulus (son of Anaxandrides), now deceased, and Tryphera, his wife, still living, with regard to the death of Eubulus, son of Chrysippus.

I ordered Asinius Gallus [proconsul of Asia], my friend, to interrogate by torture the slaves of those who were accused in the case. I learned that Philinus, son of Chrysippus, had gone three nights in a row to the home of Eubulus, son of Anaxandrides, and of Tryphera, employing violence and a kind of siege. And on the third night he was joined by his brother Eubulus, son of Chrysippus. The owners of the house, Eubulus, son of Anaxandrides, and Tryphera, since they had no dealings with Philinus and were unable to find safety in their home by barricading it against the attacks, gave orders to one of their slaves, not to commit murder, to which perhaps a person might be driven by justifiable anger, but to repel them by pouring the chamber pots over them. The slave, whether intentionally or unintentionally — for he stuck to his denial — let go the pot with its contents, with the result that Eubulus fell dead, though it would have been juster if he had been spared rather than his brother. I have also sent you their actual testimony.

I was rather surprised at the extent to which the defendants feared the examination of the slaves at your hands, unless because they deemed you to have become excessively harsh to them and to have hostile feelings toward your opponents, although they have suffered every imaginable injustice. They were annoyed at people who attacked someone else's home at night with force and violence three times, and who deprived all of you of the common safety. They suffered misfortune when they tried to protect themselves, having done no injustice at all. But now you would seem to me to be acting properly by noting my judgment in these matters, and by acknowledging my letter in your public records. Farewell.

36
AN EXILE ON THE EMPIRE'S FRONTIER

In 8 AD Ovid, at the age of fifty, was suddenly exiled for life and deported to Tomis (modern Constantza in Rumania) on the shores of the Black Sea. "Two charges ruined me," wrote Ovid, "a poem and an indiscretion." The poem was the *Art of Love;* just what the indiscretion was is unknown (perhaps it was connected with the immoral behavior of Augustus' granddaughter Julia). For such a sophisticated Roman bon vivant as Ovid, life at Tomis was repellent and monotonous: the land was bleak, the winters severe, the barbarians always close by. In this semi-barbarous place Ovid wrote his unique poems of exile, the *Tristia* (published 12 AD) and the *Letters from Pontus* (published 13–16 AD). Despite his self-abasement and his flattery of Augustus, he never was recalled, not even by Tiberius.

Ovid, *Tristia*

(Book 3 no. 10.) If there is anyone there in Rome who still remembers banished Ovid, and if my reputation still survives in the city without me, let him know that I live in the midst of a barbarian world under stars that never touch the sea. The Sarmatians surround me, a savage people, and the Bessians and Getans, names so unworthy of my talent. Yet when the breezes are mild we are protected by the intervening Danube, which repels wars with the flow of its waters. But when gloomy winter has thrust forth its ugly face, and the earth is made white with marble frost, at a time when Boreas and snow prevent one from living under the Great Bear, then it is obvious that these peoples are oppressed by the shivering pole. The snow lies there, and neither sun nor rains melt it once it has fallen. Boreas hardens it and makes it everlasting.... With skins and stitched breeches they keep out the terrible cold, and of the whole body only the face is exposed.

Often their hair, when they move it, tinkles with hanging ice, and their beards are white with matted frost. Wine that is unprotected freezes, preserving the shape of the jar, and they drink not draughts of wine, but chunks of it given to them....

Across the new bridges, over the gliding waters, Sarmatian oxen pull the wagons of the barbarians....

And whenever the cruel violence of mighty Boreas congeals the sea waters or the waters flowing out of the river, when the Danube has been made level by the freezing north winds, at once the barbarian enemy rides to the attack with his swift horses, an enemy powerful in horses and winged arrows, and he lays waste far and wide the neighboring land. Some flee, and with none to protect their fields, the unprotected resources are plundered, the small resources of the country, cattle and creaking wagons and whatever riches the poor peasant has. Part of them are driven off as captives, with their hands tied behind their backs, looking back in vain at their fields and homes; and part fall in agony, shot with barbed arrows, for there the swift steel has been dipped in poison. What they are unable to carry off with them, or lead away, they destroy, and the fire of the enemy turns into ashes the innocent huts. Even when there is peace, they still tremble with fear of war, and no one furrows the soil with down-pressed ploughshares. This place either sees or fears an enemy it does not see. The land lies idle, abandoned in its frozen expanse. This is the land discovered for my punishment.

(Book 3 no. 12 verses 25–54.) O four times happy. O countless times happy is he who is permitted to enjoy the city not forbidden to him. But it is my lot to see the snow melted by the spring sun, and waters which are not dug out hard from a lake. And the sea is not solid with ice, and the Sarmatian herdsman does not, as before, drive his creaking wagons across the Danube. Yet some ships will begin to sail here.... Rarely does a sailor cross the great sea from Italy, rarely does one visit these harborless shores. Yet if he knows how to speak with a Greek voice or a Latin one..., whoever he is..., may he, I pray, be able to tell the triumphs of to the feet of our leader. He who reports such things to me, things

I shall grieve not to have seen, will at once be a guest in my home. Woe is me! Is Ovid's home now in the Scythian world, and does my punishment now assign me its own place as a home? O gods, grant that Caesar may not will that here be my hearth and home, but only the inn of my punishment.

(Book 5 no. 7.) Naturally, as always you ask, dearest, how I am, though you can know this even when I am silent. I am miserable! This is the brief summary of my woes and will be for anyone who lives after offending Caesar.

You want to know what the people of the region of Tomis are like and under what customs I live. Though this region has a mixture of Greeks and Getans, the greater influence comes from the poorly pacified Getans. A greater number of Sarmatian and Getan people come and go on their horses along the roads. Among them there is no one who does not bear quiver and bow and weapons ghastly with viper's gall. Savage voices, grim countenances, veritable pictures of Mars, neither hair nor beards cut by any hand, with hands not slow to inflict wounds with the knife which every barbarian has fastened to his side. Among such, also, your poet now, forgetful of the loves with whom he dallied, these he sees, these he hears, my friend....

If I look upon the place, it is a place unlovable, and nothing in the whole world can be gloomier. If I look upon the men, they are hardly worthy of the name, they have more cruel savagery than wolves. They do not fear laws, but equity yields to force, and justice lies conquered beneath the aggressive sword. With skins and loose breeches they keep off the terrible cold, and their shaggy faces are protected with long hair. Among a few there remain traces of the Greek language, but this too has become barbarous with a Getic accent. There is not a single person among the people who might be able to express any common Latin words. I, the Roman poet — pardon, O Muses! — I am compelled to speak many things in Sarmatian fashion. See, I am ashamed and confess it; already from long disuse Latin words come to me with difficulty. I do not doubt that even in this book there are more than a few barbarisms — not the fault of the man but of the place....

Ovid, *Letters From Pontus*

(Book 2 no. 8 verses 1–36.) Recently I received a Caesar together with a Caesar,[28] the gods whom you sent me, Cotta Maximus. And that your gift might have the proper number, Livia is there joined with her Caesars. Blessed silver, more precious than all gold, which now has divinity in it, though it was but rough metal. Not by giving me riches could you have given me something greater than the three heavenly ones sent to my shores.

It is something to look upon gods, and to think them present, and to be able to talk, as it were, with a real divinity. Thanks to you, I have returned [to Rome], and the most remote land does not detain me, and, as before, I am staying safely in the midst of the city. I see the faces of the Caesars as I used to see them; I had scarcely had any hope of fulfilling this vow; I salute the celestial deity as I used to. You have nothing greater, I think to offer me, were I restored. What do my eyes miss except only the Palatine, a place which would be worthless if Caesar were removed? When I look upon him, I seem to see Rome, for he represents the image of our country. Am I wrong, or are the features of the image angry with me, and does the grim expression have something threatening in it? Spare me, O mightier in your virtues than the immense world, and check the reins of your just punishment. Spare me, I pray, immortal glory of our age, lord of the world under whose care it is. By the name of our country, which is dearer to you than yourself; by the gods who are never deaf to your prayers; by your consort,[29] who alone has been found equal to you, and to whom your majesty is not a burden; by your son,[30] like you a model of virtue, who can be recognized as yours by his character; by your grandsons,[31] worthy of their grandfather and father, who by your orders advance with mighty strides; reduce and restrict even in but the slightest measure my punishment, grant me a place which should be far from the Scythian enemy....

IV
A GOLDEN
AGE OF
LITERATURE

37
LITERARY PATRONAGE

The first ten years of the Augustan Age were the most brilliant decade of Roman poetry. This was partly due to the vigorous patronage of poets by such leaders as Maecenas, Pollio, and Messalla, all of whom maintained literary circles, and even directly by Augustus himself. Despite the awesome power and authority of Augustus, there was a tolerant attitude toward writers, and the authors of the age were not ordered to write propaganda.

Anonymous, *Panegyric on Piso* verses 230–245

The very poet who makes his poem on Aeneas resound among Italian peoples, who in his glorious renown touches Olympus, and in the Latin tongue challenges venerable Homer, perhaps his poetry would have remained hidden in the shadow of the grove, and, unknown to the peoples, he might have sung only on a fruitless reed if he had not had Maecenas. Yet not just to one poet only did Maecenas open his doors, and not to Vergil alone did he entrust his renown. Maecenas exalted Varius, who shook the stage with tragic gesture, and drew out his grand style, and introduced writers of repute to the people of Greece. He also made famous songs resounding on Roman strings and the Italian lyre of graceful Horace. Hail, source of fame, you who deserve to be revered for all time, protector of the choir of the Muses, under whose patronage poets were protected, never having to fear destitute old age.

Suetonius, *Life of Augustus* chapter 89

In every way Augustus sponsored men of talent of his own age; he listened with courtesy and patience to them when they recited, not only to poems and histories, but also to speeches and dialogues, too. However, he was offended by anything composed about him except in the serious treatments of distinguished writers, and he often reminded the praetors not to allow his name to be degraded in declamation contests.

38

THE CONTEMPORARY LITERARY SCENE

Authors of the Augustan Age were imbued with a sense of the high seriousness of their mission: the restoration and fostering of shared national values. They wrote with confidence that they were not only helping to create a great literature, but that they represented a new concept of the function of the poet as *vates* — the inspired spokesman for the nation. "For a time, in the principate of Augustus, poetry reads as if the world owed poets a living and they deserved it." (Gordon Williams, *Tradition and Originality in Roman Poetry* [Oxford 1968], p. 789.) As early as 35 BC, Horace, when Book 1 of his *Satires* was published, had formulated, together with other members of Maecenas' literary circle, a new programmatic theory for creating a great Roman literature. The growing individualism and aestheticism of Roman authors was to be redirected to national purposes and to a moral mission for poetry. But crude pragmatism was to be eschewed, and the new school of writers was to discipline itself in the classic perfection of form in the Greek masterpieces. Horace endorsed, and exemplified in his writings, the circle's aspiration for a literary art characterized by exquisite polish, restraint, sophistication, and good taste. Thus Greek artistry and Roman content were to be united to produce a great age of Roman literature.

Horace, *Satires*

(Book 1 no. 10 [selections].) Fundanius, you are the only one of the living able to write charming, babbling comedies, with the shrewd mistress and the slave Davus tricking the old man Chremes. Pollio sings the deeds of kings in iambic trimeter; Varius, like no one else, molds the strong, fierce epic; and the Muses rejoicing in the country have granted to Vergil tenderness and grace. What Varro of Atrax tried in vain, and some others too, I could write better; this genre [satire] is mine, but I am inferior to its inventor [i.e., Lucilius]. For I would not dare to pull down from him the crown of great honor clinging to his head. But I did say his river ran muddy, often carrying more things that should be omitted than included....

Suppose, I say, Lucilius was sophisticated and witty; suppose, likewise, that he was more polished than an inexperienced author of a poetry untouched by the Greeks, than a throng of older poets. Yet, if he should by fate's decree, drop into this our age, he would erase much and cut away all that would detract from a perfected whole, and in composing his verse he would often scratch his head and chew his fingernails down to the flesh. You often must correct with the stylus and rewrite those words worth reading a second time. Be content with a few readers, and don't labor to win the admiration of the masses. Or would you be so crazy as to prefer your poems to be dictated in bad schools? Not I! ...

May Plotius and Varius, Maecenas and Vergil, Valgius and the excellent Octavius and Fuscus approve these poems, and may both Visci. Without flattery I can mention you, Pollio, you, Messalla and your brother, and you, too, Bibulus and Servius, and with them, you, sincere Furnius,[1] and many other scholars and friends, whom I purposely fail to mention. I want these my poems, such as they are, to please these men, and I would be hurt if they are welcomed less than I expected....

Horace, *Epistles*

Horace here responds to critics of his lyric poetry who reproached it as derivative and unoriginal. Horace counters by arguing that he borrowed Greek meters, subjects, and style, adapting them to Roman themes and treatment. He concludes that his critics' attitude results from his refusal to curry favor with the masses.

(Book 1 no. 19, verses 21–41.) I was the first to plant my steps freely on untrodden ground, not following the tracks of another. Whoever puts trust in himself, will be a leader and rule the swarm. I first offered to Latium Parian iambics, following the meter and spirit of Archilochus, but not the subjects and the diction attacking Lycambes. But do not crown me with leaves too scanty because I was afraid to change the meter and his poetic technique. Masculine Sappho modelled herself on Archilochus' muse with her meter; Alcaeus did the same but differed in his subjects and arrangement. He does not seek out a father-in-law to smear in his poisonous verse nor bind a noose of scurrilous poetry for his bride. I, a Latin poet, have made widely known this lyric bard, never before mentioned by other lips. It pleases me to introduce the unheralded to be read by noble eyes and held by noble hands. Would you like to know why the ungrateful reader praises and loves my "trifles" in private but publicly unjustly criticizes them? Because I do not go hunting for votes from the capricious masses at the expense of banquets and by the bribe of some worn-out toga. I will not be a listener of famous writers and in turn retaliate [with my own readings], and it is beneath my dignity to go canvassing the tribe of critics and haunt their lecterns. It's because of this they gripe.

Horace, *Odes*

(Book 3 no. 30.) I have erected a monument more lasting than bronze and taller than the structures of the royal pyramids, a monument which neither destructive rain, nor the wild North Wind can destroy, nor the countless succession of years and the flight of time. I shall not entirely die, and a great part of me will escape the tomb; on and on I shall grow fresh with the praise of posterity. So long as the *pontifex* climbs the Capitoline together with the silent Vestal virgin, I shall be spoken of where the raging Aufidus River roars, and where King Daunus in a land poor in water ruled over farming people,[2] I, a man of importance risen from humble origins, pioneer in adapting Aeolian song to Italic measures. Accept my pride, O Melpomene, won by my merits, and graciously bind my locks with Delphic laurel.

Ovid, *Amores*

(Book 1 no. 15.) Why, gnawing Envy, do you censure those lazy years of mine and call my poetry the work of idle talent, saying that, while the vigorous stage of life sustains me, I do not, after the manner of our fathers, pursue the dusty rewards of military service, nor learn wordy laws, nor prostitute my voice in the ungrateful Forum? Mortal employment is what you ask of me, but I seek immortal fame that I may be celebrated in song forever in all the world. Homer will live as long as Tenedos and Ida stand, as long as the Simoïs sweeps its swift waters into the sea; and Hesiod will live as long as the grape swells with juice, as long as grain cut by the curved sickle falls; Callimachus will always be glorified in song all over the world — although he is not preeminent in talent, he is mighty in artistry. No loss will ever come to the buskin of Sophocles; together with the sun and moon Aratus will always live; as long as the tricky slave, the harsh father, the insolent "madame," and the enticing prostitute will live, Menander will survive; Ennius, lacking in art, and Accius with the spirited tongue have a reputation that will never vanish; what age will not learn of Varro the first ship and the golden fleece sought by Jason. The poetry of sublime Lucretius will perish when a single day brings destruction to the earth; Tityrus [i.e., the *Eclogues* of Vergil], the crops [i.e., the same poet's *Georgics*], and the armor of Aeneas will be read as long as Rome will be the capital of the world over which she has triumphed; so long as the torches and the bow are the weapons of Cupid, your verses, O elegant Tibullus, will be learned; Gallus will win renown in the West and in the East, and with Gallus his own Lycoris will be known.

Therefore, although rocks and the blade of the tough plow perish with time, poetry knows no death. Let kings and the triumphs of kings yield to poetry, and let the fertile bank of the Tagus rich in gold yield. Let the masses admire cheap things; for me, let golden-haired Apollo serve cups filled from the fountain waters of the Castalian spring; may I wear upon my hair myrtle that fears the cold, and may I be read again and again by the troubled lover. Envy feeds on the living; after death it subsides when each person's glory preserves him as he deserves. So, even when the fires of the funeral pyre have consumed me, I shall survive, and a great part of me will live on and on.

39
THE ROMAN HOMER-
VERGIL

In 28 BC, shortly after the victory of Augustus, Propertius hinted that "something greater than the *Iliad* is being born." Ten years in the making, Vergil's *Aeneid* remained unfinished in details when he suddenly died in 19 BC. His death-bed request that the poem be burned was overruled by Augustus. The *Aeneid* became at once the Roman national epic, and it has remained one of the great classics of world literature, a masterpiece of exquisite verbal art, formal perfection, and exploration of the human condition.

The *Aeneid* draws on Homer's *Iliad* and *Odyssey*, as well as numerous other works, both in Greek and Latin. It is a new kind of epic — one designed for an imperial people that had lost its way and has begun to regain its direction. The values of the Augustan Age are explored by Vergil through a fusion of myth and history. By combining the myth of Rome's beginnings with contemporary events, Vergil succeeds in giving the new age an heroic quality. He employs a conscious symbolism in the mythic material to evoke contemporary personages, events, problems. He thus invites the Romans to consider the scope of their history, the continuity with their past, and their obligations to the future. The hero is a new kind of hero — a man of destiny characterized by Roman virtues and human frailties, who is dedicated to the mission of leading his people to the "promised land," without any expectation of personal rewards.

Despite Vergil's patriotism and glorification of Augustus, the *Aeneid* is filled with doubts and a deep-seated pessimism: it has been called "the epic of grief." The high idealism which Vergil brought to the new order appears to have been disappointed by the practical compromises made by Augustus, and by the gulf between Augustus' proclaimed ideals for the new order and the patent realities of the age. There are many who do not believe that the principal theme of the *Aeneid* is "arms and the hero," or "peace," or "O Roman, remember to rule the peoples with your empire," but rather Vergil's poignant line *sunt lacrimae rerum et mentem mortalia tangunt* ("There are tears for the things of the world, and mortality touches the heart.") Rome's great national epic is, indeed, not an exultation of victory: "The poem of imperial Rome closes not with a patriotic paean or a hope of high national achievements but with the pathos of a young man's death." "Thus the *Aeneid*, that opened with a cry of trumpets, dies away with a sigh." (C.M. Bowra, *From Virgil to Milton* [London 1945], p. 47; F.M. Letters, *Virgil* [New York 1946], p. 156.)

Vergil, *Aeneid*

(Book 1 verses 1–33.) I sing of arms and a hero who was the first to come, exiled by fate, from the coasts of Troy to Italy and the Lavinian shores. Both on land and on the deep he was tempest-tossed by the power of the gods, on account of the ever-mindful wrath of savage Juno; and he suffered much in war too, while he was striving to found his city and bring in his gods to Latium, whence would come the Latin people, the fathers of Alba Longa, and the walls of lofty Rome.

Relate to me, O Muses, the reasons: how was her divinity wounded, or why did the grieving queen of the gods compel a man distinguished for his piety to undergo so many misfortunes and encounter to many laborious tests? Do celestial minds have so much angry passion?

There was an ancient city — settlers from Tyre colonized it — Carthage, facing against Italy and far away from the mouth of the Tiber, rich in resources and most fierce in the pursuits of war. More than all the other lands Juno, they say, cherished it, even holding Samos in less esteem. Here were her weapons; here she stored her chariot. Even then the goddess was striving and foster-ing the thought: this city is to be ruler of the world (if the Fates allow it). But in fact she had heard that a people springing from Trojan blood was coming to topple one day the city's citadels; from it would arise a people ruling far and wide, proud in war, and the destroyers of Carthage. Thus decreed the Fates. This she feared, the daughter of Saturn, remembering too the old war she had first and foremost waged against Troy on behalf of her dear Greeks (not yet had the causes of her anger and the fierce pains left her heart; for, buried deep in her mind remained the judg-ment of Paris, the insult to her scorned beauty, the hated race, and the honors given to stolen Ganymede). Incensed by these things in addition, the Trojans, now tossed over the whole sea —

the remnants left by the Greeks and brutal Achilles — she kept far away from Latium, and for many years driven by destiny they wandered round about all the seas. So great a task it was to found the Roman people.

When Juno causes a storm to try to sink the Trojan fleet, Neptune notices the sudden disturbance of the sea, becomes angry, and then quickly calms the turbulence. Through a famous simile, depicting the calming of the waters, Vergil portrays the ideal of a political and moral leader and his ability to control violent forces.

(Book 1 verses 148–154.) And just as when often in a large crowd a riot has started, and the base-born masses rage with passions, and presently torches and rocks begin to fly, and fury supplies arms, if then by chance they catch sight of a man distinguished by his sense of duty and his deeds, they become silent and stand wtih attentive ears as he controls their passions with his words and soothes their feelings; thus all the crashing of the sea subsided....

As Aeneas and the Trojans, after years of trials and tribulations in search of the promised land of Italy, face a new crisis, Jupiter and Venus take note of Aeneas' suffering. Venus begs Jupiter to pity her son and end the continual harassment of the Trojans. In reply, Jupiter prophesies the magnificent future of Rome and its empire, culminating in the rule of Augustus.

(Book 1 verses 223–296.) Jupiter, looking down from high upper air upon the sea studded with sails, the lands lying below, the shores and widespread peoples, stood at the summit of the sky and turned his gaze upon the realms of Africa. And as he was pondering over such troubles in his heart, Venus, her bright eyes dimmed with tears and in unusual sorrow, addressed him: "O you who govern with eternal rule the affairs of both men and gods and terrify them with lightning, what crime so sacrilegious could my Aeneas have committed against you, what could the Trojans have done to have the entire world — for Italy's sake — barred against them after already suffering so many deaths? Surely you have promised: from them as the years roll on one day would come Romans, from these would descend leaders from the blood reborn of Teucer, who would hold in their power the sea and all the lands. What motive has changed you, father? As I weighed fate against the adverse Fates, in this I found solace for the fall of Troy and its sad ruin; but now the same misfortune dogs these men who have already suffered through so many crises. What end, O great king, to these labors do you grant?... We, your own offspring, to whom you have granted the citadel of the sky, with our ships lost (how unspeakable!), are betrayed because of the resentment of a single one [i.e., Juno] and are kept far from Italy's coasts. Is this the reward for dutifulness? Is this the way you restore us to power?"

He smiled upon her with the expression by which he calms the sky and storms, and the father of men and gods then kissed his daughter and said the following: "Do not fear, Cytherea; the destiny of your children remains fixed; you will see the city and the promised walls of Lavinium, and you will carry your great-hearted Aeneas exalted to the stars of heaven. No, my mind has not changed. He — I speak out now, since this anxiety gnaws at you, and further unrolling the secrets of the fates I shall reveal them — will wage a mighty war in Italy, crush fierce peoples, and establish customs and walls for his people until he has ruled in Latium for three summers and three winters after the subjugation of the Rutulians. But his son Ascanius, who has been given the surname of Iulus (his name was Ilus, while the state of Ilium stood in power), for thirty years, month after month, he will exercise his power; he will then transfer the seat of power from Lavinium to Alba Longa, fortifying it with great strength.

Here for three hundred full years there will be rule under the line of Hector, until a royal priestess, pregnant by Mars, Ilia, will give birth to twin sons. Then, rejoicing in the tawny skin of his nurse, the she-wolf, Romulus will take up the rule, and build the walls of Mars, and call the people "Romans" from his own name. For them I set no limits of power and no time: I have granted empire without end. Yes, even fierce Juno who now wearies the sea, and the lands, and even heaven, with terror, will change her policies for the better and with me will cherish the Romans, masters of the world, the people that wears the toga. So I have decreed. With years gliding on and on, there will come an age when the house of ancient Assaracus will subjugate Phthia and famous Mycenae and will master the defeated Greeks. Trojan Caesar will be born from that distinguished line, who will limit his empire by the Ocean and his fame by the stars, Julius, a name derived from great Iulus. One day untroubled you will welcome him to heaven, laden with the spoils of the East; and he too will be invoked by prayers. Then savage ages will become tame when wars cease, venerable Faith and Vesta and Romulus with his brother Remus will dispense laws; the dreadful gates of war will be shut tight with iron bolts; within, unholy madness, sitting on brutal arms and bound behind his back by a hundred bronze knots, will roar hideously with bloody mouth.

Aeneas descends to the underworld where his father's soul prophesies the glorious future of Rome.

(Book 6 verses 756–886, selections.) Now listen to what glory awaits the Trojan line, what descendants from the Italian people await you, illustrious souls inheriting our name. I shall unfold and reveal to you your destiny.... Now look at this people, your Romans. Here is Caesar and all the offspring of Iulus destined to pass beneath the huge pole of heaven. Here is the man, this is he whom you have often heard promised, Augustus Caesar, offspring of a deified man. He will found again the Golden Age for Latium over fields that Saturn once ruled, and he will extend imperial power over Africans and Indians, in lands lying beyond the constellations, beyond the paths of the year and sun, where the heaven-bearer Atlas on his shoulder whirls the pole of heaven studded with blazing stars. Even now at his approach, the Caspian realms and Scythia shudder at the oracular warnings of gods, and the seven mouths of the Nile tremble and shake....

After pointing out many souls of men destined to be famous in Roman history, and drawing historical and moral lessons from the events connected with them, Anchises, Aeneas' father, comments on the nature of Roman national character.

Others will craft (I do believe it) bronze statues more delicate and lifelike and sculpt out of marble living features; others will plead cases better and with a pointer will trace the movements of the heavens and will describe the rising constellations. Remember, O Roman, to rule nations with your power — these will be your arts — to impose the rule of peace, to spare those who submit, and to crush the proud....

Aeneas's visit to the underworld concludes with a tribute by Vergil to the young Marcellus, son of Octavia, son-in-law of Augustus, and heir apparent until his death in 23 BC, while the composition of the *Aeneid* was in progress.

Aeneas noticed a young man, remarkable in appearance and in gleaming armor, walking with him, but his brow was quite sad and his eyes were downcast. He asked: "Who is that, father, accompanying the hero[3] during his walk? A son or some descendant from his illustrious line? What a clamor the crowd around him makes. How like the other he is. But dark night hovers around his head with gloomy shade." Then his father Anchises began, with upwelling tears: "My son, do not inquire into the bitter grief of your people. The Fates will just barely show him to earth and will not allow him to exist beyond that. The Roman stock would have seemed too powerful to you, O gods above, if these gifts had remained permanent. How many mournful cries of men the field of Mars sends to his mighty city! What funerals you will see, O Tiber, when you glide by that new tomb [i.e., Augustus' mausoleum]! No child from the Trojan people will raise so much hope in Latin ancestors, nor shall the land of Romulus ever boast so proudly of any son. O piety lost, O ancient faith, O right hand invincible in war! No one would have escaped harm meeting him armed, whether he encountered the enemy on foot or spurred the flanks of a foaming steed. Ah, pitiable boy, if you could but break the cruel bonds of your fate, you will be Marcellus! Bring lilies with generous hands, and let me scatter purple flowers, and let me at least pile gifts on the spirit of a descendant, and let me perform this duty, though in vain."

Vergil continues with the story of the outbreak of war between the Trojans and the Latins.

(Book 7 verses 601–640.) There was a custom in Latium of old, which the Alban cities carried on as a rite; now mightiest Rome practices it when they begin a war, whether they prepare to wage pitiless war with their weapons against the Getans or Hyrcanians or Arabs, or push on to India, and penetrate the East, and demand the return of the standards from the Parthians. There are two gates of war — thus they call it — sacred in religious rite and in fear of dread Mars. A hundred bronze bars keep them closed, and the deathless might of iron, and Janus is ever there as guardian of the building. When the decree of the Senate for war has been passed, the consul himself, resplendent in the mantle of Quirinus and with his toga girt up, opens up the grating doors. He himself calls forth to battle, and the rest of the people follows, and the bronze trumpets combine in a blare of assent.

Following this custom, at that time too King Latinus was bidden to declare war against the Trojans and to open up the dread gates. The old man refrained from touching them and, turning away, fled from the vile duty and concealed himself in a dark hidden place. Then the queen of the gods Juno, swooping down from heaven, herself dashed open with her hand the delaying doors and, turning them on their hinges, thrust open the iron gates of war. Italy, previously unstirred and immovable, blazes forth. Some prepare to take the field as infantry, some, dust-covered, proudly prance on their high horses. All seek arms. Some rub their shields smooth and their spears bright and sharpen their axes on flint stone with fat grease. They rejoice to carry the standards and to hear the sounds of the trumpets. Five very large cities set up anvils and manufacture new weapons: powerful Atina, proud Tibur, Ardea, Crustumerium, and towered Antemnae. They prepare hollow helmets to protect their heads and mold the willow framework of shields. Others beat out bronze breastplates or polished greaves of pliant silver. To this has come all their devotion to share, to pruning hook and plough. They forge again in furnaces their ancestral swords. And now the trumpets blare; the password goes out as signal for war. One seizes a helmet, rushing fearful from his house; another yokes his neighing horses, and puts on his shield and breastplate triple woven with gold, and girds on his trusty sword.

The early history of primitive Latium and the Golden Age under Saturn is recounted to Aeneas by Evander, ally of Aeneas against the Rutulians.

(Book 8 verses 313–332.) Native Fauns and Nymphs used to occupy these groves, and a stock of men sprung from tree trunks and hard oak. They had no order, no civilized life, nor had they learned to yoke bulls, store wealth, or ration what they produced; branches and the hunting of wild game (a hardy livelihood) furnished their nourishment. Saturn came first from heavenly Olympus, in flight from Jupiter's arms and an exile from his usurped kingdom. He organized this people, untrained and scattered about the high mountains, and gave it laws, preferring it to be called Latium because he had hidden[4] in safety along these shores. The Golden Age they tell was under his rule as king. Thus he governed the people in tranquil peace, until little by little an age more degenerate and depraved followed it, and the madness of war and the passion for possessing ensued. Then came Ausonian bands and Sicanian people, and the land of Saturn often changed its name. Then there were kings, followed by Thybris, fierce and of giant stature, from whom we Italians have since called the river by the name of Tiber.

In Homer's *Iliad* Vergil could not have failed to admire, with countless other readers, the description of the shield of Achilles, created for him by Hephaestus and portraying scenes from the world of peace, highlighting the joys and sadness of life. The shield created by Vulcan for Aeneas (cf. the "Shield of Virtue" awarded to Augustus; see no. 3 B above) features, by contrast, a panorama of Roman history, ranging from Aeneas' son Ascanius to Augustus in triumph. Vergil selects scenes that would illustrate themes central to the *Aeneid* and to Roman civilization: *furor* ("violence") as an historical necessity; the defeat of men of evil through virtue and *pietas;* the participation of the gods in Roman destiny; and the continuity of Roman history through men of destiny from Romulus to Augustus, prince of peace. The shield of Aeneas thus, through historical precedent, protects (and excuses) his use of violence for higher purposes, but also places upon him the responsibility of sacrificing himself for the future. In this sense the shield is both a justification of Augustus' methods and a call to higher ends.

(Book 8 verses 626–731.) On the shield Vulcan had portrayed Italian affairs and the triumphs of the Romans (he was not unacquainted with prophecies nor unaware of the future), and every generation of the line to come from Ascanius, and the wars fought in order. He had portrayed also the newly delivered wolf lying in the verdant cave of Mars, the twin boys playing around her udder and hanging on it, and the wolf licking the frightened boys in motherly fashion and, her slender neck turned back, smoothing them down in turn and fashioning their bodies with her tongue.

Not far from here he had added Rome and the violent rape of the Sabine women taken from amid the seated crowd while the great games of the circus were being held. And suddenly a new war rising up for the followers of Romulus and aged Tatius and the austere inhabitants of Cures. Afterwards the same kings, ending their struggle, stood armed before the altar of Jupiter, holding sacrificial bowls, and killed a pig, made a treaty. Not far from here swift four-horse chariots tore Mettius[5] apart — but you, O Alban, should have abided by the agreements — and Tullus was dragging the entrails of the lying man through a wood, and the thorn bushes were sprinkled and bedewed with his blood. Also Porsenna[6] was ordering Rome to take back expelled Tarquin[7] and attacking the city with a mighty siege. The descendants of Aeneas were rushing to arm themselves for liberty. You could see him defeated, in the guise of an angry person, a threatening one, because Cocles[8] dared to tear down the bridge, and Cloelia swam the river after bursting out of her chains.

On the top of the shield Manilius stood guard over the Tarpeian citadel in front of the temple and held the lofty Capitoline Hill, and the palace was fresh and rough with the thatch of Romulus. And here the goose of silvery whiteness flying over the gilded porticoes announced that the Gauls were at the threshold.[9] The Gauls were present in the thorn bushes and were holding the citadel, protected by darkness and the advantage of dark night. They had blond hair and gilt clothing; they were resplendent in their striped cloaks and their white necks had golden collars around them; each of them brandished two Alpine spears in his hand, their bodies protected by long shields.

Here he had portrayed Salian priests leaping, and the nude Luperci priests, and the fleecy caps, and the shields that fell from heaven.[10] Chaste matrons were conducting the sacred objects through the city in soft-cushioned carriages. Far from this he had added also the abodes of Tartarus, the lofty palace of Hades, and the punishments of crimes, and you, Catiline,[11] hanging on a rock towering over you and trembling at the mouths of the Furies, and the souls of the pious separate, and Cato holding sway over these.

Around these went a representation in gold of the sea, turbulent far and wide, but the dark blue waters foamed in a white flood, and all around dolphins of bright silver in circles skimmed the waters and cut through the tides with their tails.

In the middle of the shield were to be seen bronze fleets, the war at Actium; and you could see Leucate all ablaze with array of battle, and the waves glistening in gold. From here Augustus Caesar leading the Italians into battle together with the senators and people, the Penates and the great gods, standing on the lofty stern. From his joyous brows two flames spring forth, and the star of his father[12] dawns on his head. In another part, Agrippa proudly leads the forces, with favorable winds and gods; his head glistens with the naval crown, adorned with ships' beaks — proud symbol of war. In another part, Antony, with the help of barbarians and various arms victor over the peoples of the East and the shores of the Indian Ocean, brings Egypt and the forces of the East and farthest Bactria with him. There follows — O sinful — his Egyptian wife. All rush together in one place, and the entire sea, churned up with oars swept back and triple-beaked prows, is torn into foam. They attack the lofty ships; you would think the Cyclades Islands, torn from their foundations, were floating there, or that lofty mountains were clashing against mountains, so huge are the towered ships with which the men attack. Ropes aflame are scattered by hand, and iron darts by engines. The realm of Neptune is growing red with the fresh slaughter. The queen in the midst summons her troops with her native timbrel; not yet does she notice the twin snakes behind her;[13] and the monstrous, multiform gods, and howling Anubis bear arms against Neptune and Venus and Minerva. In the midst of the battle Mars rages, depicted in iron, and the dread Furies from heaven; and Discord, with rent robe, proceeds rejoicing, she whom the War Goddess follows with bloody whip. Observing these things, Apollo of Actium stretches his bow from above. Every Egyptian terrified by this, and the Indians, and every Arab, and all the Sabaeans turn their backs. The queen herself was seen to summon the winds and set sail, eager to release the loosened ropes. Vulcan had made her pale in the midst of the slaughter, with the intimation of approaching death, and portrayed her being carried off by the waves and the northwest wind. Opposite, however, the Nile with his mighty body, sorrowing and opening up the folds of his robe, summons the conquered into his opened garment, to his dark-blue lap and sheltering streams.

But Caesar riding into the city of Rome in triple triumph was consecrating his deathless vow to the Italian gods, three hundred immense shrines throughout the whole city. The streets roar with joy and games and applause. In all the temples a chorus of matrons, at all the temple altars; before the altars slain bullocks cover the ground. He himself, seated on the white marble threshold of the glowing Apollo, reviews the gifts of the peoples and attaches them to the proud portals. Conquered peoples march in a long line, so varied are the languages, clothing, weapons. Here Neptune had fashioned the Nomad people and the ungirdled Africans, here the Leleges and the Carians and the arrow-bearing Gelonians. The waters of the Euphrates now flowed gentler; the Morini, farthest of men, and the Rhine with its two mouths, and the indomitable Dacians and the Araxes River, which resents a bridge over it.

Aeneas marvels at all this on the shield of Vulcan, the gift of his mother, and though he does not understand the subjects, he rejoices in the representation, lifting upon his shoulders the fame and fate of his descendants.

Evander, king of the Arcadians at Pallanteum, at the site of future Rome, is an ally of Aeneas and the Trojans. He has sent a contingent of troops led by his beloved young son Pallas. It is Pallas' first day in battle.

(Book 10 verses 442–519.) "I alone am attacking Pallas; to me alone Pallas belongs. I wish his father were present as spectator."

So spoke Turnus…. Pallas marvels in amazement at Turnus, and his eyes roam over the huge body, and with fierce look scans everything from a distance, and he answers the word of the despot as follows: "Either I shall be praised presently for spoils taken from a leader, or for a glamorous death. My father can bear either lot. Away with threats." And with these words he proceeds to the level place between. Chilling fear runs through the hearts of the Arcadians. Turnus leaps down from his chariot, and prepares to fight him face to face on foot….

The dying Pallas sinks on the hostile soil with bloody face. Standing over him Turnus says: "Arcadians, remember my words and report them to Evander. I send back Pallas as he deserved. Whatever honor there is in a tomb, whatever solace in burial, I bestow. His hospitality to Aeneas will cost him dearly." And saying this he planted his left foot on the lifeless body, taking as booty the enormous, heavy sword-belt…. Now Turnus exults in this spoil and rejoices at his prize. O minds of men, ignorant of fate, and future destiny, and how to preserve moderation when raised up by prosperity! A time will come when Turnus will wish he had paid a great price to leave Pallas undefiled, and he will regret the spoils and this day.

(Book 10 lines 517–536.) [At the news of Pallas' death] Aeneas takes alive four sons of Sulmo, and as many as Ufens brought up, to slaughter them as sacrifices to Pallas' shade and pour captive blood over the flames of the funeral pyre. Then from afar he hurls his deadly spear at Magus. Craftily he ducks, and the quivering spear flies over him. And then, embracing Aeneas's knees as a suppliant, he speaks as follows: "By the spirit of your dead father and the hopes of growing Iulus, I beseech you, spare this life for my son and my father. I have a lofty palace. Deep within lies buried a large amount of engraved silver; and I have weights of wrought and unwrought gold. The victory of the Trojans does not turn on this, nor will one life make such a difference." He spoke, and in answer Aeneas said: "All the great amounts of silver and gold you mention, save them for your children. Turnus was the first to abrogate such negotiation in war, when Pallas was killed. The spirit of my father Anchises and Iulus make this judgment." Thus he spoke, and holding his helmet with his left hand, Aeneas bent back his neck and drove his sword up to the hilt into the suppliant.

In imitation of the duel between Achilles and Hector in Homer's *Iliad*, Vergil includes a duel between Aeneas and Turnus at the conclusion of the *Aeneid*. But Vergil makes a striking change. Though Achilles' rage against Hector for killing his best friend, Patroclus, brutalized him, in the end he was moved to compassion and returned Hector's body to the Trojans for burial; thus the *Iliad* ends on a note of sadness, with the funeral of Hector. In Vergil's transmutation of this scene, he has Aeneas execute the suppliant Turnus in a blaze of fury. This sudden ending of the *Aeneid* is a stroke of great artistry but raises many questions about Vergil's intent. Has Aeneas been brutalized by all the violence? Has the means he was forced to use in Italy made him into another Turnus? Do the ends justify the means? Is this meant to symbolize the triumph of violence in history? Is there in the end no room for compromise and forgiveness to enemies? Did not Vergil set forth the Roman policy of *parcere subiectis* ("spare those who surrender" — see page 207 above)? Is this but a stated ideal, while the reality of Roman policy is recognized as different? Vergil has left us with this basic enigma about Rome and Augustus himself. Vergil's acknowledgment in this way of the imperatives of historical necessity is tinged with sadness.

(Book 12 verses 919–952.) Aeneas brandishes his fateful spear at the hesitating Turnus, and, picking with his eyes the proper moment, he hurls it from afar with all the strength of his body. Never are stones hurled with such a roar against walls by an engine, nor do claps of thunder leap forth from lightning with such a sound. The spear flies like a dark whirlwind bearing dread destruction and opens up the rim of the breastplate and the outermost circles of the seven-ply shield. Roaring, it passes right through his thigh. Struck by the spear, mighty Turnus falls to earth with his leg doubled under. The Rutulians rise up with a groan.... As a suppliant Turnus lifted up his humble eyes and stretched forth his beseeching hand: "I have indeed deserved it," he said, "and I do not ask mercy. Use your fortune. If any concern for a wretched parent can touch you — you too had such a father in Anchises — pity the old age of Daunus, and restore to my people either me or my body deprived of life, as you prefer. You have conquered, and the Italians have seen me stretch out my hands in defeat. Lavinia is your wife. Do not press hatred any farther."

Aeneas stood fierce in arms, rolling his eyes, and he stayed his right hand. And already Turnus' speech was on the point of changing him as he hesitated, when high on his shoulders he spied the luckless sword-belt of the boy Pallas, glittering with the well-known bosses, the boy whom Turnus had struck down with a death blow; and he was now wearing the insignia of his enemy on his shoulders. Aeneas, after he drank in the spoils with his eyes, the reminders of his cruel grief, kindled to fury and terrible anger says: "Will you, wearing the spoils of one dear to me, now be snatched from me? Pallas it is, Pallas it is who sacrifices you with this death blow, and exacts punishment from your accursed blood." Saying this, he plunged his sword full into his breast, fiercely. And the limbs of Turnus became slack with cold death. and his life with a groan fled indignant to the shadows.

From the altar dedicated at Carthage to the imperial family. The Flight from Troy: dutiful Aeneas with Anchises and Ascanius.
From Louis Poinssot, *L'Autel de la Gens Augusta à Carthage* (Tunis 1929), Plate ix

40

HORACE
ON ROMAN LIFE

"The *Odes* of Horace are the distilled lessons of Augustan poetry...."
(David O. Rose, *Backgrounds to Augustan Poetry* [London, 1975], p. 152.)
His contributions to the Golden Age of Latin literature were indeed
remarkable — he himself was fully aware of his achievement, of his great
versatility and creativity. One of his highest ideals was the adaptation of
Greek literature to Roman national purposes. As a stylist, he exemplified
the severe poetic discipline of the Augustan poets (in contrast with the
greater striving for artistic "liberty" on the part of pre-Augustan Roman
poets). Horace aimed at perfection of art and the creation of exquisitely
polished gems of poetry. His lyric poems, a selection of which is given
below, are also vehicles for his own eclectic philosophy of life and support
the spirit of moral regeneration of the Roman people.

Horace, *Odes*

(Book 1 no. 11.) Do not ask (it is not right to know) what end for
me, what end for you, the gods have granted; and do not test,
Leuconoë, astrological tables. How much better to endure whatever will come, whether Jupiter allots more winters or has
granted this one as the last which now wearies the Tyrrhenian Sea
dashing against the opposing rocks. Be wise, drink wine, and cut
short far-reaching hopes, since life is short. While we talk envious
time has escaped. Seize the day (*carpe diem*), trusting as little as
possible in tomorrow.

Horace uses the occasion of the dedication of the magnificent temple of
Apollo to offer a prayer for moderate and temperate living.

(Book 1 no. 31.) What does the poet ask of Apollo whose shrine is
just dedicated? What does he pray for while pouring wine of

young vintage from a bowl? Not for the rich crops of fertile Sardinia, not for the pleasing herds of sweltering Calabria, not for gold or ivory from India, not for fields that the silent river Liris eats away with its calm water. Let those to whom fortune has granted the vine prune it with a hook made at Cales; and let the wealthy merchant drain from golden goblets wines bought with Syrian merchandise; he is dear to the gods, as he three or four times yearly revisits the Atlantic Ocean unharmed. Olives nourish me, endive and light mallows. I pray, Apollo, grant me the enjoyment of the things I have at hand in good health and with a sound mind, and to spend an old age that is neither shameful nor deprived of the lyre.

Horace commemorates the death of Cleopatra and the end of the disastrous civil wars. Antony's name is not mentioned.

(Book 1 no. 37.) Now is the time to drink, now is the time to dance wildly stomping the ground, now is the time, my companions, to honor the couches of the gods with banquets *extraordinaires*. Before this day it was wrong to bring out Caecuban wine from ancestral cellars, while the queen[14] was still preparing insane destruction for the Capitoline and destruction for the Empire. She, with her polluted crew, men diseased and fouled, was mad enough to hope for anything, drunk on sweet wine. But her madness soon abated with the escape of scarcely a single ship saved from the fires, and Caesar drove her mind, unbalanced by Egyptian wine, into fears of reality and pursued her with his ships as she fled from Italy, just as the hawk chases the gentle doves, or the quick hunter the hare on the snowy fields of Thessaly, to put the fateful monster in chains. But she sought to die in a more noble fashion; she did not shudder at the sword in womanly fashion, nor did she hie to secret shores with her swift fleet. Instead she had the courage to return with a calm expression on her face to her palace lying in ruins, and bravely to handle the poisonous snakes, so as to drink in the dark venom in her body. Becoming more gallant when she had resolved to die, she of course begrudged it to our tough Liburnian ships to be led, as a private citizen, in proud triumph — no ordinary woman was she!

In this poem Horace rejects Eastern luxury in favor of a modest and simple life-style.

(Book 1 no. 38.) I hate Persian excesses, boy, I do not care for flower garlands tied with linden bark. Stop searching for the spots where the late rose lingers. I do not want you to embellish plain myrtle with fuss. Myrtle suits you as you serve, and me too, as I drink beneath the thick vines.

Horace advises moderation in prosperity.

(Book 2 no. 3.) Remember to keep a level head in adverse conditions, and likewise in prosperity keep it moderated from excessive joy, as you are destined to die, Dellius, whether you live all your life in sadness or on holidays enjoy yourself reclining in a secluded grassy spot with a choice brand of Falernian wine. Why do the tall pine and white poplar love to join with their branches in making an inviting shade? Why does the hurrying water strive to bustle in the winding river? Order them to bring here wines, and perfumes, and the too-brief blossoms of the lovely rose, while circumstances and youth and the dark threads of the three sisters [i.e., the Fates] allow. You will leave the pastures you have bought up, your home, and the villa which the yellow Tiber washes, you will leave them, and some heir will get possession of the riches heaped up into the sky. It makes no difference whether you live on earth as a rich man descended from ancient Inachus, or poor and from the humblest lineage, you are still a victim of Hades that has no pity. We are all herded to the same spot. Each one's lot is being shaken in an urn, and it will come out sooner or later and embark us on the boat for the eternal exile.

After the defeat of Antony, Octavian proclaimed amnesty, allowing many of those who had fought against him to return quietly to Italy. In this poem Horace intimately conveys the result of this policy, while he includes many references to his own life and earlier political role. The Epicurean attitude and stance at the poem's conclusion are typically Horatian.

(Book 2 no. 7.) Often brought down into an extreme peril with me, when Brutus was the leader of the campaign, who, O Pompeius, has restored you your citizenship, giving you back to the gods of our country and to the Italian sky? With you, the first of my old comrades, I often broke up a lazy day with wine, wearing a wreath on my hair shining with Syrian perfume. Wtih you I experienced Philippi and the rapid retreat, ingloriously dropping my shield when my courage was broken and bragging men had to touch the inglorious ground in surrender. But Mercury carried me quickly through the enemy, in my terror, in a thick cloud; you, however, were sucked back into the war by the wave with its teeming waters. So render to Jove the feast that was vowed, and rest your body, tired from long army service, under my laurel tree, and do not spare the wine jugs reserved for you. Fill to the brim the polished cups with Massic wine that brings forgetfulness, from spacious vessels pour the perfumes. Who is seeing to the preparation, with all speed, of wreaths of moist parsley or myrtle? Whom does the Venus-throw designate as the "master of the drinks"? I shall revel more madly than the Thracians. When a friend of mine is restored, how sweet it is to act insane!

The days of wine and roses are few and brief. Enjoyment of the present is the true responsibility of man, Horace constantly reminds his reader.

(Book 2 no. 14.) Alas, how fleeting the years slip by, Postumus, my Postumus. No piety will delay wrinkles, old age in hot pursuit, and death unconquerable, not even if every day that passes you strive with three hundred bulls to placate tearless Pluto, who confines Geryon, the giant of three bodies, and Tityos by the gloomy water that all of us perforce must sail across who are nourished by the bounty of the earth, whether we be kings or poor farmers. In vain we will escape bloody Mars, and the crashing waves of the noisy Adriatic; in vain we shall fear throughout the autumn months the Scirocco that harms our bodies. You must look upon the winding Cocytus, dark and sluggish in its flow, and the infamous offspring of Danaüs, and Sisyphus, son of Aeolus, damned to labor unending. You will have to leave the earth, your home, and darling wife, and of those trees which you tend to now not a single one except the hated cypresses will follow you, their brief master. A more deserving heir will drink up the Caecuban wine that you kept locked with a hundred keys, and he will splatter the floor with a wine that is the pride of the stock, superior to the dinner wines of pontiffs.

41

THE LATIN LOVE ELEGY

Despite the regime's promotion of nationalistic-moralistic themes, the love elegy flourished in the Augustan Age. A Roman creation, this genre had a short life of about fifty years, culminating in the first decade of the principate. Love as a poetic theme was a consuming interest of many writers, and they idealized love out of all proportion to the real life of the times. The Roman elegists were anti-establishment; they rejected involvement in the standard public career, opting for a "career" of love, poetry, beauty, and art. This genre was cultivated in particular by Cornelius Gallus, Propertius, Tibullus and Ovid. A representative selection from the love elegies is given below.

Ovid, *Amores*

(Book 1 no. 1.) I was preparing to publish in stately measures arms and violent wars, with subject appropriate to the meters. The second verse was equal to the previous one, but Cupid is said to have laughed and furtively stolen one foot.[15] "Who gave you, cruel boy, this right over poetry? We are poets of the Muses, not a throng belonging to you. What if Venus should seize the arms of golden-haired Minerva, or golden-haired Minerva should fan the lighted torches? Who would approve of Ceres ruling in the woods on mountain ridges and of fields being cultivated under the authority of the maiden with the quiver? Who would equip Phoebus, distinguished by his locks, with the sharp spear, while Mars played the Aeonian lyre? You have great kingdoms, my boy, and are much too powerful; why do you ambitiously strive for a new role? Or is the whole world yours? Are the vales of Helicon yours? Is Phoebus' lyre scarcely safe any longer? Whenever a new page rises well with the first line, that next verse diminishes my strength. I do not have a subject suitable for lighter measures, for example, a boy or girl with long hair well coiffured."

I had made these complaints when he suddenly freed his quiver and chose arrows especially made for my doom. With his knee he stoutly bent the curved bow into a crescent and said, "Take this subject to sing of, O poet!" Oh poor me! The arrows of that brat hit their target. I am on fire and in my heart unfulfilled Love rules. Let my work rise in six feet and fall back in five. Good-bye to you, O iron wars, you and your meters! Crown your golden brow with myrtle from the seashore, O Muse, you who are to be proportioned in eleven melodious feet.

(Book 1 no. 7.) Every lover is a soldier, and Cupid has his own camp; believe me, Atticus, every lover is a soldier. The time of life suitable for war is also the same period ripe for love; an old man as a soldier is a shameful thing; equally disgraceful is an old man as lover. The spirit which generals look for in a brave soldier is the same which a pretty girl demands in her male companion. Both spend the night in watch, each resting on the ground; one protects the doors of his mistress, the other guards his general's. A long journey is the duty of a soldier; send the girl on, and the vigorous lover will follow continuously. He will confront mountains in his way and streams swollen from showers; he will tread on snows piled high, and, about to ride the seas, he will not plead the blustery East winds nor look for stars suitable for ploughing through the waves. Who except a soldier or lover will endure the chill of night, the snow, sleet, and pouring rain? One is sent as a spy against the dangerous enemy, the other keeps his eyes on his rival as his enemy. One besieges mighty cities, the other the threshold of a hard-hearted girl; one breaks down gates, the other doors. Often it has been an advantage to attack an enemy at sleep, and with an armed band to kill an unarmed group; in this way the wild troops of Rhesus, the Thracian, fell, and you, O captured horses, deserted your master. Lovers often take advantage of the sleep of husbands and take up arms while their enemy is in slumber. To pass through a garrison of guards and troops of watchmen is ever the soldier's and the poor lover's task. Mars is unpredictable, and Venus is uncertain; the conquered rise again, and those who you would say never could fall are brought low. Therefore, whoever used to call love lazy, let him cease. Love has a very active nature. Saddened Achilles was on fire for Briseis when she was taken from him (while it is possible, O Trojans, break the resources of the Greeks). Hector often went to battle from the embraces of Andromache, and his wife actually fitted the helmet on his head; Agamemnon, the epitome of generals, when he saw the daughter of Priam [i.e., Cassandra], is said to have been ravished at the sight of her hair, streaming like a Maenad's. Mars, too, was caught and felt the net of the blacksmith [i.e., Vulcan]; no story was better known in heaven. I myself am lazy and born for reckless leisure; a bed in the shade has softened my spirits; love for a beautiful girl has spurred me from my indolence and ordered me to earn my pay in her camp. As a result, you see me active and waging wars at night. Whoever does not wish to become indolent, let him love.

(Book 3 no. 15.) Look for a new poet, mother of tender Cupids. My elegies have now grazed the turning post for the last time. Neither the elegies that I have composed nor the *amours* I have enjoyed brought dishonor upon me, who was raised in the Paelignian countryside. If it means anything, I am an heir of ancient stock derived from great-grandfathers, not a knight suddenly created by the turmoil of war. Mantua takes pride in Vergil, Verona in Catullus. I shall be called the glory of the Paelignians, who, for the sake of their freedom, were constrained to take up honorable arms when Rome in distress feared the allied forces.[16] And some stranger looking at the walls of watery Sulmo, which occupy only a few acres of land, may say, "You who could produce such a poet, small as you are, I call you great." O venerable boy, and you, Venus, the parent of the venerable boy, pluck the golden standards from my field. Horned Bacchus has struck me with a weightier goad. Now mighty steeds must pound a mightier arena. O elegies unsuited to war, congenial Muse, farewell! My work will remain and survive after my death.

227

Propertius, *Elegies* Book 1 no. 1

Cynthia was the first, oh poor me, to captivate me with her eyes, me previously immune to any passions. But then Love cast down my resolutely disdainful eyes and bowed down my head and trampled on it, until he shamelessly taught me to hate virtuous girls and to live a completely aimless life. For an entire year now this madness has been with me, even though I am at the mercy of unfavorable gods. Milanion avoided no toil until, friend Tullus, he mastered unrelentingly hard-hearted Atalanta.... And so, he was able to tame the fleet girl. Where there is love, prayers and services count, but in my case Love is slow, does not concoct any devices, and does not remember to move on previously familiar paths. But you, whose trick is bringing down the moon, and who strive to solemnize your rites in magic fires, oh, please change my mistress's feelings, and made her face paler than my own! Then I might believe you could charm stars and rivers with the incantations of Medea. And you, my friends, who too late recall me who has gone astray, look for remedies for this sick heart. I will bravely endure both the knife and dread cautery if only there is freedom for my anger to speak out what it wants. Take me to peoples and seas at the end of the world. where no woman may learn the way I've gone. But you remain, to whom a god has nodded approval with kind ear, and be well-mated always in a faithful love. For me, our love affair brings night upon bitter night, and never does unfulfilled love desert me. I warn you, avoid this evil of mine; let each man cling to his love and not change the love to which he has become accustomed. But if anyone gives ear too slowly to my advice, ah, in what great agony will he recall my words.

Tibullus, *Elegies* Book 1 no. 1

Let another man amass for himself riches of yellow gold. And let him have many acres of cultivated soil whom continuous work does not frighten when the enemy is nearby, whose sleep the trumpet blasts of war rout. May my poverty support me in a life of leisure as long as my hearth gleams with a constant fire. I, myself a man of the country, shall plant the tender vines at the right time and large fruit trees with effortless hand. May hope not flag but always furnish heaps of fruits and thick new wine in a full vat. For I am reverent, whether a deserted stump in the fields or an old rock at the crossroads wears garlands of flowers. And whatever fruit the new year produces for me is placed before the farmer's god as an offering. Golden Ceres, may you have from our field a crown of grain spikes to hang before the doors of your shrine; let a Priapus[17] painted red be set in the fruit gardens to frighten away the birds with his ferocious hook. You too, O Lares,[18] guardians of a field once productive but now poor, carry off your gifts. At that time a slain calf purified innumerable bulls, but now a lamb is a small sacrificial victim of a scanty field. For you a lamb will fall, around which youth from the country will shout, "O grant fruitful crops and good wines." Now as for me, may I only be able to live content with a little and not always be assigned to a long march, but now may I avoid the summer risings of the Dog Star beneath the shade of a tree near streams of water flowing by. And yet may I not be ashamed sometimes to take hold of a hoe or to crack the slow oxen with a whip; may it not be displeasing to take in one's bosom a lamb or kid deserted by a forgetting mother and bring it back home. But you, both thieves and wolves, spare my meager flock; you should seek your prey from a large herd. Here I am accustomed to purify year after year my shepherd and sprinkle a calmed Pales[19] with milk. Be propitious, O gods, and do not spurn gifts from a poor table and from clean earthenware. (A farmer of old first made for himself earthenware cups, fashioning them from pitiable clay.)

I do not covet the wealth and produce of parents which a stored-up harvest handed down from grandfather of old. A small crop is sufficient; it is enough if it is possible to rest in bed and to relax the limbs on one's usual couch. How pleasant to lie down listening to fierce winds and holding a mistress in soft embrace, or, when the wintry South Wind pours its cold rains, to keep sleeping without a care during the shower. May this happen to me! Let him be rich, rightly, who can endure the fury of the sea and the saddening rains. Oh, may as much gold and emeralds as there are perish, rather than any girl weep on account of my journeys. It is fitting that you, Messalla, wage war on land and sea, so that your home may display the enemy's spoils. The bonds of a beautiful girl keep me in chains, and I sit as a doorman before her hard-hearted doors. I do not care to earn praise, my Delia, as long as I am with you, I ask to be called lazy and idle. May I be looking upon you when the final hour comes to me, and dying may I hold you with failing hand. You will weep for me when I am put upon the funeral pyre and give me kisses mixed with mournful tears. You will weep; your heart is not bound by hard steel, nor in your tender heart is there flint stone. No young man, no young girl will be able to take home dry eyes from that funeral. Do not offend my shades, but spare your hair unbound and spare, O Delia, your soft cheeks.

Meanwhile, while the Fates allow, let us join our love. Soon death with its head shrouded in darkness will come; soon that inactive period of life will creep upon us, and it will not be decent to love nor to speak sweet nothings with white-haired head. Now buoyant Venus must be taken in hand, while it is no shame to smash in doors, and it is a pleasure to start brawls. In this I am a general and a good soldier; but you, O signals and trumpet blasts, go far away, bring wounds to greedy men, and bring them wealth. Untroubled, with my heap secure, I shall despise riches and I shall despise hunger.

42
PROPERTIUS

A distinguished member of Maecenas' literary circle, Propertius expended most of his genius on erotic themes in poems to his mistress Cynthia (see no. 41 above). At the end of his career he adapted the elegiac genre to Augustan and national subjects.

Propertius, *Elegies*

(Book 1 no. 7.) While you ... write of Cadmean Thebes and the grim weapons of warfare between brothers, and (Heaven help me) you vie with revered Homer (if only the Fates are kind to your poetry), I, as usual, pursue my love affair and look for some remedy against my cruel mistress. I have no choice but to serve not so much my talent as my pain, and to bewail the harsh times of my youth. This is the way my life is wasted, this is my fame; from this I want the repute of my poetry to come. Let them praise me for being the only one to have pleased a learned girl ... and for having often endured her unfair threats. In the future let the neglected lover read me diligently, get to know my problems, and profit from them. If this boy [i.e., Love] should strike you too with his unerring bow (but I hope my gods will do otherwise), in your misery you will weep that you allowed to lie dumb, far away in eternal neglect, your camps and your seven armies, for in vain will you desire to compose gentle verse, and Love coming late will not prompt songs for you. Then you will often admire me as no mean poet; then will I be preferred among the talents; and youths will not be silent at my grave, but say: "You who lie there are the great poet of our passion." Beware that in your disdain you do not spurn my poems. Love that comes late often pays a high rate of interest.

(Book 1 no. 12.) Why do you, Rome, witness to my love, keep inventing the charge of idleness against me, as if to say that this delays me? She is separated from my bed by as many miles as the Bug River is from the Po. Cynthia no longer fosters our love as she used to in her embraces, no longer sweetly whispers in my ear. Once I pleased her; at that time there was no one whose good fortune it was to love with similar fidelity. We were the envy of all. Has some god crushed me? Or did some herb picked from the Caucasus' ridges divide us? I am not now the same person I have been; a long journey changes girls. How great was the love that has disappeared in so little time! Now for the first time I am forced to know long nights alone, and my voice is a burden to my ears. Happy is he who can weep in the presence of his girl; when tears are shed, Love rejoices for sure. Or if a rejected lover can transfer his passion, there are joys too when servitude is transferred. For me to love another or stop loving her is a sacrilege: Cynthia was the first, and Cynthia will be my last.

(Book 2 no. 10.) But now it is time to traverse Helicon with other dances, and time to permit the Thessalian horse the plain. Now would I relate the squadrons brave in battles and sing of the Roman camps of my leader [Augustus]. But if strength should fail me, still praise will surely come to me for the daring; for in great undertakings it is enough to have dared. Youth sings of loves, old age of stormy wars; now I shall sing of wars, since I have written all about my girl. Now I wish to proceed more stately with a serious expression; now my Muse is teaching me a new lyre. Up, my spirit, from the humble theme; now, my songs, take up energy; Muses, now will begin a work of mighty strain. Now the Euphrates refuses to protect the Parthian horsemen as they turn their backs, and it mourns that it detained Crassus and his men. And India, too, O Augustus, bows its neck for your triumph, and in fear of you the house of Arabia, untouched, trembles. Any land that lies far distant along the farthest borders of the world will be captured soon and feel your hand, O Caesar! I shall follow this camp; in singing of your camp I shall be a great poet; may Fate keep secure this day for me! When we can not reach the heads of tall statues, we place a garland thus at their feet; thus now, inadequate to ascend to a song of glory, I bring an inexpensive offering of incense with the rite of the poor. Not yet have my poems come to know Hesiod's fount, but Love has but dipped the them in Permessus' stream.[20]

Propertius here asserts his claim to fame for his intent of introducing Roman audiences to the sophisticated style and variety of Alexandrian lyric poetry.

(Book 3 no. 1.) Shades of Callimachus and revered relics of Philetas, allow me, I beg you, to enter your grove. I am the first to come from the pure spring, like a priest introducing Italic mysteries through Greek dances. Tell me, in what cave did you both spin your slender song? With what beat did you enter? What water did you drink? Good-bye to him who wastes Apollo's time with warfare! Let the verse flow polished by fine pumice; with this technique, fame lifts me high above the ground, and the Muse begotten by me rides in triumph behind garlanded horses, while small Cupids travel with me in a chariot, and a throng of writers follow my wheels. Why do you compete against me? It is useless to loosen your reins. The path leading to the Muses is a narrow one. Many will add in their histories to the praises of your glory, O Rome, and herald Bactria as the future border of the Empire. But my pages have brought, down from the mountain of the sister Muses on a virgin path, a work that you may read in peace.

O Muses, grant soft wreaths to your poet; a hard crown will not suit my head. But what the envious crowd has robbed me of in my life, after my death fame will restore with doubled interest; after death aging time represents all things above their reality; after the final rites greater becomes the name on the lips of men. For who would know of the citadel overcome by the wooden horse? The rivers that fought hand-to-hand with the hero Achilles? Who would have heard of the Idaean Simoïs? Of Scamander, offspring of Jove? Of Hector dragged three times over the plain and violated by the chariot? Its own soil would scarcely know Deiphobus, Helenus, Polydamas, and Paris, such as he was in arms. You now, Ilium, would have little fame, and you, Troy, twice captured by the power of the deified Hercules. Even Homer, the recounter of your fall, saw his work grow in fame in the eyes of posterity. And now me Rome shall praise among its far-off generations; after the funeral pyre, I prophesy that day. The gravestone that marks my bones will not be spurned: the god Apollo, approving my prayers, has so ordained it.

Propertius replies to Maecenas who has asked him to write on historical themes. This is an interesting poem that casts light on Propertius' poetic credo and also offers occasional glimpses of Maecenas' character and position.

(Book 3 no. 9.) Maecenas, equestrian from the blood of Etruscan kings, you who desire to live within your station, why do you send me out onto such a vast sea of writing? The sails of a tall ship do not fit my small craft. It is a disgrace to take a burden upon the back which you cannot bear, bend the knee weakened by the pressure, and then turn your back on it. All things are not equally suitable to all men.... To some comes the prize of winning the chariot race at Olympia, to others, born to run, glory won by speed; one man is born for peace, another is suited for the weapons of the war camp; each man follows his natural tendencies. I have grasped your precepts of living, Maecenas, and I am driven to defeat you by your own examples. Although you may set up the imperial axes as a Roman official and dispense justice in the middle of the Forum, although you may pass through the spears of belligerent Parthians and load your house with spoils, nailing up arms, and although Caesar may give you the power for success, and all the time wealth may come flowing in so readily — you are frugal and, keeping a low profile, withdraw to modest shadows. Of your own accord you haul down the billowing sails. Believe me, judgments of you will equal mighty Camillus, and you too will live on the lips of men; you will occupy the footprints accompanying Caesar's fame. "The loyalty of Maecanas" will be legend, your true trophies.

As for myself, I do not cleave the swelling sea in a boat under full sail; I linger entirely by a shallow stream. I shall not tell the tearful story of the citadel of Cadmus fallen in the ashes of the fathers, and the seven battles with the same number of disasters,[21] nor shall I bring up again the Scaean gates, and Pergama, Apollo's towers, nor the return of Greek ships in the tenth spring,[22] when the victorious wooden horse constructed by the cunning of Athena plowed under Neptune's walls. I will be content to have found favor among the books of Callimachus, and to have sung, O poet Philetas, in your measures. May these writings inflame boys, set girls afire; let them acclaim me a god and bear me sacrifices. Under their guidance I shall sing of Jove's arms and the giants who threatened heaven.... I shall compose the song of the lofty Palatine grazed by Roman bulls, and the walls established after Remus' murder. I shall sing of the two kings (equal then) nourished by the teats of the wild wolf. Under your instructions my talent will increase; I shall celebrate chariots triumphing from East and West. I shall sing of the weapons of the Parthians cleverly shot in flight, and the Nile camps overrun by Roman sword, and Antony, whose grim hand sealed his own fate. But, O kindly sponsor of my youthful undertaking, take the reins, and give me auspicious signs as my wheels spin on. You grant, Maecenas, this honor to me, and it is from you that I shall be reputed to have followed a way of thinking.

(Book 4 no. 1.) All this which you now view, O stranger, where mighty Rome now stands, before Trojan Aeneas was but hill and grass; and where the Palatine sacred to Phoebus of the ships is now, Evander's exiled cattle once lay. These golden temples grew from gods of clay, and a house constructed without skill was then not a source of disdain; the Tarpeian father used to thunder from a bare cliff, and the Tiber was strange to our oxen. There, where that house of Remus rises on a flight of steps, once was a single hearth, the mighty kingdom of the two brothers. The Senate House, which now looms high glistening with senators clad in purple-bordered togas, once held the Fathers (those rustic souls) clothed in animal skins. A trumpet brought the citizens of old to debate; one hundred in the meadow often made a Senate. No billowing awnings hung over the hollow theater, and the stage did not smell of the now usual saffron. No one thought to seek foreign gods when the throng trembled in suspense at their ancestral ritual; straw was set afire to celebrate the yearly festival to Pales,[23] purificatory rites which nowadays are renewed by the cropping of a horse. Vesta in poverty was happy with garlanded asses, and skinny cattle pulled cheap sacred emblems. Fat pigs purified small crossroad shrines, and the shepherd to the sound of reed pipes offered the entrails of a sheep. The plowman dressed in hides snapped the shaggy whips, whence the festival of the Lupercal[24] maintains its unrestrained rites. The rude soldiers did not glitter in threatening armor; they engaged in battles unprotected, with burnt stake for weapon....

The Roman of today keeps nothing of his forefathers except the name; he would not believe that the she-wolf was the nurse of his bloodline. It was better, O Troy, that you sent here the exiled gods; oh what an augury it was under which Trojan ships sailed! Even then the omens promised success, considering that the opened belly of the wooden horse has not really harmed Troy, while the father clung trembling on the back of his son and the flame feared to burn those devoted shoulders. Then came the dauntless Decii, the consular axes of Brutus, and Venus herself brought the armor of her own Caesar, carrying the victorious arms of resurgent Troy. A favorable land, O Iulus, received your gods.... Wolf of Mars, the very best nurse of our affairs, what great walls sprang from your milk. Let me describe in reverent verse those walls — but, oh, how puny the sound from my mouth; and yet however narrow the stream flowing from my puny heart, all of it will serve my country. Let Ennius crown his works with a shaggy wreath, but you, Bacchus, extend to me the leaves from your ivy, that my books may make Umbria swell with pride — Umbria, home of the Roman Callimachus! Let anyone upon seeing the towers rising out of the valley esteem those walls because of my special talent. O Rome, favor me; this work is erected for you. Citizens, give me favorable signs of omen, and may a bird from the right side sing auspiciously upon my undertakings.

43

TIBULLUS

Among those who had experienced the turmoil of the civil war was Tibullus. In the Augustan Age he remained a private person, belonging to the literary circle of Messalla. He was generally neutral toward the regime, and in all his poetry there is not a single mention of Augustus. The focus of his love poetry is the country, where he yearns for a life of simplicity and peace.

Tibullus, *Elegies*

(Book 1 no. 10.) What kind of man was he who first invented horrid swords? How barbaric and really iron-hearted was he! For then murder arose for the human race, then battles began, then a shorter plan for dreadful death lay open. Did that wretch deserve nothing? That which he gave for savage wild beasts we have turned to our own destruction. This is the fault of enriching gold: there were no wars when a cup made of beechwood stood before the feast; there were no citadels, no palisade; the shepherd without a concern amid different flocks sought sleep. I would have had an ordinary life then, I would not have known mournful arms, and I would not have heard the blast of trumpet with leaping heart; but now I am drawn toward wars, and perhaps now some enemy is carrying weapons meant for my breast.

O protecting gods of the country, save me, as you nourished me when as a youngster I ran about before your feet. Let there be no shame that you were made from an old stump; thus you honored the houses of a grandfather of old. In time past, men kept faith better, when in a small shrine a wooden image of a god stood revered by the poor. He was appeased, whether anyone offered a grape cluster or gave garlands of ears of grain for his reverend hair. And some other, granted his wish, used himself to carry his sacrificial cakes, and behind him in accompaniment a small daughter carried pure honey. O protecting deities, keep those bronze weapons from me! [I offer] as sacrifice a pig from a full sty. I shall follow it in clean dress, and I shall carry baskets garlanded with myrtle; my head too will be garlanded with myrtle. In this manner may I appease you. Let some other man be brave in arms, and let him rout enemy leaders under a favorable Mars, so as to be able to tell me, as I drink, of his deeds as a soldier and with wine mark out the camp on the table. What madness is it to summon dark death by wars! It threatens and comes in secrecy upon silent foot. There is no crop below the earth, no cultivated vineyard, but violent Cerberus and the filthy sailor [Charon] of the river Styx. There the ghostly crowd with marred cheeks and burned hair wander along shadowy lakes.

No, rather should this man be praised who has provided an offspring and obtains in his small house an inactive old age. He pursues his own sheep, and his son tends to the lambs, and his wife prepares warm water for him when he is tired. May I be like him, may my hair grow white on my head, and may I, when an old man, recall the deeds of an earlier age. In the meantime, may peace tend the fields. Radiant peace first brought oxen to plow beneath the curved yokes; peace nourished the vines and stores the juice of the grape, so that the urn of a father might pour wine for a son. In time of peace the hoe and plow glisten; on the other hand, in the dark places rust takes possession of the mournful weapons of the tough soldier. In peacetime the man of the country, far from sober, drives his wife and children home in a wagon from the sacred grove. Then the wars of love rage; the wife complains of torn hair and smashed doors; she weeps, her tender cheeks bruised, and he, the winner, weeps that his hands were so furious. Lascivious Love supplies the curses in a brawl, but then unbiased sits between both when they are angered. Ah, he is stone and iron who strikes his girl; he drags the gods right out of heaven. Let it be enough to rip thin clothing off her body; let it be enough to muss her coiffured hair; let it be enough to move her to tears. Four times blessed is he who by his anger can make his gentle girl weep. But let him who will use violent hands carry shield and pike, and let him keep far away from gentle Venus.

Come to us, O nourishing Peace, and take hold of the grain stalk; may your radiant bosom pour forth fruits before us.

The central theme of this poem is that wealth and greed foster and control love in Rome. After a brief description of Venus' reputation and worship during the Golden Age, Tibullus begins his view that the Iron Age has corrupted the elegiac Utopia.

(Book 2 no. 3 verses 35–80.) Now the Iron Age praises not Venus but booty. Yet booty carries in its train many evils; booty arms beastly armies with discordant weapons; because of it gore, carnage, and death come ever closer. At the bidding of booty, the dangers of a restless sea were doubled, when it offered war-like beaks to hesitant ships. The plunderer desires to besiege vast fields in order to feed countless sheep on numerous acres. He has to have imported stone, and in the uproar of the city he transports a column with a thousand strong, yoked oxen. A causeway blockades the sea, up to now untamed, so that indifferent fish within may ignore the presence of winter's threats. But for me, Samian jugs lengthen joyful parties and slippery clay made into earthenware by a Cumaean wheel. Alas, alas, I see girls enjoying rich men. Now let booty come, if Venus desires wealth, so that Nemesis may swim in luxury and parade through the city to be eyed in my gifts. May she wear delicate clothing which a woman from Cos has woven and which she has tricked out with gold stripes. May her attendants be dark-skinned men whom India tans and the fire of the sun with his goaded horses colors. May African and Tyre vie to furnish to her choice dyes, either red or purple. I say what is well known. He now has a kingdom whom the barbarian slave-block often compelled to endure chalked feet.

But for you, O harsh crop, who has drawn Nemesis away from the city, may earth keeping faith repay no seeds. And you, O tender Bacchus, planter of the pleasant grape, yes, you, O Bacchus, leave the cursed vats. Not with impunity may you conceal beautiful girls in gloomy fields; your vintages are not that valuable, O father Bacchus. May fruits thrive if only girls are absent from the country. May the acorn serve as food, and, as in the old

239

days, may water be the drink. The acorn nourished the ancients, and they made love everywhere and always. What harm did it do not to have seeded furrows? At that time gentle Venus openly supplied in a shady valley joys which love favored. There was no guard, no door to exclude the love sick; if there is divine justice, I pray that custom return.... They covered ugly bodies in shaggy hides. But now, if I am barred from my girl, if opportunity of seeing her is rare, O poor me, what use is a broad toga? Lead on: at the command of a mistress we shall plow fields. I shall not refuse her chains and whips.

44
OVID

Belonging to the second generation of the principate, one which had no personal experience of the upheavals of the civil wars, Ovid did not share the fervor of such poets as Vergil and Horace for the new regime. Ovid's heart was not in the political world; his outlook was un-Augustan, and he flaunted his irreverence toward the spirit of Augustus' moral program. He had nothing but contempt for the concept of the poet's function as supporter of the establishment. Ovid was a sophisticated, brilliant literary virtuoso, a truly versatile craftsman — but the last great poet of the age.

Ovid, *Art of Love*

The work that helped send Ovid into exile, in 8 AD, is a titillating, tongue-in-cheek "handbook," ostensibly written to instruct the uninitiated into the mysteries of love. A very polished and sophisticated poem, the *Art of Love* crowns Ovid's great interest in the theme and poetic treatment of love. Included in this witty, mock-serious handling of a traditional subject there are many allusions and brief treatments of various myths, carefully woven into the fabric of the work. Underneath the poetry and mythology Ovid portrays the social texture of the capital city, offering glimpses of its public buildings, its shrines, its theaters, some of its people and their manners. Augustus, however, regarding the poem as an affront and threat to the spirit of his moral legislation, took offense, and eventually had the poet exiled — partly because of this poem, but principally because of a serious indiscretion on Ovid's part (see no. 36 above).

(Book 1 verses 1 – 166, selections.) If any man in this population does not know the art of loving, let him read this work and then, instructed by this poem, let him love. It is by art that ships are propelled quickly by sail and by oar; art also makes chariots fleet. Love, too, must be guided by art....

Your Rome has as many girls as the sky has stars. His mother, Venus, has become a fixture in the city of her own Aeneas. If you are enraptured by those in their early and still-growing years, the right girl will appear before your eyes; or if you wish for a young lady, a thousand young ladies will please you, and you will not know your own desire. Or perhaps you enjoy a middle-aged (and somewhat wiser) woman; believe me, here, too, there will be a crowd more numerous than the other. Leisurely stroll now in the shade of Pompey's portico when the sun approaches the back of Hercules' lion, or where his mother Octavia has added her public building to that of her son Marcellus; do not avoid the portico which bears the name of Livia, its builder, and which is dotted with old paintings; go where the Danaids[25] have ventured to plot the murder of their hapless cousins and their savage father stands with sword drawn; and do not pass by the shrine of Adonis lamented by Venus, and the precincts worshipped on the Sabbath by the Jews from the East; and do not shun the temple of the heifer of Memphis[26] shrouded in linen (she makes many women become what she herself was to Jupiter); even the Forums (who could believe it?) are suitable for love, and the fires of passion are often found in the shrill Forum....

But especially do your hunting in the various round theaters. In those locales are fertile opportunities beyond your wish; there you will find someone to love, someone to play with, or someone to fondle just once, or someone you want to keep.... And do not let the competition of thoroughbreds escape you: the stadium filled to capacity offers many opportunities. There is no need of speaking through hand signals to send secret messages, nor of exchanging signs by nods....

These are the approaches that the race track will offer you for a new love, as will the melancholy sand spread upon the ground of the busy Forum.[27] At this arena the child of Venus has often fought, and the spectator who saw the wounds got wounded himself....

Ovid, *Metamorphoses*

The *Metamorphoses,* Ovid's compendium of ancient mythology, is artificially unified by the theme of change. Beginning with *chaos,* in rough chronological sequence Ovid continued his treatment down to his own day, culminating in the praise of Augustus. Most of Ovid's poem (the only Augustan poem comparable in length to the *Aeneid*) is, however, completely irrelevant to Rome and Augustus. His ending — a eulogy of Augustus — seems to be an artificial afterthought.

(Book 1 verses 1 – 162.) My design is to tell of forms changed into new bodies. O gods, inspire my undertakings (for you yourselves have wrought these changes), and from the very beginning of the world down to my times weave a continuous poem.

Before there was sea and land and sky (which covers everything), the appearance of nature in the entire universe was the same. They called it Chaos, a raw and orderless mass. It was nothing but mass, inert, and piled up together in the same place were warring seeds of disconnected substances....

Thus when the god, whoever he was, divided and arranged the massive heap and reduced what he had divided into parts, he first fashioned the earth into the shape of a large sphere, to make it even on every side. He then ordered the waters to spread and to swell up before the brisk winds and to surround and encircle the shores of the earth. He added the springs, the huge ponds, and lakes, and he dammed up the down-flowing rivers with sloping banks. Some streams in different areas are absorbed by earth, some flow into the sea, and, collected in an open expanse with a freer water, strike against shores instead of banks. Under his orders the fields extended, valleys subsided, forests became covered with foliage, and rocky mountains arose .... .

Until then there was lacking an animal more august, more capable than the others of lofty thought, and one which could be master over all the rest. So man was born, whether that creator of all things, the originator of a better world, made him from divine seed, or the young earth, recently separated from the lofty air, retained the seeds of its kindred heaven. Prometheus mixed earth with rain water and fashioned him in the image of gods who control all things, and whereas the other animals are prone and look upon the earth, he gave man an uplifted face and bade him look at the heaven and lift his erect features toward the stars....   .

The Golden Age was born first, which of its own accord, without any compulsion, without law, maintained faith and justice.

Fear of punishment was absent; there were no threatening words to be read on bronze tablet, and no supplicating throng feared the face of its judge, but people were secure without a judge. Not yet were pine trees felled from their mountians and brought down upon clear waters to visit foreign parts of the world; men knew no shores except their own. Not yet did steep ditches surround towns; there was no trumpet made of straight bronze, no horn of curved bronze; there were no helmets, no swords; without the use of soldiers the peoples lived securely in gentle leisure. The earth itself also, without compulsion, untouched by the hoe, suffering no hurt from any plows, produced everything spontaneously. Men were content with the foods produced by no one's effort. They gathered the fruits from the trees, the mountain strawberry, the cornel cherry, the mulberry that clung to prickly brambles, and the acorns that fell from the spreading tree of Jove [i.e., oak]. Spring was everlasting, and gentle zephyrs with their balmy breezes caressed the flowers grown from no seed. Soon also the earth, unplowed, produced fruits, and a field though untilled, grew white with heavy wheat. Now streams of milk flowed, now streams of nectar, and golden honey dripped from the verdant oak.

After Saturn had been driven to the shadowy realm of Tartarus, the world came under Jove's domination, and the Silver Age crept in, inferior to the Golden Age but more precious than tawny Bronze. Jupiter shortened the old-time season of spring and divided the year into four measured periods, with winter, summer, variable autumn, and a brief spring. Then, for the first time, the air grew hot, burned and dried by heat, and icicles hung down, congealed by the cold winds. Then, for the first time, men sought shelter in houses; previously homes had been caves, dense thickets, and twigs interlaced with bark. Then, for the first time, seeds of grain were planted in long furrows, and oxen groaned beneath the yoke.

The third Age that succeeded this one was of Bronze, more brutal in nature and more prompt to rush to grim arms, yet the age was not criminal. The last age is of hard Iron. Immediately every sin of the baser vein broke forth forever; shame, truth, and faith fled, and in their place came deceit, treachery, plots, violence, the cursed love of property. Men set sails to the winds, which until that time the sailor did not know well; the wood that previously stood on high mountain leaped as boats upon waves hitherto unknown. The careful surveyor marked off with extensive boundaries the ground once, like the rays of the sun and the air, common to all. Not only did men demand of the earth the crops and the required sustenance, but also they penetrated into the entrails of the earth; they dug up the resources, the instigator of evils, which earth had removed and hidden in Stygian shadows. Now baneful iron, and gold more baneful than iron, came forth; war came, which fights with both and brandishes in its bloody hand the clashing arms. Men lived on plunder; no host was safe from a guest; no father-in-law from a son-in-law, rare, too, was affection among brothers. A husband threatens his wife with death, the wife her husband; dreadful step-mothers mix ghastly poisons, and a son inquires into the years left to his father. Piety lies beaten, and the maiden Astraea [goddess of justice] was the last of the divinities to leave the blood-soaked earth.

(Book 10 verses 1−63.) From there Hymen, dressed in saffron clothing, traveled through the boundless air and made his way to the Ciconian shores. The voice of Orpheus had called him in vain. Yet he came there, but brought with him no auspicious words, no happy face, no lucky omen. The torch, too, which he was holding was continually sputtering and smoking, causing tears and caught no fire when it was shaken. The outcome was even more serious than the beginning. For while the young bride was strolling through the grass, accompanied by a group of nymphs, she was bitten on her ankle by a snake and died. After the bard Orpheus had bewailed to the full in the upper world, he ventured, so as not to leave the shades untried, to descend to the Styx through the Taenarian gate. Passing the insubstantial population and the buried ghosts, he approached Persephone and the ruler of that unpleasant kingdom, the lord of the shades. Strumming the chords of the lyre, he sang the following: "O gods of the world beneath the earth, to which we, whoever are born, come, if it is possible, permit me to speak the truth, laying aside the deceitful snares of lying speech. I have descended here not to seek dark

245

Tartarus, not to bind the three necks shaggy with snakes of Medusa's monster.[28] The reason for my journey is my wife, whose budding years were snatched away by the poison shot from a viper upon which she stepped. I wanted to be able to endure this loss, and I will not deny that I tried. Love has conquered! This god is well known in the upper region; I doubt whether he is here, too. I suppose he is known here, too, if the story of that old rape is not a lie, and that Love has joined you, too. By these places full of fear, by this huge chaos, and by the silence of this vast kingdom, I pray, reverse the untimely fates of Eurydice! All things are owed to you; some of us delay a little longer, others hurry sooner to this one abode. All of us make our way here, this is our final home, and you rule the longest over the human race. When in maturity she has lived her rightful years, this woman, too, will be under your jurisdiction; not as a gift but on loan, we beg her. But if the Fates deny dispensation for my wife, I refuse to return. My decision is final. Rejoice in the death of two!"

As he spoke thus and accompanied his words with the strings, the lifeless phantoms wept: Tantalus did not strive to catch the receding water, Ixion's wheel was struck silent; the vultures did not tear at the liver [of Tityos]; the Danaïds took time off from their urns; and you, O Sisyphus, sat on your rock. It is reported that for the first time the Furies were overcome by song, and their cheeks became wet with tears. Neither the royal consort nor the ruler of the nether regions could endure his pleading nor deny him. They called Eurydice. She was there among the latest phantoms, and she approached limping from the recent wound. Orpheus the Thracian received her and, at the same time, accepted the stipulation that he not turn his eyes back until he should go forth from the valleys of Avernus, otherwise the gift would be voided. In mutual silence they press on up the steep path, high up, dark and thick with clouding mist. They were not far from the edge of upper earth, when here he, out of love, and fearing that she might fail, and eager to see her, turned his gaze upon her. Immediately she faded, extending her arms and struggling to be caught and clasp him. She unfortunately caught nothing but receding air. Dying now for the second time, she made no complaint against her husband (what could she complain of except that she was loved?). His ears barely caught her final word "good-bye" before she disappeared again below.

(Book 10 verses 243–297.) When Pygmalion saw women living a life of sin, he was offended by their vices which nature had furnished to the female character in abundance. A bachelor, he lived without a partner, and for some time his bed lacked a consort. Meanwhile, he successfully sculpted a snow-white ivory statue executed with marvelous skill, and he gave it a beauty which no woman could possess by nature, and he fell in love with his own work. In appearance she was a real girl; you would think she was alive and, if modesty did not prevent it, wanted to move. So art then conceals art. Pygmalion marvels and in his heart derives passionate fires from the body he has fashioned. He often applies his hands to test the work if it be a body or only ivory; he swears it is no longer ivory. He gives it kisses and imagines they are returned, he speaks to it, holds it; he believes at his touch his fingerprints remain stamped upon her limbs, and he fears that a bruise may appear upon the spot that he has pressed. Sometimes he uses sweet words, and sometimes he brings her the gifts usually pleasing to girls: shells, polished stones, small birds, flowers of a thousand colors, lilies, painted balls, and amber drops. He adorns her body with dresses, he puts gemmed rings upon her fingers and hangs long necklaces from her neck; small earrings hang upon her ears, and ribbons lie across her breast. All these things become her, and she seems no less beautiful nude. He lays her down on covers dyed with Phoenician purple, calls her his bed partner, and places her reclining head on soft, feathery pillows as if she could feel it.

Venus' holiday came, the most popular festival in all of Cyprus. Heifers, their curved horns covered in gold, took the sacrificial blow on their snowy necks and fell. Incense was burning, when he, having duly made his sacrifice, stood before the altars and reverently prayed: "O Gods, if you have the power to grant all things, I pray my wife may be like my ivory statue." (He did not dare say "ivory girl.") Golden Venus, who was present at her festival, perceived what those prayers meant, and, as a sign of favorable omen, three times a flame blazed, the tip darting into the air. When he returned home he went straight to the image of his girl, and lying down on a couch he kissed it. She seems to grow warm; again he applies his lips, and feels her breasts too with his hands. At this touch the ivory softens, and the stiffness disappears, the fingers sink in, the flesh yields, just as Hymettian wax melted by the sun is molded into numerous shapes by the fingers, and becomes useful through this very application.... Pygmalion is surprised, he doubts, he is happy and yet fears it is all a trick; again he fondles it, once more with his hand he examines the object of his desire. It was flesh. At the touch of a finger, veins pulsate. Then the Paphian hero poured out copious words in giving Venus thanks. At length with his lips he presses her (not at all unreal). The girl felt the kisses, she blushed, and cautiously lifting her eyes to the light, she saw at once her lover and the sky. The goddess attends the marriage which she has made. And when the lunar crescent had formed nine full spheres she gave birth to a girl, Paphos, from whom the island got its name.

Book 15 opens with Numa Pompilius, the second king of Rome, traveling to Croton to receive counsel from the philosopher Pythagoras (chronologically impossible). In his statement to Numa, Pythagoras discloses many tenets of his philosophy and also prophesies, in the manner of Jupiter in Book 1 of Vergil's *Aeneid* (see no. 39 above), the coming glory of Rome and the Augustan Age.

(Book 15 verses 431–449.) Now too there is the story that Rome is rising from Trojan descent and is laying massive and extensive foundations for her power near by the waters of the Tiber, arising from the Apennines. In her growth her appearance changes, and one day will she be the capital of the measureless world. So prophets and mantic oracles have declared, so people say. As far as I can recall, when the Trojan state was falling, Helenos, a son of Priam, spoke to Aeneas, who was weeping and in doubt of his safety: "Goddess-born, if you keep sufficiently in mind my soul's prophecies, with you surviving Troy will not totally fall. Fire and sword will offer you a way; you will leave and catch up and carry Troy with you, until it is your good fortune to find a foreign land more hospitable to you and Troy than your fatherland. I see a city rendering its debt of Phrygian grandsons; there is none so great, nor will be, nor existed in previous years. Other leaders will make her powerful through the long centuries, but it is an offspring of the blood of Iulus who will make her the mistress of the world. After the earth has used him, the abodes of the sky will enjoy him, and heaven will be his final end.

Ovid ends the *Metamorphoses* with an account of the deification of Julius Caesar and a prophetic encomium of Augustus. Venus, anticipating the murder of Julius Caesar, confronts Jupiter and complains of unjust disaster destined for him. Jupiter soothes her and unfolds the future of Rome under Augustus.

(Book 15 verses 807–870.) Her father Jupiter spoke to her as follows: "You alone, my daughter, try to disturb unconquerable fate. You may enter the halls of the three sisters [i.e., the Fates], and there you will view the records of events on tablets made of bronze and hard iron, a vast undertaking. These records fear no shaking of the heaven, no wrath of lightning, nor any destruction. They are protected and eternal. There you will find engraved and everlasting on adamant the recorded fates of your offspring. I myself have read them, etched them in my mind, and shall recite them so that you, too, may know the future. The man on whose behalf you grieve, O Cytherea, has fulfilled his time, completing the years which he owed to the earth. You will cause him to enter heaven as a god and be worshipped in shrines, you and his son, who upon inheriting his name will bear the burden imposed upon him, and as the most valiant avenger of his murdered parent will have us as his allies for wars. Under his command the conquered city of besieged Mutina will seek peace. Pharsalia will feel his presence, and Macedonian Philippi will once again flow red with blood; a mighty name will be beaten in Sicilian waters [i.e., Sextus Pompey]; the Egyptian wife of a Roman general will fall, trusting in the union without success — in vain will she make threats that our Capitoline will serve her Canopus. Why should I list for you the barbarian territory and the tribes living near each Ocean? Whatever inhabitable land the earth contains will be his realm. The sea, too, will be subservient to him. After he establishes peace on earth, he will direct his attention to civil justice, and as a most righteous legislator will promulate laws, and by his own example he will guide behavior. Looking forward to a future time and the generations to come, he will order that a child born from a chaste wife [i.e., Tiberius, from Livia] assume both his name and his responsibilities. He will not reach the abodes of heaven nor meet kindred stars [i.e., the deified Julius Caesar] until, as an old man, he has equaled in age the years of Nestor. In the meantime, catch up this spirit from his slain body and make it into a constellation, so that the deified Julius from his lofty abode may look down upon our Capitoline and Forum."

He had scarcely finished his prophecy, when nourishing Venus, visible to none, came to stop in the middle of the Senate House, and from the body of her own Caesar she snatched his fresh soul. Not allowing it to dissipate in the air, she brought it to the celestial stars. As she carried it, she felt it catch light and begin to burn, and then she released it from her bosom. Up higher than the moon it flew, and dragging in its long path a flaming stream it flashed, a star! And seeing it, Venus confessed that the accomplishments of her son were greater than her own, happy to be outdone by him.

Although Augustus forbids his own accomplishments to be exalted above those of his father, yet fame is unrestrained, submissive to no orders, and glorifies him against his will and resists him in this one respect. Thus great Atreus yielded to the honors of Agamemnon; thus Theseus surpassed Aegeus, as Achilles did Peleus; and, as a final case, if I may use as examples those who equaled their fathers, Saturn is less than Jupiter. Jupiter controls the citadels of the sky and the kingdoms of the tripartite world. The earth is beneath Augustus' power; each is both a father and a ruler. O gods, I pray — O companions of Aeneas to whom the sword and fire gave way; O native gods; O Romulus, father of the city; O Mars, father of the unconquered Romulus, O Vesta, worshipped among Caesar's household gods, and you, Apollo, god of the home along with Caesar's Vesta, and you, O Jupiter on high, who occupy the Tarpeian citadels [i.e., the Capitoline Hill]; and all you other gods to whom a poet in religious propriety and devotion may appeal: May that day be slow in coming and later than our own time when the person of Augustus enters heaven, leaving behind the world which he now rules, and from afar is propitious to our prayers.

EPILOGUE
45
POSTERITY'S JUDGEMENT
OF AUGUSTUS

Strabo, *Geography* Book 6 chapter 4.2

It is difficult ... to administer such a great dominion in any other way than by entrusting it to one man as father. At any rate, never have the Romans and their allies been so prosperous in peace and plenty as that which Caesar Augustus has provided, from the time he assumed absolute power.

Velleius, *Roman History* Book 2 chapter 89

There is nothing that men can hope for from the gods, nothing that the gods can grant to men, nothing that can be conceived of in a wish, nothing that can be consummated by good fortune, that Augustus, after his return to the city [28 BC], did not bestow upon the country, the Roman people, and the whole world. After twenty years the civil wars were ended, foreign wars suppressed, peace restored, the madness of arms everywhere laid to rest, validity restored to the laws, authority to the courts, prestige to the Senate, the *imperium* of the magistrates reduced to its former limits.... The old traditional form of the Republic was restored. Cultivation of the fields revived; respect for religious ceremonies, security to men, property rights were secured for each. As for the laws, some were amended advantageously, others passed for the public good. The Senate's roll was revised without difficulty but not without severity. The chief men who had held triumphs and the most distinguished offices were induced by the exhortation of the *princeps* to adorn the city.... To write of the wars waged under his command, and the pacification of the whole world by his victories, and of the numerous works outside Italy and at home would tire a writer intent on spending his whole life on this subject alone.

Philo, *Embassy to Gaius* chapters 143–149

Philo of Alexandria (ca. 30 BC to 45 AD). Jewish leader and intellectual of his native city, is the author of a body of writing combining Jewish theology and Greek philosophy. In 39/40 AD he was sent to Rome to seek from the emperor Caligula reaffirmation of freedom of worship for the Jews. His pamphlet *Embassy to Gaius* was written in connection with that embassy.

He who surpasssed human nature in all the virtues, who because of the greatness of his imperial power, together with his noble character, was the first to be named Augustus — a title he assumed not through succession in his family, as a kind of inheritance, but because he himself became the source of veneration that devolved upon his successors; he who gave his attention to turbulent and chaotic conditions from the moment he assumed the administration of the state. For islands contested with the mainlands for supremacy, and the mainlands with islands, having for their leaders and champions those Romans who were most eminent in office. Morover, the great divisions of the world, Asia against Europe, and Europe against Asia, contended for sovereign power, European and Asiatic peoples rising up from the ends of the earth, waging grievous wars throughout all the land and sea in infantry and naval combats. As a result the whole human race, exhausted by mutual slaughter, was little short of being totally destroyed, but for one man and leader, Augustus, whom they rightly called averter of evil. This is the Caesar who calmed the storms pouring down everywhere, who healed the common diseases of Hellas and the barbarians, diseases which came down from the South and the East, sped to the West and North, scattering uncontrolled evils over the lands and seas between. This is he who not only loosened and broke the chains with which the world was shackled and oppressed; this is he who eliminated both the open and the covert wars coming from the attacks of brigands. This is he who emptied the seas of pirate vessels and filled it with merchant ships. This is he who restored every city to freedom, who brought order out of disorder, who civilized and harmonized all the savage and brutish peoples, who enlarged Hellas by many Hellases and Hellenized the barbarian world in the most necessary regions, the guardian of peace, the dispenser of all that is due to each, who did not hoard his blessings but offered them openly, who did not conceal anything good or excellent throughout his entire life....

He was the first and greatest and common benefactor, in that he entrusted the ship of the commonwealth to the steering of one pilot instead of the rule of many, that is, to himself, a remarkable expert in government.... And the whole world voted him honors like to those given to the Olympian gods.

Tacitus, *Annals* Book 1 chapters 8–10

Another portion of this appraisal by Tacitus will be found in no. 2 above.

On the day of Augustus' funeral soldiers were stationed as if to protect him, while there was much joking on the part of those who had themselves seen, or had heard from their parents of that day when slavery was still fresh and liberty was unsuccessfully sought again, when the assassination of the dictator Caesar seemed to some the foulest, to others the most glorious, crime. People said that now an aged *princeps,* who had held power for a long time and had also provided the resources for his heirs to retain the state, needed military assistance to assure that his burial would be peaceful.

There was much talk then about Augustus himself, with many marveling at idle things, such as that the day he first received the *imperium* was the same as the last day of his life; that he died at Nola in the house and bedroom in which his father Octavius had died. The number of his consulates was also commented on, for he had in this equalled the total of Valerius Corvus and Gaius Marius combined. His tribunician power was continuous for thirty-seven years, the title imperator he won twenty-one times, and his other offices were manifold and novel....

[Some spoke in favorable terms of Augustus; some took the opposite view].

Soon, when by a decree of the Senate he had made his way to the *fasces* and the power of a praetor, when Hirtius and Pansa were killed (whether the enemy had removed them, or Pansa's wound was sprinkled with poison and his own soldiers, together with Caesar, the contriver of treachery, had removed Hirtius), he seized the troops of both. The consulship was extorted from an unwilling Senate. the troops which he had received against Antony were turned against the state. The proscriptions of citizens, the distributions of lands were not praised even by those who administered them. It is true that the destruction of Cassius and the Brutuses was granted on account of vengeance for his father, although it would be proper to discard private feuds for the utility of the state. But [Sextus] Pompey was deceived under the pretence of peace, Lepidus of friendship. Afterwards Antony, enticed by the treaties of Tarentum and Brundisium and marriage to Octavian's sister and a deceitful marriage alliance, paid the penalty with death. There was doubtless peace after this, but a bloody one — witness the destruction of a Lollius, a Varus, a Varro killed at Rome, an Egnatius, an Iullus. And he did not abstain from domestic crime: the wife of Nero was taken from him, and a mockery was made of consulting the pontiffs to see whether it was proper for the marriage to take place when there was a pregnancy but the offspring was not yet born.... The extravagance of a Vedius Pollio; finally Livia, a harsh mother for the state, a harsh stepmother for the house of the Caesars. There were no honors left to the gods, since he desired that he himself be worshipped with temples and cult statues through flamens and priests....

Orosius, *History Against the Pagans* Book 6 chapter 22

Publius Orosius (early fifth century AD), pupil of St. Augustine, is the author of *History Against the Pagans,* in seven books, the first Christian universal history.

And so in the 752nd year from the founding of the city, Caesar Augustus, having organized all peoples under one peace from the East to the West, from the North to the South and throughout the whole circuit of the Ocean, closed the gates of Janus himself for the third time. From that time for almost twelve years it was ever very peaceful, so that rust marked the gates bathed in peace.... And so, having closed the gates of Janus, zealous to nourish and enlarge the state, which he had sought after in war, he promulgated many laws through which the human race might live morally with self-disciplined reverence.... And so at that time, that is in the year in which Caesar had established the most secure and truest peace by the dispensation of God, Christ was born, for whose advent this peace was shaped....

Francis Bacon (1561–1626), "Of Honor and Reputation," in *Essays and New Atlantis* (New York, 1942; first published 1597), pp. 222–223

The true marshalling of the degrees of sovereign honor are these. In the first place are *conditores imperiorum,* founders of states and commonwealths; such as were Romulus, Cyrus, Caesar, Ottoman, Ismael. In the second place are *legislatores,* lawgivers, which are also called second founders, or *perpetui principes,* because they govern by their ordinance after they are gone; such were Lycurgus, Solon, Justinian, Edgar, Alphonsus of Castile, the Wise.... In the third place are *deliverers* or *preservers (liberatores* or *salvatores),* such as compound the long miseries of civil wars, or deliver their countries from servitude of strangers of tyrants, as Augustus Caesar, Vespasian, Aurelianus, Theodoricus, King Henry the Seventh of England, King Henry the Fourth of France. In the fourth place are *extenders* or *defenders of the empire, (propagatores* or *propugnatores imperii),* such as in honorable wars enlarge their territories, or make noble defenses against invaders. And, in the last place are *fathers of their country (patres patriae),* which reign justly, and make the times good wherein they live.

Laurence Echard, *The Roman History.* 5th Ed. (London, 1702), Vol. 1, pp. 450–452

Thus Augustus Caesar became supreme Governour of the

Roman People, neither by Inheritance, nor Usurpation, nor Conquest, nor Election, yet by means of them all....

Here ended the greatest Commonwealth in the World, and at the same time began the greatest Monarchy; a Monarchy so well fixed, and firmly settled, that not all the tyrannical carriages of those Monsters of men who succeeded Augustus, could shake it; a Monarchy, which if it be considered with others, as to its Power and Riches, together with its Extent and Continuance, there is scarce any room left for comparison, and a Monarchy which the Romans, for many years, believed Indissoluble and Immortal....

As for the Romans themselves, they had now nothing so elevated a Temper, either for the Greatness of Genius, or the Force of the Soul, as in some time in the Republick; but had something more Polite and Sociable; and never were more glorious, or at least, more pleasant times than now, all Wars and Conquests ceasing, all Arts and Sciences flourishing, and all Riches and Pleasures increasing.

Charles Rollin, *The Roman History*, 3rd Ed. (London, 1768), Vol. x, pp. 314–317

In this manner, Octavius congratulated himself in the view of the whole world, on being arrived at the height of his wishes. The methods by which he attained them have been considered by his contemporaries in very different lights, and Tacitus has furnished us with a double view of it.... It is evident that the monarchical government was at that time the only recourse of the Roman republic....

The vast extent of the Roman empire, in connecting together, by a free and constant commerce, all the parts of the then known world, opened all the ways for the preachers of the Gospel; to which the terrible calamities of the civil wars would have been a very great obstacle. The "Prince of Peace" must then be born in the bosom of peace; and thus God raised up Octavius to put an end to all dissensions, and establish a lasting tranquillity in the empire....

Oliver Goldsmith, *Roman History* (London, 1769), p. 211

Such were the honours paid to Augustus, whose power began in slaughter, and terminated in the happiness of his subjects; so that it was said of him "that it had been good for mankind if he had never been born, or if he had never died." It is very probable, that the cruelties exercised in his triumvirate, were suggested by his colleagues; and perhaps, he thought, in the case of Caesar's death, that revenge was virtue. Certain it is, that these severities were, in some measure, necessary to restore public tranquility; for until the Roman spirit was entirely eradicated, no monarchy could be secure. He gave the government an air suited to the disposition of the times; he indulged his subjects in the pride of seeing an appearance of a republic, while he made them really happy in the effects of a most absolute monarchy, guided by the most consummate prudence. In this last virtue he seems to have excelled most monarchs, and, indeed, could we separate Octavius from Augustus, he was one of the most faultless princes in history....

Edward Gibbon, *The Decline and Fall of the Roman Empire* (New York, 1932; first published 1776) Vol. I, pp. 1–3, 63–64

It was reserved for Augustus to relinquish the ambitious design of subduing the whole earth, and to introduce a spirit of moderation into the public councils. Inclined to peace by his temper and situation, it was easy for him to discover that Rome, in her present exalted situation, had much less to hope than to fear from the chance of arms....

Happily for the repose of mankind, the moderate system recommended by the wisdom of Augustus, was adopted by the fears and vices of his immediate successors....

The tender respect of Augustus for a free constitution which he destroyed, can only be explained by an attentive consideration of the character of that subtle tyrant. A cool head, an unfeeling heart, and a cowardly disposition, prompted him, at the age of

nineteen, to assume the mask of hypocrisy, which he never afterwards laid aside.... His virtues, and even his vices, were artificial;
and according to the various dictates of his interest, he was at first
the enemy, and at last the father, of the Roman world. When he
framed the artful system of the Imperial authority, his moderation was inspired by his fears.... Augustus was sensible that mankind is governed by names; nor was he deceived in his expectation, that the senate and people would submit to slavery, provided
they were respectfully assured that they still enjoyed their ancient
freedom....

Thomas De Quincy, "Historical Essays and
Researches" in *The Collected Writings,* ed. David Masson
(London, 1897), Vol. vi, pp. 268–281

The qualities in which he really excelled, the gifts of intrigue,
patience, long-suffering, dissimulation, and tortuous fraud were
...allowed their full value.... Augustus, having finally triumphed,
has met with more than justice from succeeding ages. Even Lord
Bacon says that, by comparison with Julius Caesar, he was *"non
tam impar quam dispar"* ("not so much unequal but dissimilar") —
surely a most extravagant encomium, applied to whomsoever....

The cruelties of Augustus were perhaps equal in atrocity to any
which are recorded.... He once actually slaughtered upon an altar
a large body of his prisoners.... Every friend to Augustus must
have wished that the twelve years of his struggle might for ever be
blotted out from human remembrance. During the forty-two
years of his prosperity and triumph, being above fear, he showed
his natural or prudential lenity....

That prosperity in a public sense, has rarely been equalled....

He made himself master of the world, and against the most
formidable competitors, his power was absolute, from the rising
to the setting sun... He was loved by nobody....

Ronald Syme, *The Roman Revolution* (Oxford, 1939),
pp. 2, 9, 524

For power Augustus had sacrificed everything.... The new dispensation ... was the work of fraud and bloodshed, based upon the seizure of power and redistribution of property by a revolutionary leader.... During the Civil Wars every party and every leader professed to be defending the cause of liberty and of peace. Those ideals were incompatible. When peace came, it was the peace of despotism.

Arnaldo Momigliano, "Augustus," *Oxford Classical Dictionary.* 2nd Ed. (London, 1970) p. 151

When he entered political life, republican liberty was already dead. He tried to establish a government in which an accurate balance of classes and of countries gave the predominance to Roman tradition and Italian men without offending the provinces and without diminishing Greek culture. He gave peace, as long as it was consistent with the interests of the empire and with the myth of his glory. But he intended especially that the peace was to be the internal peace of the State. He assured freedom of trade and wealth to the upper classes. He did his enormous work in a simple way, living a simple life, faithful to his faithful friends. His superstition did not affect the strength of his will. Yet, as he never thought of real liberty, so he never attained to the profound humanity of the men who promote free life.

CHRONOLOGICAL
TABLE

BC

63 September 23, birth of Octavius (later Augustus).

44 March 15, assassination of Julius Caesar; Octavius adopted in Caesar's will, henceforth known as Octavian(us).

43 January 1, reception of *imperium* by Octavian; in August, election as consul; autumn, formation of Second Triumvirate; proscriptions.

42 January 1, recognition of Caesar as *divus;* November, battles at Philippi; defeat of Caesar's assassins.

40 Autumn, Treaty of Brundisium; marriage of Antony and Octavia.

38 Octavian's marriage to Livia.

38 to 36 War with Sextus Pompey.

33 Aedileship of Agrippa; December 1, end of Second Triumvirate; election of Octavian as consul for second time.

31 Consul III; September, Battle of Actium.

30 Consul IV; suicides of Antony and Cleopatra; annexation of Egypt.

29 Consul V; triple triumph.

28 Consul VI.

27 Consul VII; January 13 to 16, "restoration of the Republic"; title of Augustus bestowed.

26 Consul VIII.

25 Consul IX; marriage of Marcellus and Julia.

24 Consul X.

23 Consul XI; death of Marcellus; constitutional reorganization; July 1, beginning of tribunician power.

21 Marriage of Agrippa and Julia.

20 Diplomatic settlement with Parthia.

19 Death of Vergil and Tibullus.

17 Adoption of grandsons, Gaius and Lucius Caesar; Secular
   Games.
12 Death of Lepidus; Augustus becomes *pontifex maximus;* death
   of Agrippa.
9 Death of Drusus.
8 Death of Horace and Maecenas.
5 Consul XII.
2 Consul XIII; named *pater patriae;* exile of Julia.

AD

2 Death of Lucius Caesar.
4 Death of Gaius Caesar; adoption of Tiberius.
8 Exile of Ovid.
14 August 19, death of Augustus; September 17, deification.

FOR FURTHER READING

History and Culture of the Augustan Age

Baker, George P. *Augustus, The Golden Age of Rome.* New York, 1937.

Bauman, Richard A. *The Crimen Maiestatis in the Roman Republic and Augustan Principate.* Johannesburg, 1967.

Bowersock, Glen W. *Augustus and the Greek World.* Oxford, 1966.

Broch, Hermann. *The Death of Virgil* [a novel]. New York, 1945.

Brunt, P.A., and Moore, J.M. *Res Gestae Divi Augusti: Introduction, Commentary and Translation.* London, 1967.

Buchan, John. *Augustus.* Boston, 1937.

Cambridge Ancient History, Vol. x. Cambridge, 1934.

Earl, Donald C. *The Age of Augustus.* London and New York, 1968.

Hammond, Mason. *The Augustan Principate in Theory and Practice during the Julio-Claudian Period.* 2nd Ed. New York, 1968.

Holmes, Thomas R.E. *The Architect of the Roman Empire, 27 BC to AD 14.* 2 Vols. Oxford, 1928 to 1931.

Jones, A.H.M. *Augustus.* New York, 1970.

Marsh, Frank B. *The Founding of the Roman Empire.* 2nd Ed. London, 1927.

Momigliano, Arnaldo D. "Augustus," *Oxford Classical Dictionary.* 2nd Ed., pp. 149–151. Oxford, 1970.

Ogilvie, Robert M. *The Romans and Their Gods in the Age of Augustus.* New York, 1970.

Reinhold, Meyer. *Marcus Agrippa. A Biography.* Geneva, N.Y., 1933.

Rowell, Henry T. *Rome in the Augustan Age.* Norman, 1962.

Simon, Erika. *Ara Pacis Augustae.* New York, 1967.

Syme, Ronald. *The Roman Revolution.* Oxford, 1939.

Taylor, Lily Ross. *The Divinity of the Roman Emperor.* Middletown, 1931.

Williams, John E. *Augustus* [a novel]. New York, 1972.

Winspear, Alban D., and Geweke, Lenore K. *Augustus and the Reconstruction of Roman Government and Society.* Madison, 1935.

Wirszubski, Chaim. *Libertas as a Political Idea at Rome during the Late Republic and Early Principate.* Cambridge, 1950.

Wiseman, Timothy P. *New Men in the Roman Senate, 139 BC to AD 14.* London, 1971.

Literature of the Augustan Age

Anderson, William S. *The Art of the Aeneid.* Englewood Cliffs, N.J., 1969.

Binns, J.W., ed. *Ovid.* London, 1973.

Commager, Steele, *A Prolegomenon to Propertius.* Norman, 1974.

───── *The Odes of Horace. A Critical Study.* New Haven, 1962.

───── ed., *Virgil, A Collection of Critical Essays.* Englewood Cliffs, N.J., 1966.

Costa, Charles D.N., ed. *Horace.* London, 1973.

Di Cesare, Mario A. *The Altar and the City: A Reading of Vergil's Aeneid.* New York, 1974.

Dudley, Donald R., ed. *Virgil.* London, 1969.

Fraenkel, Eduard. *Horace.* Oxford, 1957.

Fraenkel, Hermann F. *Ovid: A Poet between Two Worlds.* Berkeley, 1945.

Galinsky, G. Karl. *Ovid's Metamorphoses: An Introduction to the Basic Aspects.* Oxford, 1975.

Hubbard, Margaret. *Propertius.* New York, 1975.

Johnson, W.R. *Darkness Invisible. A Study of Vergil's Aeneid.* Berkeley, 1976.

Knight, William F.J. *Roman Virgil.* Rev. Ed. Harmondsworth, 1966.

Luck, Georg. *The Latin Love Elegy.* 2nd Ed. New York, 1969.

McKay, Alexander. *Vergil's Italy,* Greenwich, Conn. 1970.

Mendell, Clarence W. *Latin Poetry: The New Poets and the Augustans.* New Haven, 1965.

Newman, J.K. *Augustus and the New Poetry*. Brussels, 1967.

Otis, Brooks, *Ovid as an Epic Poet*. 2nd Ed. Cambridge, 1970.

—— *Virgil: A Study in Civilized Poetry*. Oxford, 1963.

Perret, Jacques. *Horace*. New York, 1964.

Pöschl, Viktor. *The Art of Vergil*. Ann Arbor, 1962.

Putnam, Michael C.J. *The Poetry of the Aeneid*. Cambridge, Mass., 1966.

—— *Tibullus: A Commentary*. Norman, 1973.

——*Virgil's Pastoral Art: Studies in the Eclogues*. Princeton, 1970.

Reckford, Kenneth J. *Horace*. New York, 1969.

Ross, David O. *Backgrounds to Augustan Poetry: Gallus, Elegy, and Rome*. New York, 1975.

Sellar, William Y. *The Roman Poets of the Augustan Age*. 2nd Ed. Oxford, 1892.

Sullivan, J.P. *Propertius: A Critical Introduction*. Cambridge, 1976.

Thibault, John C. *The Mystery of Ovid's Exile*. Berkeley, 1964.

Wilkinson, L.P. *The Georgics of Virgil*. New York, 1970.

—— *Golden Latin Artistry*. Cambridge, 1963.

—— *Horace and his Lyric Poetry*. 2nd Ed. London, 1968.

—— *Ovid Recalled*. Cambridge, 1955.

Williams, Gordon. *Horace*. Oxford, 1972.

Williams, Robert D. *Vergil*. Oxford, 1967.

NOTES

PREFACE

1 F.E. Adcock, *Cambridge Ancient History*, Vol. x, p. 583.
2 Arnaldo Momigliano, *Oxford Classical Dictionary*. 2nd Ed. (Oxford 1970), p. 151.
3 *Considerations on Representative Government* (New York 1958), p. 42.

PROLOGUE

1 Horace alludes to the Social War of 91 to 88 BC in which these people fiercely opposed Rome.
2 A southern Italic city that went over to Hannibal after the Roman defeat at Cannae in 216 BC and aspired to the hegemony of all Italy.
3 The Allobroges were drawn into and betrayed the Catilinarian conspiracy of 63 BC.
4 Greek city in Ionia that, in 534 BC, emigrated *en masse*, rather than submit to Persian domination, and settled in the west, in Corsica.
5 On the eastern coast of Apulia, Italy.
6 A reference to the ship Argo and the famous voyage of Jason and the Argonauts.
7 I.e., Medea, the archetypal sorceress.
8 A reference to Theocritus and pastoral poetry.
9 A reference to the prophecy of the Sibyl, an aged prophetess of Apollo, who had a shrine near Cumae.
10 Astraea, goddess of Justice, who left the earth in the Iron Age.
11 Goddess of childbirth often identified or associated (as here) with Diana.
12 Gaius Asinius Pollio, consul in 40 BC, author of tragedies and of a history of the civil wars. In the year after his consulship, he celebrated a triumph.
13 Helmsman of the Argo.

14 Often associated with Apollo as rival or son, he is connected with the lyre, song and teaching.

15 Muse of epic poetry.

16 A god of the woods and shepherds, hence associated with pastoral poetry.

PART I

1 I.e., possess proconsular power in a form that superseded the power of all governors of provinces.

2 The *pomerium* was the sacred boundary around the inner city of Rome.

3 Augustus regularly used this title, but after him it did not become an official title of the emperors until the reign of Vespasian.

4 This was not true in the time of Augustus. Dio Cassius is retrojecting a power that devolved upon the emperors two centuries later.

5 I.e., makes them sacrosanct, so that no violence may be done to them on penalty of religious defilement.

6 This, too, is an anachronism on Dio's part.

7 On *Pater Patriae* see no. 3C of this volume.

8 On the *consilium* of Augustus (a sort of rotating cabinet) see no. 5 of this volume.

9 Such nomination and commendation of candidates for office by Augustus were tantamount to election.

10 This was most unusual, since he had already held the consulship, in 37 BC. Agrippa undertook this office to mobilize public opinion on the side of Octavian in the coming showdown with Antony.

11 This is an error; this aqueduct was completed in 19 BC. Pliny seems to have confused this with the new Aqua Julia, opened in 33 BC.

12 The inscription (*CIL*, Vol. VI no. 6896) on the facade of the Pantheon reads: "Marcus Agrippa, son of Lucius, consul three times, made it."

13 He did this because a *pontifex* was forbidden by Roman religion to behold a dead body.

14 Tiberius was married to Agrippa's daughter Vipsania Agrippina. Publius Quinctilius Varus was married either to a sister of Vipsania, or a daughter of Agrippa by his second wife, Claudia Marcella.

15 Gamaliel the Elder is said to have been a grandson of the great Jewish rabbi Hillel; he was a Pharisee and a member of the Sanhedrin. The genuineness of his conversation with Agrippa is not wholly without question. Gamaliel is usually put in the Apostolic Age (30–40 AD). St. Paul is said to have been his pupil (*Acts* xxii. 3).

16 I.e., demobilized veterans after the civil war with Antony. The date is 31 BC.

17 I.e., Antony and Cleopatra.

18 This region, up to the second cataract (ca. 165 miles), thus became a Roman protectorate with an Ethiopian client-king. A decade later this area was restructured into a permanent buffer zone of about 66 miles.

19 There were indeed twenty-five legions in existence at the time of Augustus' death, 14 AD.

20 The Roman armies had about 150,000 auxiliary troops, in addition to about 150,000 citizen soldiers in the legions.

21 After the death of Julius Caesar, Lepidus acquired the post of *pontifex maximus*, previously held by Caesar. In 36 BC Lepidus was deposed from the Second Triumvirate, but Augustus allowed him to retain the priestly office, though he remained in virtual house arrest in a small town in Italy, until his death in 12 BC.

22 A ceremony observed in time of peace to determine whether the consuls should offer prayers to the "Public Safety."

23 A priesthood of Jupiter which tended to be left unfilled because of the numerous taboos associated with it.

24 An old festival celebrating a fertility god (Lupercus) in which men dressed in goat-skins (Luperci) struck women with thongs to stimulate fertility.

25 Games in honor of guardian gods of the crossroads.

26 The Sibylline Books.

27 Members of the Board of Fifteen.

28 Greek goddesses of childbirth.

29 Greek sacrificial cakes.

30 Manumission "by the rod" was a formal symbolic method of freeing a slave; it took place before a public official. The manumission councils set up by this law consisted of five Senators and five Equestrians chosen by lot in Rome, and twenty in the provinces.

31 The reference is to a flood in Greek mythology from which Deucalion and Pyrrha were the sole survivors.

32 Headquarters of the *pontifex maximus* in the Forum.

33 Muse of history.

34 Helicon and Pindus are celebrated haunts of the Muses.

35 Mt. Haemus, in Thrace, is associated with Orpheus.

36 Second king of Rome, purported to be the founder of the ancestral Roman religious institutions.

37 The last of the seven kings of Rome; he was deposed in 509 BC.

38 Famous great Roman leaders during various periods of the Roman Republic.

39 Horace refers to Marcus Claudius Marcellus, conqueror of Syracuse in 212 BC. There is thus here a compliment to Augustus' nephew and son-in-law Marcellus, his chosen successor; he died in 23 BC.

40 By pouring a libation of wine.

41 This was a tribe in Thrace, in a client-kingdom subject to Augustus' jurisdiction.

42 This Marcellus is not likely to be Augustus' nephew and son-in-law Marcellus, but perhaps Marcus Claudius Marcellus Aeserninus, consul for 22 BC.

43 That is, republican. Labienus committed suicide rather than have his freedom to write suppressed.

44 Cassius Severus was exiled for life.

45 A festival of Mars the Avenger, first held in 2 BC. Augustus may be referring to the festival of Mars held in 12 AD.

46 I.e., Germanicus.

47 Thirteen miles southeast of Rome. There was a venerable temple of Jupiter there, the focal point of the age-old Latin Games.

48 Mother of Claudius. She was the widow of Tiberius' brother Drusus, who died in 9 BC.

49 Festival of Minerva.

50 Both Gaius and his brother Lucius Caesar are meant.

51 Popularly believed to be a protection against lightning.

52 That is, the negative implication of the sound "no."

53 This is a typical barb of Tacitus, who had a conspiratorial view of history and assumed the existence of intrigue, especially in court circles.

54 Augustus adopted Tiberius in 4 AD, four months after the death of Gaius Caesar.

55 The last child of Agrippa and Julia, born after his father's death in 12 BC. At the age of fifteen he was adopted by Augustus, along with Tiberius, in 4 AD. A youth of rebellious character and a focus of dynastic intrigues, he was disinherited by Augustus and permanently exiled in 7 AD.

56 It is difficult to identify this member of the famous Cornelius Scipio family. *Quaestor pro praetore* designates him as administrator of the provincial district.

57 Gaius assumed the consulship in 1 AD, when he was actually in Syria.

58 The reference is to a stream, eleven miles north of Rome, where the Gauls in 390 or 387 BC overwhelmed the Romans. The anniversary of the defeat became a day of national mourning.

59 An earlier theory, based on an attempt to reconstruct a previous inscription — that the Maison Carrée was originally dedicated to Marcus Agrippa in 16/15 BC — has been disproven. See Robert Amy, "L'Inscription de la Mason Carrée de Nîmes," *Comptes Rendus de l'Académie des Inscriptions et Belles-Lettres,* 1970, pp. 670–686.

60 The destruction of Hasdrubal's army in 207 BC by consular armies, one headed by Claudius Nero.

61 At Colchis the golden fleece was protected by a serpent, and Jason had to yoke fire-breathing bulls; at Thebes Cadmus was confronted by a "dragon" in the form of a water serpent.

62 The elder Marcella.

63 In the Forum, at a spot where business transactions were conducted.

64 Antony and his supporters are meant. Antony was then consul.

65 I.e., it proclaimed martial law through the so-called "ultimate decree of the Senate."

66 Julius Caesar, his adoptive father. Noteworthy is that Augustus does not name his natural father or his mother in this document.

67 The battles at Philippi, in 42 BC.

68 Warships captured in the naval victories over Sextus Pompey, off Sicily, and over Antony and Cleopatra, at Actium.

69 The unprecedented triple triumph, on August 13 to 15, 29 BC, over Dalmatia, Actium, and Egypt.

70 Roman symbol of power *(imperium),* consisting of a bundle of rods tied together, with the head of an ax protruding.

71 His friend, son-in-law, and presumptive successor, Marcus A-grippa, two times; his stepson, son-in-law, and designated heir, Tiberius, three times.

72 Of these seven priestly offices, all Roman emperors subsequently held the first four.

73 A purification ceremony traditionally performed after each census.

74 Lepidus is meant; see note 21 above.

75 I.e., the traditional Roman ceremony at puberty, when Roman boys assumed the "man's toga."

76 "Crown gold," originally an offering of golden crowns by communities to rulers and generals, became during the empire a tax imposed annually and on special occasions.

77 Antony is meant.

78 Sextus Pompey is meant.

79 Actually they were restored as the result of diplomatic negotiations (see no. 31 of this volume).

80 The tradition was that Julius Proculus, a Roman senator in the reign of Romulus, claimed that Romulus had appeared to him shortly after his death as the god Quirinus.

PART II

1 On other building construction of the Augustan Age see no. 22B of this volume.

2 Cf. Strabo, *Geography* Book 5 chapter 3.8: "Augustus and his sons and friends and wife and sister exceeded all zeal and expense in adorning Rome."

3 See also no. 23 of this volume for other statements on the moral rededication of Roman society.

4 Parthian leaders.

5 Myrtle was sacred to Venus, mythical ancestress of the Julian line.

6 Octavian's birthday was September 23, for which the natal sign was Libra, symbolizing Justice. But Augustus early in his career published his horoscope as Capricorn. The reason is not known; perhaps the sign denoted the position of the sun at Augustus' conception; or Capricorn was the birth sign of the sun; or it symbolized Augustus' role as avenger of Caesar; or — an attractive possibility — Capricorn is the symbol of plenty.

7 The Greek author (eighth century BC) of *Works and Days,* a poem on agricultural life.

8 The reference is to the victory of Publius Cornelius Scipio Aemilianus over Numantia in Spain in 133 BC.

9 Cf. no 10 of this volume for Augustus' legislation on marriage.

10 The triumvir.

11 See note 21 to Part I.

12 Protecting spirits of the dead in Roman religion.

13 A well-known orator and declaimer; he was consul *(suffectus)* in 5 BC.

14 Adherents of Julius Caesar; they were consuls in 43 BC. Both died during their consulship, and Octavian was suspected of having had them eliminated.

15 Roman senator, unyielding defender of the Republic against Caesar. Rather than surrender to Caesar in the civil war, he committed suicide at Utica in North Africa.

16 One of the most distinguished teachers of oratory in the Augustan Age. He died in 4 AD.

17 Famous teacher of rhetoric in the Augustan Age; Ovid was his pupil.

18 Janus was a god with a double-faced head.

19 The event referred to is the "Restoration of the Republic" in 27 BC (see no. 2 of this volume). Augustus is here called the grandfather of Germanicus, adopted by Tiberius.

20 The civic crown awarded to Augustus for "saving the citizens."

21 Tiberius.

22 The rape of the Sabine Women under Romulus' rule is referred to here.

23 The *Manes* are meant, spirits of the dead ancestors.

24 Caesar was *pontifex maximus.*

25 A reference to a Greek myth, the battle of the Centaurs and Lapiths that erupted at the wedding feast of Pirithous and Hippodamia when the Centaurs got drunk and tried to rape Hippodamia and the other women.

26 Lines marked off the seats in the stadium.

27 The displeasure of the fans might result in the race being scratched.

28 A fashionable seaside resort on the Bay of Naples frequented by wealthy Romans and the capital's smart set.

PART III

1 On the privileges under the Julian Law and the Papian-Poppaean Law, see no. 10 of this volume.

2 An African people renowned as serpent charmers.

3 The date is 30 BC.

4 See no. 6B of this volume.

5 He was apparently appointed administrator of the region with the title "prefect"; later in 44 AD, he assumed the title of king, which his father had borne.

6 She died in 7/8 AD.

7 Husband of Queen Dynamis.

8 King of Thrace; he died in 12 AD.

9 Cf. no 16D of this volume.

10 "White Village," on the Red Sea.

11 This would be several years later, when Augustus was in Asia Minor in 20 BC.

12 In 20 BC Augustus also met envoys from India: "Nicolaus of Damascus says that at Antioch near Daphne Augustus met the ambassador of the Indians, who had arrived to see Caesar Augustus.... Although King Porus was ruler over 600 kings, nevertheless he was eager to be a friend to Caesar, and was ready to provide a passage wherever he

wished, and also to cooperate in whatever was suitable." (Strabo, *Geography* Book 15 chapter 1.73.)

13 Cf. Augustus's comments on Parthia in the *Res Gestae*, no. 18 of this volume.

14 Passed in 42 BC, this law was apparently intended to reward provincials who supported the triumvirate against Caesar's assassins.

15 Proconsul of Province of Asia, 2–3 AD.

16 I.e., from the first to the last day of the Egyptian calendar year.

17 The continuation of the birthday celebration of Augustus for a second day was unofficial. This may have been one way the Equestrian Order devised to show its loyalty to the imperial house. ("The Roman Equestrians on their own initiative and by consensus always celebrated his birthday for two days." [Suetonius, *Life of Augustus* chapter 57.])

18 Augustus was first admitted to the Senate at Rome on January 1.

19 The date on which, in 43 BC, he first received *imperium*.

20 Lepidus held the consulship during the first part of the year 11 AD; he was then replaced by Lucius Cassius Longinus mentioned in the caption of the inscription. The practice under the emperors, beginning with Augustus, was to appoint consuls for part of a year, both to reward more men with this high honor and to provide a sufficient number of ex-consuls for high administrative posts.

21 The minimum property qualification for jury duty at Rome was 100,000 denarii.

22 The jurors were chosen by placing balls with names marked on them in a container or by dropping them in a lottery "machine" to ensure random selection. They were weighed before the lottery to check that they were all the same.

23 Augustus's clemency to these Roman citizens was intended as a conciliatory measure to balance concessions made to Greeks in Cyrene.

24 As, for example, in the case of Seleucus of Rhosus (see no. 32 C of this volume).

25 On Augustus' consilium, a sort of cabinet, see no. 5 of this volume.

26 For example, Gaius and Lucius Caesar (see no. 16 of this volume).

27 Passed in 17 BC, this law regulated the criminal courts.

28 Ovid is referring to a coin or medallion depicting Augustus, Tiberius, and Livia.

29 Livia.

30 Tiberius.

31 Germanicus, son of Tiberius' brother Drusus, and Drusus II, son of Tiberius. At Augustus' order Germanicus was adopted by Tiberius.

PART IV

1 Not much is known of the writers and statesmen mentioned here, except for Maecenas, Vergil, Pollio, Messalla.

2 Horace here refers to the country around Venusia, his birthplace in southern Italy.

3 I.e., the famous Roman general Marcellus.

4 An effort to derive "Latium" from the Latin verb *latere* ("to lie hidden"). It is thought that "Latium" meant "flat land," since *Latium* is a plain (cf. Via Lata in Rome, "Broad-Way").

5 Treacherous Mettius Fuffetius, dictator of Alba Longa.

6 Lars Porsenna, Etruscan king of Clusium, who sought to restore the Etruscan royal family of the Tarquins to the throne of Rome.

7 The last of the Tarquins, who had ruled Rome for about a hundred years. They were expelled about 510 BC and replaced by two elected consuls in the Roman Republic.

8 Horatius Cocles, who held off the army of Porsenna by guarding a bridge over the Tiber River single-handedly and then escaped after the bridge was torn down behind him by his fellow Romans.

9 The Gauls invaded central Italy, seizing Rome about 390 BC.

10 Sacred shields said to have been droped from heaven.

11 A Roman noble and senator who, in 63 BC, attempted to overthrow the government and seize power. His conspiracy was detected and suppressed by Cicero, who was then consul.

12 The "star of Julius," a comet which appeared after Caesar's death and was thought to have carried his soul to heaven.

13 A reference to the two asps which Cleopatra used to commit suicide in Alexandria.

14 Cleopatra.

15 I.e., the elegiac couplet, consisting of one hexameter and one pentameter.

16 A reference to the Social War of 91−87 BC, in which various Italian towns and regions revolted against Rome.

17 A fertility god protecting gardens and vineyards.

18 Protecting spirits of farm land and homes.

19 Shepherd goddess, whose holiday was on April 21, the day celebrated as the foundation of Rome.

20 Small stream in Greece associated with the Muses.

21 A reference to the myth of the Seven Against Thebes.

22 The Trojan War was recorded to have lasted ten years.

23 See note 17 above.

24 A festival for the god Pan, in which Luperci (men dressed in skins) struck women with thongs of goat hide to stimulate fertility.

25 Fifty sisters, all but one of whom slew their bridegrooms. The scene was represented on the temple of Apollo on the Palatine.

26 The Egyptian goddess Isis, whose cult was popular during the Augustan Age. The Roman poets often identified her with the mythic Greek princess Io, who, in her wandering, spent some time in Egypt.

27 Gladiatorial shows were sometimes given here.

28 The three-headed dog Cerberus is meant.

INDEX